MEMOIRS

THE OTHER VOICE IN EARLY MODERN EUROPE

A Series Edited by Margaret L. King and Albert Rabil, Jr.

RECENT BOOKS IN THE SERIES

Hortense Mancini
and
Marie Mancini

MEMOIRS

꒰꒱

Edited and Translated by
Sarah Nelson

THE UNIVERSITY OF CHICAGO PRESS
Chicago & London

Hortense Mancini (1646–1699)
Marie Mancini (1639–1715)

Sarah Nelson is associate professor of French
at the University of Idaho.

The University of Chicago Press, Chicago 60637
The University of Chicago Press, Ltd., London
© 2008 by The University of Chicago
All rights reserved. Published 2008
Printed in the United States of America

17 16 15 14 13 12 11 10 09 08   1 2 3 4 5

ISBN-13: 978-0-226-50278-6 (cloth)
ISBN-13: 978-0-226-50279-3 (paper)
ISBN-10: 0-226-50278-3 (cloth)
ISBN-10: 0-226-50279-1 (paper)

The University of Chicago Press gratefully acknowledges the generous support of
James E. Rabil, in memory of Scottie W. Rabil, toward the publication of this book.

Library of Congress Cataloging-in-Publication Data

Memoirs / Hortense Mancini and Marie Mancini ;
edited and translated by Sarah Nelson.
p.   cm. — (The other voice in early modern Europe)
Includes bibliographical references and index.
ISBN-13: 978-0-226-50278-6 (cloth : alk. paper)
ISBN-10: 0-226-50278-3 (cloth : alk. paper)
ISBN-13: 978-0-226-50279-3 (pbk. : alk. paper)
ISBN-10: 0-226-50279-1 (pbk. : alk. paper)
1. Mazarin, Hortense Mancini, duchesse de, 1646–1699—Diaries. 2. Mancini,
Maria, 1639–1715—Diaries. 3. France—History—Louis XIV, 1643–1715—Sources.
4. France—Court and courtiers—Diaries. I. Nelson, Sarah. II. Mazarin, Hortense
Mancini, duchesse de, 1646–1699. Mémoires. English. III. Mancini, Maria,
1639–1715? Apologie. English.
DC130.A2M4613   2008
944'.0330922—dc22
2007050574

CONTENTS

ACKNOWLEDGMENTS

In July 2003, I had the good fortune to take part in the National Endowment for the Humanities Summer Institute, A Literature of Their Own? Women Writing—Venice, London, Paris—1550–1700. I am profoundly grateful to the director of the institute, Albert Rabil, Jr., for his organization of that extraordinary experience, for his creation and oversight, along with Margaret L. King, of the Other Voice in Early Modern Europe series and for the opportunity he afforded me to edit this volume. I thank Janet Rabil for her contributions to running the institute, and I thank the distinguished scholars who served as faculty for it. I am especially grateful to the French specialists, Elizabeth Goldsmith and Erica Harth, who brought into the institute the memoir of Marie Mancini in its seventeenth-century English translation; and I thank Elizabeth Goldsmith for her scholarship on the Mancinis, which was tremendously valuable to me as I prepared this volume. Finally, I express my hearty thanks to the twenty-four other participants in the institute, including Monique Nagem, Carrie Klaus, and Nathalie Hester, who read drafts, offered advice, and furnished helpful information on this project.

My work on this volume was supported by a University of Idaho Seed Grant and also by a grant-in-aid from the Friends of the University of Wisconsin–Madison Libraries. I am particularly grateful to Tom Garver for his kind assistance at the University of Wisconsin. I would also like to thank Katherine Aiken, James Reece, and Joan West at the University of Idaho for helping me carve out the time to complete this project. Many other Idaho colleagues were generous in their assistance: Cecelia Luschnig read multiple drafts of both memoirs; Sandra Reineke tracked down volumes at the Bibliothèque nationale; Ellen Kittell, Louis Perraud, and Sean Quinlan were invaluable consultants on historical and linguistic questions; and a great many people, including Michael O'Rourke, Bill McLaughlin, Debbie McLaughlin, Irina Kappler-Crookston, and Anne Perriguey, provided precious advice and support. I am also grateful to colleagues and mentors from outside of Idaho who kindly advised me on specific points: Ellen Millender, Ullrich Langer, Christopher Kleinhenz, and Kirk Read. I owe a great debt to a number of people whom I have never met but whose careful genealogical documentation made much of my annotation of this volume possible: Alain de Carné, Davide Shamà, Salvador Miranda, and Nicolas Hobbs. And I am very grateful to Alison Folk for the illustrations she created, as well as to freelance copyeditor Susan Tarcov, and Randy Petilos and his colleagues at the University of Chicago Press for their expertise and generosity.

Finally, I thank the friends and family whose constant interest in this project made working on it such a pleasure for me: many dear friends in Moscow, Idaho, and Coeur d'Alene, Idaho; the Madison group—Nancy Virtue, Dolly Weber, Kathleen Suchenski, Tim Scheie, Loren Ringer, Elise Leahy, Cheryl Krueger, Rebecca Karoff, and Rebecca Saunders; my parents, Corinne and Harland Nelson; and of course, my son Luke Gresback and my husband Tim Gresback, who (unlike the husbands of Hortense and Marie Mancini) always sent me on my research travels with a smile and never, never sought legal means to detain me or had agents tail me.

Sarah Nelson

THE OTHER VOICE IN
EARLY MODERN EUROPE:
INTRODUCTION TO THE SERIES

Margaret L. King and Albert Rabil Jr.

THE OLD VOICE AND THE OTHER VOICE

In western Europe and the United States, women are nearing equality in the professions, in business, and in politics. Most enjoy access to education, reproductive rights, and autonomy in financial affairs. Issues vital to women are on the public agenda: equal pay, child care, domestic abuse, breast cancer research, and curricular revision with an eye to the inclusion of women.

These recent achievements have their origins in things women (and some male supporters) said for the first time about six hundred years ago. Theirs is the "other voice," in contradistinction to the "first voice," the voice of the educated men who created Western culture. Coincident with a general reshaping of European culture in the period 1300–1700 (called the Renaissance or early modern period), questions of female equality and opportunity were raised that still resound and are still unresolved.

The other voice emerged against the backdrop of a three-thousand-year history of the derogation of women rooted in the civilizations related to Western culture: Hebrew, Greek, Roman, and Christian. Negative attitudes toward women inherited from these traditions pervaded the intellectual, medical, legal, religious, and social systems that developed during the European Middle Ages.

The following pages describe the traditional, overwhelmingly male views of women's nature inherited by early modern Europeans and the new tradition that the "other voice" called into being to begin to challenge reigning assumptions. This review should serve as a framework for understanding the texts published in the series The Other Voice in Early Modern Europe. Introductions specific to each text and author follow this essay in all the volumes of the series.

TRADITIONAL VIEWS OF WOMEN, 500 B.C.E.–1500 C.E.

Embedded in the philosophical and medical theories of the ancient Greeks were perceptions of the female as inferior to the male in both mind and body. Similarly, the structure of civil legislation inherited from the ancient Romans was biased against women, and the views on women developed by Christian thinkers out of the Hebrew Bible and the Christian New Testament were negative and disabling. Literary works composed in the vernacular of ordinary people, and widely recited or read, conveyed these negative assumptions. The social networks within which most women lived—those of the family and the institutions of the Roman Catholic Church—were shaped by this negative tradition and sharply limited the areas in which women might act in and upon the world.

GREEK PHILOSOPHY AND FEMALE NATURE. Greek biology assumed that women were inferior to men and defined them as merely childbearers and housekeepers. This view was authoritatively expressed in the works of the philosopher Aristotle.

Aristotle thought in dualities. He considered action superior to inaction, form (the inner design or structure of any object) superior to matter, completion to incompletion, possession to deprivation. In each of these dualities, he associated the male principle with the superior quality and the female with the inferior. "The male principle in nature," he argued, "is associated with active, formative and perfected characteristics, while the female is passive, material and deprived, desiring the male in order to become complete."[1] Men are always identified with virile qualities, such as judgment, courage, and stamina, and women with their opposites—irrationality, cowardice, and weakness.

The masculine principle was considered superior even in the womb. The man's semen, Aristotle believed, created the form of a new human creature, while the female body contributed only matter. (The existence of the ovum, and with it the other facts of human embryology, was not established until the seventeenth century.) Although the later Greek physician Galen believed there was a female component in generation, contributed by "female semen," the followers of both Aristotle and Galen saw the male role in human generation as more active and more important.

In the Aristotelian view, the male principle sought always to reproduce itself. The creation of a female was always a mistake, therefore, resulting

---

1. Aristotle, *Physics* 1.9.192a20–24, in *The Complete Works of Aristotle*, ed. Jonathan Barnes, rev. Oxford trans., 2 vols. (Princeton, 1984), 1:328.

from an imperfect act of generation. Every female born was considered a "defective" or "mutilated" male (as Aristotle's terminology has variously been translated), a "monstrosity" of nature.[2]

For Greek theorists, the biology of males and females was the key to their psychology. The female was softer and more docile, more apt to be despondent, querulous, and deceitful. Being incomplete, moreover, she craved sexual fulfillment in intercourse with a male. The male was intellectual, active, and in control of his passions.

These psychological polarities derived from the theory that the universe consisted of four elements (earth, fire, air, and water), expressed in human bodies as four "humors" (black bile, yellow bile, blood, and phlegm) considered, respectively, dry, hot, damp, and cold and corresponding to mental states ("melancholic," "choleric," "sanguine," "phlegmatic"). In this scheme the male, sharing the principles of earth and fire, was dry and hot; the female, sharing the principles of air and water, was cold and damp.

Female psychology was further affected by her dominant organ, the uterus (womb), *hystera* in Greek. The passions generated by the womb made women lustful, deceitful, talkative, irrational, indeed—when these affects were in excess—"hysterical."

Aristotle's biology also had social and political consequences. If the male principle was superior and the female inferior, then in the household, as in the state, men should rule and women must be subordinate. That hierarchy did not rule out the companionship of husband and wife, whose cooperation was necessary for the welfare of children and the preservation of property. Such mutuality supported male preeminence.

Aristotle's teacher Plato suggested a different possibility: that men and women might possess the same virtues. The setting for this proposal is the imaginary and ideal Republic that Plato sketches in a dialogue of that name. Here, for a privileged elite capable of leading wisely, all distinctions of class and wealth dissolve, as, consequently, do those of gender. Without households or property, as Plato constructs his ideal society, there is no need for the subordination of women. Women may therefore be educated to the same level as men to assume leadership. Plato's Republic remained imaginary, however. In real societies, the subordination of women remained the norm and the prescription.

The views of women inherited from the Greek philosophical tradition became the basis for medieval thought. In the thirteenth century, the supreme Scholastic philosopher Thomas Aquinas, among others, still echoed

---

2. Aristotle, *Generation of Animals* 2.3.737a27–28, in *The Complete Works*, 1: 1144.

Aristotle's views of human reproduction, of male and female personalities, and of the preeminent male role in the social hierarchy.

ROMAN LAW AND THE FEMALE CONDITION. Roman law, like Greek philosophy, underlay medieval thought and shaped medieval society. The ancient belief that adult property-owning men should administer households and make decisions affecting the community at large is the very fulcrum of Roman law.

About 450 B.C.E., during Rome's republican era, the community's customary law was recorded (legendarily) on twelve tablets erected in the city's central forum. It was later elaborated by professional jurists whose activity increased in the imperial era, when much new legislation was passed, especially on issues affecting family and inheritance. This growing, changing body of laws was eventually codified in the *Corpus of Civil Law* under the direction of the emperor Justinian, generations after the empire ceased to be ruled from Rome. That *Corpus*, read and commented on by medieval scholars from the eleventh century on, inspired the legal systems of most of the cities and kingdoms of Europe.

Laws regarding dowries, divorce, and inheritance pertain primarily to women. Since those laws aimed to maintain and preserve property, the women concerned were those from the property-owning minority. Their subordination to male family members points to the even greater subordination of lower-class and slave women, about whom the laws speak little.

In the early republic, the *paterfamilias*, or "father of the family," possessed *patria potestas*, "paternal power." The term *pater*, "father," in both these cases does not necessarily mean biological father but denotes the head of a household. The father was the person who owned the household's property and, indeed, its human members. The *paterfamilias* had absolute power—including the power, rarely exercised, of life or death—over his wife, his children, and his slaves, as much as his cattle.

Male children could be "emancipated," an act that granted legal autonomy and the right to own property. Those over fourteen could be emancipated by a special grant from the father or automatically by their father's death. But females could never be emancipated; instead, they passed from the authority of their father to that of a husband or, if widowed or orphaned while still unmarried, to a guardian or tutor.

Marriage in its traditional form placed the woman under her husband's authority, or *manus*. He could divorce her on grounds of adultery, drinking wine, or stealing from the household, but she could not divorce him. She could neither possess property in her own right nor bequeath any to her children upon her death. When her husband died, the household property passed not to her but to his male heirs. And when her father died, she had no claim to any family inheritance, which was directed to her brothers or more remote male relatives. The effect of these laws was to exclude women from civil society, itself based on property ownership.

In the later republican and imperial periods, these rules were significantly modified. Women rarely married according to the traditional form. The practice of "free" marriage allowed a woman to remain under her father's authority, to possess property given her by her father (most frequently the "dowry," recoverable from the husband's household on his death), and to inherit from her father. She could also bequeath property to her own children and divorce her husband, just as he could divorce her.

Despite this greater freedom, women still suffered enormous disability under Roman law. Heirs could belong only to the father's side, never the mother's. Moreover, although she could bequeath her property to her children, she could not establish a line of succession in doing so. A woman was "the beginning and end of her own family," said the jurist Ulpian. Moreover, women could play no public role. They could not hold public office, represent anyone in a legal case, or even witness a will. Women had only a private existence and no public personality.

The dowry system, the guardian, women's limited ability to transmit wealth, and total political disability are all features of Roman law adopted by the medieval communities of western Europe, although modified according to local customary laws..

CHRISTIAN DOCTRINE AND WOMEN'S PLACE. The Hebrew Bible and the Christian New Testament authorized later writers to limit women to the realm of the family and to burden them with the guilt of original sin. The passages most fruitful for this purpose were the creation narratives in Genesis and sentences from the Epistles defining women's role within the Christian family and community.

Each of the first two chapters of Genesis contains a creation narrative. In the first "God created man in his own image, in the image of God he created him; male and female he created them" (Gn 1:27). In the second, God created Eve from Adam's rib (2:21–23). Christian theologians relied principally on Genesis 2 for their understanding of the relation between man and woman, interpreting the creation of Eve from Adam as proof of her subordination to him.

The creation story in Genesis 2 leads to that of the temptations in Genesis 3: of Eve by the wily serpent and of Adam by Eve. As read by Christian theologians from Tertullian to Thomas Aquinas, the narrative made Eve responsible for the Fall and its consequences. She instigated the act; she deceived her husband; she suffered the greater punishment. Her disobedience made it necessary for Jesus to be incarnated and to die on the cross. From the pulpit, moralists and preachers for centuries conveyed to women the guilt that they bore for original sin.

The Epistles offered advice to early Christians on building communities of the faithful. Among the matters to be regulated was the place of women. Paul offered views favorable to women in Galatians 3:28: "There is neither Jew nor Greek, there is neither slave nor free, there is neither male nor female; for you are all one in Christ Jesus." Paul also referred to women as his coworkers and placed them on a par with himself and his male coworkers (Phlm 4:2–3; Rom 16:1–3; 1 Cor 16:19). Elsewhere, Paul limited women's possibilities: "But I want you to understand that the head of every man is Christ, the head of a woman is her husband, and the head of Christ is God" (1 Cor 11:3).

Biblical passages by later writers (although attributed to Paul) enjoined women to forgo jewels, expensive clothes, and elaborate coiffures; and they forbade women to "teach or have authority over men," telling them to "learn in silence with all submissiveness" as is proper for one responsible for sin, consoling them, however, with the thought that they will be saved through childbearing (1 Tm 2:9–15). Other texts among the later Epistles defined women as the weaker sex and emphasized their subordination to their husbands (1 Pt 3:7; Col 3:18; Eph 5:22–23).

These passages from the New Testament became the arsenal employed by theologians of the early church to transmit negative attitudes toward women to medieval Christian culture—above all, Tertullian (*On the Apparel of Women*), Jerome (*Against Jovinian*), and Augustine (*The Literal Meaning of Genesis*).

THE IMAGE OF WOMEN IN MEDIEVAL LITERATURE. The philosophical, legal, and religious traditions born in antiquity formed the basis of the medieval intellectual synthesis wrought by trained thinkers, mostly clerics, writing in Latin and based largely in universities. The vernacular literary tradition that developed alongside the learned tradition also spoke about female nature and women's roles. Medieval stories, poems, and epics also portrayed women negatively—as lustful and deceitful—while praising good housekeepers and loyal wives as replicas of the Virgin Mary or the female saints and martyrs.

There is an exception in the movement of "courtly love" that evolved in southern France from the twelfth century. Courtly love was the erotic love between a nobleman and noblewoman, the latter usually superior in social rank. It was always adulterous. From the conventions of courtly love derive modern Western notions of romantic love. The tradition has had an impact disproportionate to its size, for it affected only a tiny elite, and very few women. The exaltation of the female lover probably does not reflect a higher evaluation of women or a step toward their sexual liberation. More likely it gives expression to the social and sexual tensions besetting the knightly class at a specific historical juncture.

The literary fashion of courtly love was on the wane by the thirteenth century, when the widely read *Romance of the Rose* was composed in French by two authors of significantly different dispositions. Guillaume de Lorris composed the initial four thousand verses about 1235, and Jean de Meun added about seventeen thousand verses—more than four times the original—about 1265.

The fragment composed by Guillaume de Lorris stands squarely in the tradition of courtly love. Here the poet, in a dream, is admitted into a walled garden where he finds a magic fountain in which a rosebush is reflected. He longs to pick one rose, but the thorns prevent his doing so, even as he is wounded by arrows from the god of love, whose commands he agrees to obey. The rest of this part of the poem recounts the poet's unsuccessful efforts to pluck the rose.

The longer part of the *Romance* by Jean de Meun also describes a dream. But here allegorical characters give long didactic speeches, providing a social satire on a variety of themes, some pertaining to women. Love is an anxious and tormented state, the poem explains: women are greedy and manipulative, marriage is miserable, beautiful women are lustful, ugly ones cease to please, and a chaste woman is as rare as a black swan.

Shortly after Jean de Meun completed *The Romance of the Rose*, Mathéolus penned his *Lamentations*, a long Latin diatribe against marriage translated into French about a century later. The *Lamentations* sum up medieval attitudes toward women and provoked the important response by Christine de Pizan in her *Book of the City of Ladies*.

In 1355, Giovanni Boccaccio wrote *Il Corbaccio*, another antifeminist manifesto, although ironically by an author whose other works pioneered new directions in Renaissance thought. The former husband of his lover appears to Boccaccio, condemning his unmoderated lust and detailing the defects of women. Boccaccio concedes at the end "how much men naturally surpass women in nobility" and is cured of his desires.[3]

---

3. Giovanni Boccaccio, *The Corbaccio, or The Labyrinth of Love*, trans. and ed. Anthony K. Cassell, rev. ed. (Binghamton, N.Y., 1993), 71.

WOMEN'S ROLES: THE FAMILY. The negative perceptions of women expressed in the intellectual tradition are also implicit in the actual roles that women played in European society. Assigned to subordinate positions in the household and the church, they were barred from significant participation in public life.

Medieval European households, like those in antiquity and in non-Western civilizations, were headed by males. It was the male serf (or peasant), feudal lord, town merchant, or citizen who was polled or taxed or succeeded to an inheritance or had any acknowledged public role, although his wife or widow could stand as a temporary surrogate. From about 1100, the position of property-holding males was further enhanced: inheritance was confined to the male, or agnate, line—with depressing consequences for women.

A wife never fully belonged to her husband's family, nor was she a daughter to her father's family. She left her father's house young to marry whomever her parents chose. Her dowry was managed by her husband, and at her death it normally passed to her children by him.

A married woman's life was occupied nearly constantly with cycles of pregnancy, childbearing, and lactation. Women bore children through all the years of their fertility, and many died in childbirth. They were also responsible for raising young children up to six or seven. In the propertied classes that responsibility was shared, since it was common for a wet nurse to take over breast-feeding and for servants to perform other chores.

Women trained their daughters in the household duties appropriate to their status, nearly always tasks associated with textiles: spinning, weaving, sewing, embroidering. Their sons were sent out of the house as apprentices or students, or their training was assumed by fathers in later childhood and adolescence. On the death of her husband, a woman's children became the responsibility of his family. She generally did not take "his" children with her to a new marriage or back to her father's house, except sometimes in the artisan classes.

Women also worked. Rural peasants performed farm chores, merchant wives often practiced their husbands' trades, the unmarried daughters of the urban poor worked as servants or prostitutes. All wives produced or embellished textiles and did the housekeeping, while wealthy ones managed servants. These labors were unpaid or poorly paid but often contributed substantially to family wealth.

WOMEN'S ROLES: THE CHURCH. Membership in a household, whether a father's or a husband's, meant for women a lifelong subordination to others. In western Europe, the Roman Catholic Church offered an alternative to the career of wife and mother. A woman could enter a convent, parallel in function to the monasteries for men that evolved in the early Christian centuries.

In the convent, a woman pledged herself to a celibate life, lived according to strict community rules, and worshiped daily. Often the convent offered training in Latin, allowing some women to become considerable scholars and authors as well as scribes, artists, and musicians. For women who chose the conventual life, the benefits could be enormous, but for numerous others placed in convents by paternal choice, the life could be restrictive and burdensome.

The conventual life declined as an alternative for women as the modern age approached. Reformed monastic institutions resisted responsibility for related female orders. The church increasingly restricted female institutional life by insisting on closer male supervision.

Women often sought other options. Some joined the communities of laywomen that sprang up spontaneously in the thirteenth century in the urban zones of western Europe, especially in Flanders and Italy. Some joined the heretical movements that flourished in late medieval Christendom, whose anticlerical and often antifamily positions particularly appealed to women. In these communities, some women were acclaimed as "holy women" or "saints," whereas others often were condemned as frauds or heretics.

In all, although the options offered to women by the church were sometimes less than satisfactory, they were sometimes richly rewarding. After 1520, the convent remained an option only in Roman Catholic territories. Protestantism engendered an ideal of marriage as a heroic endeavor and appeared to place husband and wife on a more equal footing. Sermons and treatises, however, still called for female subordination and obedience.

THE OTHER VOICE, 1300–1700

When the modern era opened, European culture was so firmly structured by a framework of negative attitudes toward women that to dismantle it was a monumental labor. The process began as part of a larger cultural movement that entailed the critical reexamination of ideas inherited from the ancient and medieval past. The humanists launched that critical reexamination.

THE HUMANIST FOUNDATION. Originating in Italy in the fourteenth century, humanism quickly became the dominant intellectual movement in

Europe. Spreading in the sixteenth century from Italy to the rest of Europe, it fueled the literary, scientific, and philosophical movements of the era and laid the basis for the eighteenth-century Enlightenment.

Humanists regarded the Scholastic philosophy of medieval universities as out of touch with the realities of urban life. They found in the rhetorical discourse of classical Rome a language adapted to civic life and public speech. They learned to read, speak, and write classical Latin and, eventually, classical Greek. They founded schools to teach others to do so, establishing the pattern for elementary and secondary education for the next three hundred years.

In the service of complex government bureaucracies, humanists employed their skills to write eloquent letters, deliver public orations, and formulate public policy. They developed new scripts for copying manuscripts and used the new printing press to disseminate texts, for which they created methods of critical editing.

Humanism was a movement led by males who accepted the evaluation of women in ancient texts and generally shared the misogynist perceptions of their culture. (Female humanists, as we will see, did not.) Yet humanism also opened the door to a reevaluation of the nature and capacity of women. By calling authors, texts, and ideas into question, it made possible the fundamental rereading of the whole intellectual tradition that was required in order to free women from cultural prejudice and social subordination.

A DIFFERENT CITY. The other voice first appeared when, after so many centuries, the accumulation of misogynist concepts evoked a response from a capable female defender: Christine de Pizan (1365–1431). Introducing her *Book of the City of Ladies* (1405), she described how she was affected by reading Mathéolus's *Lamentations:* "Just the sight of this book . . . made me wonder how it happened that so many different men . . . are so inclined to express both in speaking and in their treatises and writings so many wicked insults about women and their behavior."[4] These statements impelled her to detest herself "and the entire feminine sex, as though we were monstrosities in nature."[5]

The rest of *The Book of the City of Ladies* presents a justification of the female sex and a vision of an ideal community of women. A pioneer, she has received the message of female inferiority and rejected it. From the four-

---

4. Christine de Pizan, *The Book of the City of Ladies,* trans. Earl Jeffrey Richards, foreword by Marina Warner (New York, 1982), 1.1.1, pp. 3–4.

5. Ibid., 1.1.1–2, p. 5.

teenth to the seventeenth century, a huge body of literature accumulated that responded to the dominant tradition.

The result was a literary explosion consisting of works by both men and women, in Latin and in the vernaculars: works enumerating the achievements of notable women; works rebutting the main accusations made against women; works arguing for the equal education of men and women; works defining and redefining women's proper role in the family, at court, in public; works describing women's lives and experiences. Recent monographs and articles have begun to hint at the great range of this movement, involving probably several thousand titles. The protofeminism of these "other voices" constitutes a significant fraction of the literary product of the early modern era.

THE CATALOGS. About 1365, the same Boccaccio whose *Corbaccio* rehearses the usual charges against female nature wrote another work, *Concerning Famous Women*. A humanist treatise drawing on classical texts, it praised 106 notable women: ninety-eight of them from pagan Greek and Roman antiquity, one (Eve) from the Bible, and seven from the medieval religious and cultural tradition; his book helped make all readers aware of a sex normally condemned or forgotten. Boccaccio's outlook nevertheless was unfriendly to women, for it singled out for praise those women who possessed the traditional virtues of chastity, silence, and obedience. Women who were active in the public realm—for example, rulers and warriors—were depicted as usually being lascivious and as suffering terrible punishments for entering the masculine sphere. Women were his subject, but Boccaccio's standard remained male.

Christine de Pizan's *Book of the City of Ladies* contains a second catalog, one responding specifically to Boccaccio's. Whereas Boccaccio portrays female virtue as exceptional, she depicts it as universal. Many women in history were leaders, or remained chaste despite the lascivious approaches of men, or were visionaries and brave martyrs.

The work of Boccaccio inspired a series of catalogs of illustrious women of the biblical, classical, Christian, and local pasts, among them Filippo da Bergamo's *Of Illustrious Women*, Pierre de Brantôme's *Lives of Illustrious Women*, Pierre Le Moyne's *Gallerie of Heroic Women*, and Pietro Paolo de Ribera's *Immortal Triumphs and Heroic Enterprises of 845 Women*. Whatever their embedded prejudices, these works drove home to the public the possibility of female excellence.

THE DEBATE. At the same time, many questions remained: Could a woman be virtuous? Could she perform noteworthy deeds? Was she even, strictly speaking, of the same human species as men? These questions were debated over four centuries, in French, German, Italian, Spanish, and English, by authors male and female, among Catholics, Protestants, and Jews, in ponderous volumes and breezy pamphlets. The whole literary genre has been called the *querelle des femmes*, the "woman question."

The opening volley of this battle occurred in the first years of the fifteenth century, in a literary debate sparked by Christine de Pizan. She exchanged letters critical of Jean de Meun's contribution to *The Romance of the Rose* with two French royal secretaries, Jean de Montreuil and Gontier Col. When the matter became public, Jean Gerson, one of Europe's leading theologians, supported de Pizan's arguments against de Meun, for the moment silencing the opposition.

The debate resurfaced repeatedly over the next two hundred years. *The Triumph of Women* (1438) by Juan Rodríguez de la Camara (or Juan Rodríguez del Padron) struck a new note by presenting arguments for the superiority of women to men. *The Champion of Women* (1440–42) by Martin Le Franc addresses once again the negative views of women presented in *The Romance of the Rose* and offers counterevidence of female virtue and achievement.

A cameo of the debate on women is included in *The Courtier,* one of the most widely read books of the era, published by the Italian Baldassare Castiglione in 1528 and immediately translated into other European vernaculars. *The Courtier* depicts a series of evenings at the court of the duke of Urbino in which many men and some women of the highest social stratum amuse themselves by discussing a range of literary and social issues. The "woman question" is a pervasive theme throughout, and the third of its four books is devoted entirely to that issue.

In a verbal duel, Gasparo Pallavicino and Giuliano de' Medici present the main claims of the two traditions. Gasparo argues the innate inferiority of women and their inclination to vice. Only in bearing children do they profit the world. Giuliano counters that women share the same spiritual and mental capacities as men and may excel in wisdom and action. Men and women are of the same essence: just as no stone can be more perfectly a stone than another, so no human being can be more perfectly human than others, whether male or female. It was an astonishing assertion, boldly made to an audience as large as all Europe.

THE TREATISES. Humanism provided the materials for a positive counterconcept to the misogyny embedded in Scholastic philosophy and law and inherited from the Greek, Roman, and Christian pasts. A series of humanist treatises on marriage and family, on education and deportment, and on the nature of women helped construct these new perspectives.

The works by Francesco Barbaro and Leon Battista Alberti—*On Marriage* (1415) and *On the Family* (1434–37)—far from defending female equality, reasserted women's responsibility for rearing children and managing the housekeeping while being obedient, chaste, and silent. Nevertheless, they served the cause of reexamining the issue of women's nature by placing domestic issues at the center of scholarly concern and reopening the pertinent classical texts. In addition, Barbaro emphasized the companionate nature of marriage and the importance of a wife's spiritual and mental qualities for the well-being of the family.

These themes reappear in later humanist works on marriage and the education of women by Juan Luis Vives and Erasmus. Both were moderately sympathetic to the condition of women without reaching beyond the usual masculine prescriptions for female behavior.

An outlook more favorable to women characterizes the nearly unknown work *In Praise of Women* (ca. 1487) by the Italian humanist Bartolommeo Goggio. In addition to providing a catalog of illustrious women, Goggio argued that male and female are the same in essence, but that women (reworking the Adam and Eve narrative from quite a new angle) are actually superior. In the same vein, the Italian humanist Mario Equicola asserted the spiritual equality of men and women in *On Women* (1501). In 1525, Galeazzo Flavio Capra (or Capella) published his work *On the Excellence and Dignity of Women.* This humanist tradition of treatises defending the worthiness of women culminates in the work of Henricus Cornelius Agrippa *On the Nobility and Preeminence of the Female Sex.* No work by a male humanist more succinctly or explicitly presents the case for female dignity.

THE WITCH BOOKS. While humanists grappled with the issues pertaining to women and family, other learned men turned their attention to what they perceived as a very great problem: witches. Witch-hunting manuals, explorations of the witch phenomenon, and even defenses of witches are not at first glance pertinent to the tradition of the other voice. But they do relate in this way: most accused witches were women. The hostility aroused by supposed witch activity is comparable to the hostility aroused by women. The evil deeds the victims of the hunt were charged with were exaggerations of the vices to which, many believed, all women were prone.

The connection between the witch accusation and the hatred of women is explicit in the notorious witch-hunting manual *The Hammer of Witches* (1486) by two Dominican inquisitors, Heinrich Krämer and Jacob Sprenger. Here the inconstancy, deceitfulness, and lustfulness traditionally associated with women are depicted in exaggerated form as the core features of witch behavior. These traits inclined women to make a bargain with the devil—

sealed by sexual intercourse—by which they acquired unholy powers. Such bizarre claims, far from being rejected by rational men, were broadcast by intellectuals. The German Ulrich Molitur, the Frenchman Nicolas Rémy, and the Italian Stefano Guazzo all coolly informed the public of sinister orgies and midnight pacts with the devil. The celebrated French jurist, historian, and political philosopher Jean Bodin argued that because women were especially prone to diabolism, regular legal procedures could properly be suspended in order to try those accused of this "exceptional crime."

A few experts such as the physician Johann Weyer, a student of Agrippa's, raised their voices in protest. In 1563, he explained the witch phenomenon thus, without discarding belief in diabolism: the devil deluded foolish old women afflicted by melancholia, causing them to believe they had magical powers. Weyer's rational skepticism, which had good credibility in the community of the learned, worked to revise the conventional views of women and witchcraft.

WOMEN'S WORKS. To the many categories of works produced on the question of women's worth must be added nearly all works written by women. A woman writing was in herself a statement of women's claim to dignity.

Only a few women wrote anything before the dawn of the modern era, for three reasons. First, they rarely received the education that would enable them to write. Second, they were not admitted to the public roles—as administrator, bureaucrat, lawyer or notary, or university professor—in which they might gain knowledge of the kinds of things the literate public thought worth writing about. Third, the culture imposed silence on women, considering speaking out a form of unchastity. Given these conditions, it is remarkable that any women wrote. Those who did before the fourteenth century were almost always nuns or religious women whose isolation made their pronouncements more acceptable.

From the fourteenth century on, the volume of women's writings rose. Women continued to write devotional literature, although not always as cloistered nuns. They also wrote diaries, often intended as keepsakes for their children; books of advice to their sons and daughters; letters to family members and friends; and family memoirs, in a few cases elaborate enough to be considered histories.

A few women wrote works directly concerning the "woman question," and some of these, such as the humanists Isotta Nogarola, Cassandra Fedele, Laura Cereta, and Olympia Morata, were highly trained. A few were professional writers, living by the income of their pens; the very first among them was Christine de Pizan, noteworthy in this context as in so many others. In addition to *The Book of the City of Ladies* and her critiques of *The Romance of the Rose,* she wrote *The Treasure of the City of Ladies* (a guide to social decorum for women), an advice book for her son, much courtly verse, and a full-scale history of the reign of King Charles V of France.

WOMEN PATRONS. Women who did not themselves write but encouraged others to do so boosted the development of an alternative tradition. Highly placed women patrons supported authors, artists, musicians, poets, and learned men. Such patrons, drawn mostly from the Italian elites and the courts of northern Europe, figure disproportionately as the dedicatees of the important works of early feminism.

For a start, it might be noted that the catalogs of Boccaccio and Alvaro de Luna were dedicated to the Florentine noblewoman Andrea Acciaiuoli and to Doña María, first wife of King Juan II of Castile, while the French translation of Boccaccio's work was commissioned by Anne of Brittany, wife of King Charles VIII of France. The humanist treatises of Goggio, Equicola, Vives, and Agrippa were dedicated, respectively, to Eleanora of Aragon, wife of Ercole I d'Este, duke of Ferrara; to Margherita Cantelma of Mantua; to Catherine of Aragon, wife of King Henry VIII of England; and to Margaret, Duchess of Austria and regent of the Netherlands. As late as 1696, Mary Astell's *Serious Proposal to the Ladies, for the Advancement of Their True and Greatest Interest* was dedicated to Princess Anne of Denmark.

These authors presumed that their efforts would be welcome to female patrons, or they may have written at the bidding of those patrons. Silent themselves, perhaps even unresponsive, these loftily placed women helped shape the tradition of the other voice.

THE ISSUES. The literary forms and patterns in which the tradition of the other voice presented itself have now been sketched. It remains to highlight the major issues around which this tradition crystallizes. In brief, there are four problems to which our authors return again and again, in plays and catalogs, in verse and letters, in treatises and dialogues, in every language: the problem of chastity, the problem of power, the problem of speech, and the problem of knowledge. Of these the greatest, preconditioning the others, is the problem of chastity.

THE PROBLEM OF CHASTITY. In traditional European culture, as in those of antiquity and others around the globe, chastity was perceived as woman's quintessential virtue—in contrast to courage, or generosity, or leadership, or rationality, seen as virtues characteristic of men. Opponents of women charged them with insatiable lust. Women themselves and their defenders—without disputing the validity of the standard—responded that women were capable of chastity.

The requirement of chastity kept women at home, silenced them, isolated them, left them in ignorance. It was the source of all other impediments. Why was it so important to the society of men, of whom chastity was not required, and who more often than not considered it their right to violate the chastity of any woman they encountered?

Female chastity ensured the continuity of the male-headed household. If a man's wife was not chaste, he could not be sure of the legitimacy of his offspring. If they were not his and they acquired his property, it was not his household, but some other man's, that had endured. If his daughter was not chaste, she could not be transferred to another man's household as his wife, and he was dishonored.

The whole system of the integrity of the household and the transmission of property was bound up in female chastity. Such a requirement pertained only to property-owning classes, of course. Poor women could not expect to maintain their chastity, least of all if they were in contact with high-status men to whom all women but those of their own household were prey.

In Catholic Europe, the requirement of chastity was further buttressed by moral and religious imperatives. Original sin was inextricably linked with the sexual act. Virginity was seen as heroic virtue, far more impressive than, say, the avoidance of idleness or greed. Monasticism, the cultural institution that dominated medieval Europe for centuries, was grounded in the renunciation of the flesh. The Catholic reform of the eleventh century imposed a similar standard on all the clergy and a heightened awareness of sexual requirements on all the laity. Although men were asked to be chaste, female unchastity was much worse: it led to the devil, as Eve had led mankind to sin.

To such requirements, women and their defenders protested their innocence. Furthermore, following the example of holy women who had escaped the requirements of family and sought the religious life, some women began to conceive of female communities as alternatives both to family and to the cloister. Christine de Pizan's city of ladies was such a community. Moderata Fonte and Mary Astell envisioned others. The luxurious salons of the French *précieuses* of the seventeenth century, or the comfortable English drawing rooms of the next, may have been born of the same impulse. Here women not only might escape, if briefly, the subordinate position that life in the family entailed but might also make claims to power, exercise their capacity for speech, and display their knowledge.

THE PROBLEM OF POWER. Women were excluded from power: the whole cultural tradition insisted on it. Only men were citizens, only men bore arms, only men could be chiefs or lords or kings. There were exceptions that did not disprove the rule, when wives or widows or mothers took the place of men, awaiting their return or the maturation of a male heir. A woman who attempted to rule in her own right was perceived as an anomaly, a monster, at once a deformed woman and an insufficient male, sexually confused and consequently unsafe.

The association of such images with women who held or sought power explains some otherwise odd features of early modern culture. Queen Elizabeth I of England, one of the few women to hold full regal authority in European history, played with such male/female images—positive ones, of course—in representing herself to her subjects. She was a prince, and manly, even though she was female. She was also (she claimed) virginal, a condition absolutely essential if she was to avoid the attacks of her opponents. Catherine de' Medici, who ruled France as widow and regent for her sons, also adopted such imagery in defining her position. She chose as one symbol the figure of Artemisia, an androgynous ancient warrior-heroine who combined a female persona with masculine powers.

Power in a woman, without such sexual imagery, seems to have been indigestible by the culture. A rare note was struck by the Englishman Sir Thomas Elyot in his *Defence of Good Women* (1540), justifying both women's participation in civic life and their prowess in arms. The old tune was sung by the Scots reformer John Knox in his *First Blast of the Trumpet against the Monstrous Regiment of Women* (1558); for him rule by women, defects in nature, was a hideous contradiction in terms.

The confused sexuality of the imagery of female potency was not reserved for rulers. Any woman who excelled was likely to be called an Amazon, recalling the self-mutilated warrior women of antiquity who repudiated all men, gave up their sons, and raised only their daughters. She was often said to have "exceeded her sex" or to have possessed "masculine virtue"—as the very fact of conspicuous excellence conferred masculinity even on the female subject. The catalogs of notable women often showed those female heroes dressed in armor, armed to the teeth, like men. Amazonian heroines romp through the epics of the age—Ariosto's *Orlando Furioso* (1532) and Spenser's *Faerie Queene* (1590–1609). Excellence in a woman was perceived as a claim for power, and power was reserved for the masculine realm. A woman who possessed either one was masculinized and lost title to her own female identity.

THE PROBLEM OF SPEECH. Just as power had a sexual dimension when it was claimed by women, so did speech. A good woman spoke little. Excessive speech was an indication of unchastity. By speech, women seduced men. Eve had lured Adam into sin by her speech. Accused witches were commonly accused of having spoken abusively, or irrationally, or simply too much. As enlightened a figure as Francesco Barbaro insisted on silence in a woman, which he linked to her perfect unanimity with her husband's will and her unblemished virtue (her chastity). Another Italian humanist, Leonardo Bruni, in advising a noblewoman on her studies, barred her not from speech but from public speaking. That was reserved for men.

Related to the problem of speech was that of costume—another, if silent, form of self-expression. Assigned the task of pleasing men as their primary occupation, elite women often tended toward elaborate costume, hairdressing, and the use of cosmetics. Clergy and secular moralists alike condemned these practices. The appropriate function of costume and adornment was to announce the status of a woman's husband or father. Any further indulgence in adornment was akin to unchastity.

THE PROBLEM OF KNOWLEDGE. When the Italian noblewoman Isotta Nogarola had begun to attain a reputation as a humanist, she was accused of incest—a telling instance of the association of learning in women with unchastity. That chilling association inclined any woman who was educated to deny that she was or to make exaggerated claims of heroic chastity.

If educated women were pursued with suspicions of sexual misconduct, women seeking an education faced an even more daunting obstacle: the assumption that women were by nature incapable of learning, that reasoning was a particularly masculine ability. Just as they proclaimed their chastity, women and their defenders insisted on their capacity for learning. The major work by a male writer on female education—that by Juan Luis Vives, *On the Education of a Christian Woman* (1523)—granted female capacity for intellection but still argued that a woman's whole education was to be shaped around the requirement of chastity and a future within the household. Female writers of the following generations—Marie de Gournay in France, Anna Maria van Schurman in Holland, and Mary Astell in England—began to envision other possibilities.

The pioneers of female education were the Italian women humanists who managed to attain a literacy in Latin and a knowledge of classical and Christian literature equivalent to that of prominent men. Their works implicitly and explicitly raise questions about women's social roles, defining problems that beset women attempting to break out of the cultural limits that had bound them. Like Christine de Pizan, who achieved an advanced education through her father's tutoring and her own devices, their bold questioning makes clear the importance of training. Only when women were educated to the same standard as male leaders would they be able to raise that other voice and insist on their dignity as human beings morally, intellectually, and legally equal to men.

THE OTHER VOICE. The other voice, a voice of protest, was mostly female, but it was also male. It spoke in the vernaculars and in Latin, in treatises and dialogues, in plays and poetry, in letters and diaries, and in pamphlets. It battered at the wall of prejudice that encircled women and raised a banner announcing its claims. The female was equal (or even superior) to the male in essential nature—moral, spiritual, and intellectual. Women were capable of higher education, of holding positions of power and influence in the public realm, and of speaking and writing persuasively. The last bastion of masculine supremacy, centered on the notions of a woman's primary domestic responsibility and the requirement of female chastity, was not as yet assaulted—although visions of productive female communities as alternatives to the family indicated an awareness of the problem.

During the period 1300–1700, the other voice remained only a voice, and one only dimly heard. It did not result—yet—in an alteration of social patterns. Indeed, to this day they have not entirely been altered. Yet the call for justice issued as long as six centuries ago by those writing in the tradition of the other voice must be recognized as the source and origin of the mature feminist tradition and of the realignment of social institutions accomplished in the modern age.

ॐ

We thank the volume editors in this series, who responded with many suggestions to an earlier draft of this introduction, making it a collaborative enterprise. Many of their suggestions and criticisms have resulted in revisions of this introduction, although we remain responsible for the final product.

PROJECTED TITLES IN THE SERIES

Ana de San Bartolomé, *Autobiography and Other Writings*, edited and translated by Darcy Donahue

Catharina Regina von Greiffenberg, *Meditations on the Life of Christ*, edited by Lynne Tatlock

Emilie du Châtelet, *Selected Writings of an Enlightenment Philosophe*, edited by Judith Zinsser, translated by Isabelle Bour

Christine de Pizan, *Debate over the "Romance of the Rose,"* edited and translated by David F. Hult

Christine de Pizan, *Early Defense of Women Poems*, edited and translated by Thelma Fenster

Christine de Pizan, *Life of Charles V*, edited and translated by Nadia Margolis

Christine de Pizan, *The Long Road of Learning*, edited and translated by Andrea Tarnowski

Vittoria Colonna, Chiara Matraini, and Lucrezia Marinella, *Who is Mary? Three Early Modern Women on the Idea of the Virgin Mary*, edited and translated by Susan Haskins

Pernette du Guillet, *Complete Poems*, edited with an introduction by Karen James, translated by Marta Finch Koslowsky

Sister Margaret of the Mother of God, *Autobiography*, edited with an introduction by Cordula van Wyhe, translated by Paul Arblaster and Susan Smith

Marguerite de Navarre, *Selected Writings*, edited and translated by Rouben Cholakian and Mary Skemp

Lucrezia Marinella, *Enrico, or Byzantium Conquered*, edited and translated by Maria Galli Stampino

Valeria Miani, *Celinda: A Tragedy*, edited with an introduction by Valeria Finucci, translated by Julia Kisacky

Cecilia del Nacimiento, *Autobiography and Poetry*, edited with an introduction by Sandra Sider, translated by Kevin Donnelly and Sandra Sider

Sister Giustina Niccolini, *Chronicle of Le Murate*, edited and translated by Saundra Weddle

Antonia Tanini Pulci, *Saints' Lives and Biblical Stories for the State (1483–1492)*, edited by Elissa Weaver, translated by James Cook (a revised edition of *Florentine Drama for Convent and Festival*, published in the series in 1997)

Madeleine de Scudéry and Madame de Villedieu, *Amorous Letters and The Letter Case*, edited and translated by Sharon Nell and Aurora Wolfgang

Gaspara Stampa, *Complete Poems*, edited and translated by Jane Tylus

Sara Copio Sullam, *Jewish Poet and Intellectual in Early Seventeenth-Century Venice*, edited and translated by Don Harrán

Maria Vela y Cueto, *Autobiography*, edited with an introduction by Susan Laningham, translated by Jane Tar

Women Religious in Late Medieval and Early Modern Italy, edited and translated by Lance Lazar

Maria de Zayas y Sotomayor, *Exemplary Tales of Love and Tales of Undeceiving*, edited and translated by Margaret R. Greer and Elizabeth Rhodes

THE MEMOIRS OF HORTENSE
AND MARIE MANCINI

THE OTHER VOICE

Like all members of French courtly society, Marie and Hortense Mancini lived in a world where keeping track from minute to minute of the dips and swells in one's own and in others' social status came as naturally as breathing. For them, the calculus was particularly complicated, though, since they were not born into French society, and their standing there was thus less fixed; rather, it was entirely dependent on the power and wealth of their uncle, Cardinal Mazarin, and on the marriage alliances he managed to forge between their family and the leading families of France. Conversely, the continuance of the cardinal's power and wealth depended at least in part on the status he was able to establish for his nieces through strategic marriages.

Because of their uncle's prominence, the Mancinis lived on intimate terms with Louis XIV and those closest to him; Marie became famous as the king's first great love and was recognized as a *précieuse* with considerable wit and a passable knowledge of literature; and Hortense was acclaimed as the court's great beauty, whose charm opened nearly as many doors for her as her uncle's influence. The marriages that Mazarin negotiated for these two nieces were brilliant—Hortense's for the vast fortune with which the cardinal endowed it, and Marie's for the exalted birth and wealth of her Roman husband—but from another point of view both were disappointing compromises. After the glorious time when both she and Louis had believed that Marie could one day be his queen, her Italian marriage was perceived by her and by others as a form of exile; and when Mazarin resorted in the last weeks of his life to the unspectacular match he made for Hortense, the court wondered and sneered, since it was well known that she had come close to marriages with sovereigns such as Charles II of England

and Charles-Emmanuel II of Savoy. The court continued to watch and comment as Hortense began legal proceedings against her husband, and then she caused a sensation when she made a clandestine run to Italy disguised as a man; but when both sisters fled together from Rome to France, the scandal was tremendous, and observers like Madame de Sévigné eventually began using their names as generic terms for women who ran away from their husbands.[1]

Neither Hortense nor Marie expressed philosophical objections to the institution of marriage in her memoir, and neither of them conceived herself to be presenting a tract for the autonomy of married women in general when she published the account of her own quest for independence from her husband. Indeed, the exquisite privilege in which they were raised, to which both of them repeatedly call attention in their memoirs, clearly conditioned their perspectives on their situations. They could hope that the normal rules of marriage might be suspended for them, precisely because they could appeal directly to the king of France as an old and intimate friend, and later, to the sovereigns of Savoy, of Spain, and of England.

The exceptionality of their positions may help to explain why they dared to take the unprecedented step of publishing their memoirs—Hortense's was the first piece of life-writing published by a French woman under her own name and during her lifetime—and it certainly also helps to account for the strong interest in their books by the reading public. Both women undertook the writing of their life stories as maneuvers in their respective struggles to win the right to live independently, and for each, the ability to determine her own destiny depended at least in some measure on her defining her own public image. Exceptional though they may be, the life stories of Hortense and Marie Mancini represent an important phase in the evolution of the "other voice" in seventeenth-century France and Europe. In their content, they recount the efforts by two prominent women to assert legal claims and negotiate for the right of self-determination; and in the very act of committing their accounts to print, the authors claim and exercise the right to define their own public image.

---

1. In a letter to her daughter, Madame de Sévigné said, about the arrival in Paris of the grand duchess of Tuscany (daughter of Louis XIII's brother Gaston), who had left her husband to come and live in a convent in France, "We are expecting her here like a sort of Colonna or Mazarin, because of the folly of having left her husband after fifteen years of marriage." Madame de Sévigné to Madame de Grignan, Paris, July 3, 1675, in *Correspondance*, ed. Roger Duchêne, 3 vols. (Paris: Gallimard, 1972–78), 1: 748. Unless otherwise noted, all translations are my own.

BIOGRAPHY

Marie Mancini lived from 1639 to 1715—almost exactly the dates of Louis XIV, with whom she had a famous love affair before his marriage—and Hortense, from 1646 to 1699. They were two of the eight children of Cardinal Mazarin's younger sister Hieronyma (or Geronima or Girolama) Mazzarini and a Roman nobleman named Lorenzo Mancini. Another of the cardinal's sisters also had two daughters, so in all, he had ten nieces and nephews, whom he brought from their native Rome to the French court in three "shipments." Marie and Hortense came in the second group, in the spring of 1653. Mazarin had not asked for Hortense to be brought, since she was only six years old at the time, but (according to Marie's memoir) the girls' mother favored Hortense because she was extremely beautiful, and she brought her along anyway; the cardinal approved of her decision when he saw Hortense, who eventually became his favorite niece and his choice as principal heiress for his vast fortune.

Marie tells the early part of her life in France as a Cinderella story, in which her wicked mother and "stepfather" (the cardinal) put her away in convents or kept her in her mother's apartment while her sisters Hortense and Olympe (who later became the influential comtesse de Soissons) were allowed to partake of all the pleasures of court life. Then, as Marie attended her dying mother in late 1656, she was "discovered" by the young king, who made daily visits to her mother's bedside. He was struck by her lively wit; love blossomed and so did Marie herself; and for two years she lived a life of idyllic romance. Hortense's memoir also features a sort of fairy-tale beginning, filled with anecdotes aimed at emphasizing the close terms on which they all interacted with the king, the queen mother, and the other greats of the court; these vignettes culminate in a scene where Hortense, having received a cabinet filled with gold coins and rich baubles after her marriage contract was signed, amuses herself with her brother and sisters by throwing handfuls of coins into the courtyard of the Palais Mazarin in Paris, just for the fun of watching the valets scramble after them (36).

However, marriage marked the end of the fairy-tale period and the entry into real life for both sisters. First of all, it was Louis XIV's marriage to the infanta Marie-Thérèse of Spain in 1660 that crushed Marie's dream of actually reigning as his queen. After a tumultuous and wrenching end to their affair which took nearly two years to play itself out, Marie gave in to the reality of her situation and accepted a marriage with Lorenzo Onofrio Colonna, who was probably the preeminent nobleman of Rome. They were married by proxy in the king's chapel of the Louvre in April 1661, six weeks after Hortense's marriage to Armand-Charles de La Porte de La Meilleraye, the fairly unprepossessing son of a respected French military leader who was also cousin to Louis XIII's minister Cardinal Richelieu. In the interval between the two sisters' weddings, Cardinal Mazarin died, leaving the lion's share of his wealth to Hortense and her new husband, whom he had selected for her and who took on the title of Duc Mazarin. Marie made the journey to Italy, where she met her husband and adjusted as best she could to the culture and mores of Rome; by her own and others' accounts, she became quite attached to Lorenzo, and they lived happily together until after the birth of their third son in 1665, at which time she determined to have no more children and demanded a *separazione di letto* from her husband. Their relations soured from that point on. Hortense, meanwhile, was being kept away from court and dragged all over France by her intensely jealous and fanatically religious husband, who obliged her to come with him as he traveled from one to another of the many governorships he had inherited from Cardinal Mazarin. She too bore several children—three daughters and then a son—during this time, although she makes no mention of them in her memoir except to note that she was often made to travel while pregnant, and that she was finally pushed to lodge a public complaint against her husband when it became clear to her that he was dissipating the inheritance that was to go to her son.

In her memoir, Hortense recounts her various attempts to leave her husband and to obtain a formal separation through the *parlement* of Paris or from the king, beginning some time after her son's birth in 1666. By 1668, matters had come to such a pass that Hortense fled Paris in the dark of night, her maid and she dressed in men's clothing; they traveled to Italy and were received by Marie and her husband. There the sisters were joined by their brother Philippe, duc de Nevers, with whom they amused themselves in grand style, hosting elaborate balls and constantly planning their next journey to Venice for the carnival season. This only added to the displeasure of certain Roman men, who thought Lorenzo Colonna was setting a bad example by allowing his wife the kind of freedom of movement and association that she had enjoyed in France but was not customary in Italy. Hortense remarks in her memoir that "the poor opinion which he [Lorenzo], like all Italians, held of the freedom that women have in France" was changed when he found Marie to be a virgin at their marriage; Hortense concludes that "he desired that she enjoy the same freedom in Rome, since she knew how to make such good use of it" (38). Philippe and Hortense made a journey back to Paris in 1670–71—he to be married to the niece of the king's favorite

Madame de Montespan, and she to pursue her efforts toward legal separation and to obtain a pension from her husband which would allow her to live comfortably in Italy. She obtained neither, but she did get the king's blessing and a promise of a small (quite insufficient for her style of life) pension from the royal coffers. She returned to Rome, where relations between Marie and her husband were ever more strained; by the spring of 1672, the two sisters had determined to flee together and to return to France in the hope of winning Louis XIV's protection and being allowed to live independently from their husbands.

They had reason to hope that this might be possible because of the king's promises of enduring support for Marie. Indeed, when he was informed that Marie believed her husband might be trying to poison her (a charge which she was politic enough to leave out of her memoirs), he sent word that if she should feel it necessary to flee, she would find a letter of safe conduct for her and her suite at their arrival in Marseille. Thus, she expected to be welcomed back to court, or at least allowed to live quietly in Paris, and she was shocked when first the queen and then the king himself forbade her to come near the capital. From that time on, both Marie and Hortense, each following her own path, sought to subsist independently, cachet-rich but cash-poor.

Hortense accepted the hospitality of one former suitor, the duke of Savoy, and settled in the château of Chambéry from 1672 until the duke's sudden death in 1675; little did she know, as she ended her memoir on a note of peace and contentment, that within months she would be forced to go in search of a new haven. She moved to England at the invitation of Charles II, who also had once aspired to marry her. There, at her house next to Saint James's Palace, she began to receive all the most illustrious people in literature, philosophy, and politics; her faithful friend from then until her death was another French expatriate, the writer and courtier Saint-Evremond, who was thirty years her senior. Successive French ambassadors expressed their concern to Louis XIV that Hortense would eventually supplant Louise de Kéroualle, the royal mistress who had been put in place to represent French interests with Charles II; they urged Louis to grant Hortense what she required in order to live separately from her husband in France. Meanwhile, the Duc Mazarin continued his efforts to force her back to him; extraordinarily litigious throughout his life—he was party to hundreds of lawsuits—he made one final legal sally against his wife in 1689, following the Glorious Revolution of 1688, which caused the Catholic monarch James II and his consort Mary of Modena, who was Hortense's cousin, to flee to France. The Duc Mazarin asked the court to deprive Hortense of her dowry and order her either to return unconditionally to him or to be confined to a convent. The court ruled in his favor and ordered Hortense to return to France, but her lawyer argued that English law prevented her from leaving the country until her very considerable debts had been paid; the Duc Mazarin refused to recognize those debts, saying that a wife had no legal authority to contract them without her husband's permission, and so matters were at an impasse. In the end, Hortense remained in England until her death in 1699, after which her husband finally managed to regain possession of her, so to speak: he settled her debts in England and had her remains shipped to him in France. For nearly a year, he traveled back and forth across France to his various lands, bringing his wife in her coffin along with him. Finally, he left her remains at the village church of Notre Dame de Liesse, near one of his châteaux in Picardy. He eventually had her entombed next to Cardinal Mazarin at the Collège des Quatre Nations, which today houses the Institut de France, on the left bank of the Seine in Paris; and after the duke's own death in 1713, according to his wishes, he was laid next to her. (Their bones were thrown into the Seine by revolutionaries in 1793.)

Marie never returned to live with her husband either, but she was less successful than Hortense in creating a bubble of freedom around herself. Her memoirs recount her progress through southern France, Savoy, northern Italy, Switzerland, Germany, Flanders, and finally Spain. As she explains in her account, and as her extant letters demonstrate, she remained in regular contact with her husband, informing him of her movements, justifying herself to him, calling for items to be sent to her from Italy, requesting permission to make changes to her living arrangements, asking that he allow one of their sons to travel to her, or offering strategic advice on the marriages to be sought for their sons. The tone of her letters was often petulant and reproachful, but it could also be cordial and almost tender at times. It was an intricate chess match that they played, each of them declaring one set of motivations, intentions, and actions, while often harboring and pursuing another. Lorenzo had his wife constantly followed and observed by his agents, who sent him regular reports; and he relied on his great influence to back his appeals to the French king, as well as to the various sovereigns and governors through whose lands Marie traveled, to have her confined to convents or fortresses and to limit her freedom of movement as much as possible.

Marie's memoir and her letters together offer an intriguing window on her calculations (or miscalculations) as she tried to navigate the turbulent waters of patronage and influence among the mighty of France and of Europe. Through a long series of rash and, from the memoir reader's point of view, predictably disastrous choices, she seemed to find herself ever less free, although she struggled mightily for the opposite result. Marie's biographer Claude Dulong expresses some frustration at what she sees as Marie's lamentable lack of judgment: "The historian sometimes feels disheartened when facing heroes and heroines whose character and destiny [s]he, unlike the novelist, cannot alter. Every time Marie opens her mouth, you want to shout, 'Watch out!' before she says a word. But alas! . . ."[2] And yet, as Patricia Cholakian observes, the main reason why we perceive Marie's actions as hopelessly rash or ill-advised is that she is unflinching in the frankness of her account; she is incisive and forthright in her self-description.[3] She owns up to the character traits that seem to contribute to her confounding: she is unwilling to compromise and loath to abandon a plan once she has formulated it; she bridles at opposition or thwarting; she largely ignores reprimands; she is less easygoing, less optimistic, and less hardy than Hortense—also less beautiful, as everyone including Marie herself regularly remarks; she insists on the recognition of her high status; and of course, she is incapable of not speaking the truth as she sees it.

In early 1677, when Marie was composing *La Vérité dans son jour*, Don Juan of Austria marched on Madrid and took over the government as chief minister to his half-brother, Charles II, forcing out the minister Valenzuela and the queen mother whose favorite the latter was. Marie refers to these events in the final pages of her memoir. Don Juan soon named Lorenzo Colonna to replace him as viceroy of Aragon, and in July 1678 Colonna arrived in Spain with his three sons to take up his post in Saragossa and also to begin marriage negotiations for the eldest son, Filippo, with the daughter of a Spanish dignitary, the duke of Medinaceli, who would later become chief minister after the death of Don Juan in September 1679. Lorenzo was low on liquid assets, and he needed capital to bring to the table for the marriage talks; he wanted to use some of Marie's dowry, but Roman law and their marriage contract obliged him to obtain her authorization.[4] Marie agreed to his request for the dowry, but she declined to go and live with him in Saragossa; nevertheless, she did live under the same roof with him in Madrid—although in separate apartments—for several months in 1680, as preparations were being made for Filippo's wedding. Apparently, the duke

---

2. Claude Dulong, *Marie Mancini. La première passion de Louis XIV* (Paris: Perrin, 1993, 2002), 222.

3. Patricia Francis Cholakian, *Women and the Politics of Self-Representation in Seventeenth-Century France* (Newark: University of Delaware Press, 2000), 119–21.

4. Dulong, *Marie Mancini*, 278.

of Medinaceli was not pleased to be linked by this marriage to as scandalous a woman as Marie, no matter how wealthy she was or how high her status: she had repeatedly caused a sensation by running away from the convent where she lived, and it seems to have been an open secret that she had taken a lover right under the nose of her husband.[5] In October 1680, soldiers broke into Marie's room in the house she had been sharing with her husband (who had since returned to Saragossa) and took her to be imprisoned in the *alcazar* of Segovia; though it is not clear by whose order this was done, it could not have happened without the consent of the chief minister. In any case, Marie remained in that prison until February 1681, when she agreed to become a nun, a course of action which seemed unbelievable to all who knew her and which indicated to them her state of desperation. Thus, when Filippo was married in April 1681, his mother was not present.

Marie stayed as a novice in the Hieronymite convent of the Conception, without ever taking her vows, until 1686, when the pope became aware of the situation and forced her to leave. She then moved to a very posh religious establishment, where she was finally granted the freedom to go out twice a week. She continued steadfastly to refuse Lorenzo's requests that she return to Rome; his health began to fail, and he died in April 1689. After his death, her sons pressed her to return to Rome, and in the fall of 1691, she did. However, she was unhappy there and left again after only a few months. She returned to Spain, where she stayed for the next ten years, spending part of each year in Barcelona and the rest in Madrid. She was intensely concerned with furthering the political and protocolary interests of her sons, and she appears to have been in the service of Queen Mariana of Neuburg, probably for that reason. Unfortunately for Marie, she remained loyal to the queen even after the death of the king, Charles II, and soon after the arrival in 1701 of his Bourbon successor, the grandson of Louis XIV, she was discreetly asked to leave Spain.

Marie had been allowed to pass through southern France in 1691–92, and in 1702–3 she stayed eighteen months in Lyon, Nevers, and especially Avignon. She made two more trips to France, in 1705 and 1706, and during

---

5. The wife of the French ambassador in Madrid, Madame de Villars, wrote to her friend Madame de Coulanges that she had even met the man in question: "She has a lover here; she tries to get me to agree that he is pleasing, that there is something clever and roguish about his eyes. He is horrible; but that is not what ought to curb her penchant for him or put her off, compared to another small thing that's hardly worth mentioning, namely, that this lover does not care a bit for her, from what she has told me. And yet she is quite pleased with him that way; because if he returned her feelings in the slightest, it would cause an even greater scandal." Madrid, August 15, 1680, in *Lettres de Madame de Villars à Madame de Coulanges (1679–1681)*, ed. Alfred de Courtois (Paris: Plon, 1868), 139.

the 1705 trip she even stayed near Paris, in Passy; reportedly, Louis XIV invited her to visit Versailles, but she declined. Claude Dulong lays out the details that can be established regarding Marie's involvement in a tale of intrigue surrounding a defrocked young Capuchin monk called Father Florent and asserts that Marie's various stays in France during this period must certainly have been connected to this.[6] Be that as it may, Marie spent the remaining years of her life traveling from one to another of the Colonna estates in Italy and occupying herself with the interests of the family. She died in May 1715—just four months before Louis XIV's death—in Pisa, where she had come in order to amend her will in the wake of her eldest son's death. She famously requested the simple inscription on her tombstone, which can still be viewed at the church of the Holy Sepulcher in Pisa: "Maria Mancinia Columna, Pulvis et cinis" (Marie Mancini Colonna, Dust and ashes).

EDITIONS OF THE MEMOIRS OF HORTENSE AND OF MARIE MANCINI

Hortense was the first of the two sisters to publish an account of her life. In 1675, a book called *Mémoires D.M.L.D.M.*—some copies bore the full title, *Mémoires de Madame la Duchesse de Mazarin*—appeared under the imprint of "Pierre du Marteau, Cologne," which was a fictitious imprint used for works at risk of being censored. The book sold well, and translations into English (1676) and Italian (1678) followed quickly. At the time of her memoirs' first publication in 1675, Hortense had been living in the château of Chambéry for nearly three years under the protection of the duke of Savoy, who maintained his own residence in Turin. In Chambéry, she became acquainted with the writer and historian César Vichard, abbé de Saint-Réal, who was a native of that city, and critics have often asserted that he had either a small or a large part in the composition of Hortense's memoirs. Indeed, eighteenth-century editions of the works of Saint-Réal regularly included the text. Since no autograph manuscript of the memoirs exists, or any evidence from letters concerning the precise authorship of the work, we cannot know with certainty what, if anything, Saint-Réal had to do with the writing of Hortense's life story. However, it is entirely reasonable to expect that he may have acted as secretary and editor for her in the same way that educated young men commonly served nobles, whose formal education was often patchy at best. Beyond that, I am generally persuaded by the critics

6. Dulong, *Marie Mancini*, 351–58.

who note the very different (and livelier) style of these memoirs from that of other works whose attribution to Saint-Réal is certain. The voice that comes through seems to be much more Hortense's than Saint-Réal's, although the question of their respective roles in the composition is certainly an open one, and it highlights the complexity of discussing women's life-writing at this period.

The story of Marie's text is much more convoluted. After the success of *Mémoires D.M.L.D.M.* in 1675, some enterprising editor brought out in the following year, also under the imprint of Pierre du Marteau, the similarly titled *Mémoires de M.L.P.M.M. Colonne, G. Connétable du Royaume de Naples* (meaning *Mémoires de Madame la Princesse Marie Mancini Colonne, Grande Connétable du Royaume de Naples*). This work lifted sentences directly out of Hortense's memoir and seemed calculated to capitalize on the public's appetite for behind-the-scenes accounts of the lives of these two famously scandalous women. It appeared in Italian translation in 1678, also from Pierre du Marteau—or rather "Pietro del Martello"; Hortense's memoir came out in Italian in the same year and under the same imprint.

Marie was incensed when she learned of *Mémoires de M.L.P.M.M. Colonne*. In response, she wrote and had published in Madrid the text presented in English translation in the present volume: *La Vérité dans son jour, ou les véritables mémoires de M. Manchini, Connétable Colonne*, which appeared in 1677. In the opening paragraph of this work, Marie expresses outrage over the spurious memoirs which were circulating under her name, and she contends that their publication forced her to write her own account of her life in order to set the public record straight. At several points in her text, she refers scornfully to details presented in *Mémoires de M.L.P.M.M. Colonne* and counters them, either with ridicule or with contrary evidence. Whereas *La Vérité dans son jour* recounts Marie's whole life up until the time of its publication, including her childhood and youth, and also the years of travel between her flight from Rome and her writing of the memoirs in Madrid, *Mémoires de M.L.P.M.M. Colonne* covers only her time in Rome in any depth. However, it does include many anecdotes and details which suggest that its author had intimate knowledge of the Colonna household. It has been variously speculated that its contents might have come from letters written by Marie to a friend which could have fallen into other hands, or that its publication was arranged by Paolo Vincenzo Spínola y Doria, marquis de los Balbases, a brother-in-law of Marie's husband who harbored a longstanding resentment toward her. In any case, it is clear that Marie was not the author of *Mémoires de M.L.P.M.M. Colonne* and that she objected vehemently to the image of her that those memoirs projected, which was one of frivolity, loose morality, and frequent escapades in the company of various men, such as Cardinal Flavio Chigi (who was indeed her close friend and neighbor in Rome). On the other hand, it is equally clear that Marie was the author of *La Vérité dans son jour*. Two extant letters written by her to her husband Lorenzo in March and April of 1677 report her anger over the pseudo-memoir, her decision to write her own true account of her life, and the publication of that account.[7] A letter to Lorenzo from his half-brother, Fernando Colonna, dated August 9, 1677, from Madrid also confirms that the complete Spanish translation of the work was sent to Lorenzo (he did not read French well), in two parts, in July and August. Finally, on September 15, 1677, Marie wrote to her husband, "I am pleased that the book has been to your liking. It is much better in Spanish."[8]

There was indeed a Spanish version of Marie's memoir published in Saragossa in 1677, under the title *La Verdad en su luz, o las verdaderas memorias de Madama Maria Manchini, Condestablesa Colona*. As Marie's comment to Lorenzo suggests, it went beyond merely translating the French version—it included certain emendations to the text itself. Clearly, she knew of this publication, and she approved. It is less clear to what extent she was involved with, or even aware of, a second French version of her text, which was prepared by a writer named Sébastien Bremond and appeared in 1678 as *Apologie, ou les Véritables mémoires de Mme Marie Mancini, connétable de Colonna, écrits par elle-même*.[9] This version followed the content of *La Vérité dans son jour* very closely, but Bremond thoroughly rewrote it, so that the narrative voice of the original was substantially altered. There is no indication in Marie's extant letters that she knew Bremond, that she requested his help in editing her work, or that she even knew he was working on it. He was living in England at the time *La Vérité dans son jour* appeared, and he may possibly have become aware of it because of Hortense's presence there; he moved to the Netherlands soon after, and it was the printer Jean van Gelder in Leiden who produced the 1678 edition of *Apologie*.[10] In 1679, J. Magnes and R. Bentley in London

7. Patricia Francis Cholakian and Elizabeth C. Goldsmith, eds., introduction, in Marie Mancini, *La Vérité dans son jour* (Delmar, NY: Scholars' Facsimiles and Reprints, 1998), 10–11.

8. Cholakian and Goldsmith quote from unpublished letters housed in Subiaco, Italy, at the Benedictine monastery of Santa Scolastica. The translation into English is theirs; the original letters were in Spanish.

9. This writer has at times been confused with another, Gabriel de Brémond, or has erroneously been called Saint-Brémont, but Edwin Paul Grobe has demonstrated that the man responsible for *Apologie* was indeed Sébastien Bremond. See "Sébastien Bremond: His Life and His Works" (Ph.D. diss., Indiana University, 1954), 1–6; and his article, "Gabriel and Sébastien Bremond," *Romance Notes* 4, no. 2 (1963): 132–35.

10. Cholakian and Goldsmith, introduction 11–12.

brought out an English version of Bremond's text, with the title *The Apology: or, The Genuine Memoires of Madam Maria Manchini, Constabless of Colonna, eldest Sister to the Duchess of Mazarin.*[11]

From 1677 until 1998, when Patricia Cholakian and Elizabeth Goldsmith produced a new edition of *La Vérité dans son jour,* this version of Marie's life—the only one which clearly seems to have been written by her—was forgotten. There are only three known copies of the original edition, two at the Bibliothèque Nationale de France in Paris and the other at the Madrid National Library. Nineteenth- and twentieth-century editors regularly reproduced Bremond's text; Gérard Doscot's Mercure de France edition, *Mémoires d'Hortense et de Marie Mancini,* is the most recent and most widely available of these, with copyrights in 1965, 1987, and 2003. Even the very assuredly spurious *Mémoires de M.L.P.M.M. Colonne* has seen a recent modern edition. In 1997, Le Comptoir des Historiens reissued it under the title *Cendre et poussière;* the editor, Maurice Lever, recognized that its authenticity is contested but preferred it because he found it "more independent, more free, and more trustworthy" than the other, by which he meant Bremond's version. Bremond, in his dedicatory letter to the duke of Zell, congratulated himself on how true to life his "portrait" of Marie was, and he went on at some length about her inimitable style of expression, but then he proceeded to rewrite everything so as to flatten and deaden that style. Meanwhile, nobody read Marie's text anymore. By returning to *La Vérité dans son jour* as the basis for the present English translation, I hope to give the English-speaking reader the best possible idea of Marie's own voice.

ANALYSIS: THE NEGOTIATION OF FEMININE "GLOIRE"

> I know that a woman's *gloire* lies in not giving rise to gossip, and those who know me know well enough that I do not care for making a public sensation; but one cannot always choose the kind of life one wishes to lead, and there is fate even in the very things that seem to depend most on conduct.
>
> Hortense Mancini, *Memoirs*

> As there are no actions upon which the light of public scrutiny shines more harshly than upon those of people in high places, there are also none that are more exposed to

---

11. Cholakian and Goldsmith observe that the English translation contained passages from *La Vérité dans son jour* which were dropped or changed in the 1678 Leiden edition of *Apologie.* Their speculative explanation for this is that the translation may have been prepared using a draft of *Apologie* left behind in England with Bremond's friend Richard Bentley, who published the English edition; then, Bremond may have made further revisions in the French text before having it published in Leiden. Introduction, 12. Cholakian adds to this that the English edition also appears to be based in part on the Spanish *La Verdad en su luz. Women and the Politics of Self-Representation,* 105.

censure, nor more easily the target of malicious gossip, and especially in France, where the lampoons meant to libel and to blacken the reputations of those of our sex sell very well, and pass for works of court gallantry.

Marie Mancini, *The Truth in Its Own Light*

When they were summoned to France by their uncle, Cardinal Mazarin, Marie and Hortense Mancini were thirteen and six years old, respectively. Although Mazarin had amassed an immense personal fortune, and although by 1653 he was gathering the reins of power back into his hands, he was still reviled as a foreigner and a parvenu by many of the leading nobles in France; indeed, he had only just emerged triumphant from the four-year period of revolt led by certain princes—and princesses—of the blood, called the Fronde. Mazarin was in dire need of means by which to shore up his position in France. Having no children of his own (he was a prelate), Mazarin made use of his nieces and nephews and went to work to consolidate his power by contracting strategic marriages between his family and the greatest families of the French nobility.

Thus, from their childhood Hortense and Marie were placed in the inherently contradictory position of being female and being high French nobles, and they were forced by this situation to grapple with the meaning of *gloire* and to imagine what shape it could take for them. The term encompassed opposing meanings in the seventeenth century. On one hand, it meant "glory," widespread celebrity based on remarkable achievements or heroic acts, and the thirst for this kind of glory was often opposed to true "honor." On the other hand, the word *gloire* was frequently used in the seventeenth century as a synonym for "honor"—it could refer to a person's good reputation and claim to esteem. Using the aphorism cited above, which appears in the first paragraph of her memoir, Hortense points to the peculiar nature of *gloire* as it applies to those of her sex: a woman's *gloire* (second sense of the word) depended precisely on her avoidance of the other type of *gloire*, which was reserved for the public actions of men. However, their prominent birth and the designs of their uncle meant that although Hortense and Marie did not engage overtly in politics, their very existence and their every act were public and could have repercussions in affairs of state. This, of course, was true of all women of high birth, but very few "resolved" the dilemmas of their status in ways like those of these two "illustrious adventuresses." (The epithet was applied by various nineteenth- and early twentieth-century male editors and commentators of their writings.)

Hortense and Marie's formulation of feminine *gloire* was original because unlike the legions of other unhappily married women of their social condition, they did not shy away from creating a public spectacle and doing the unthinkable. They were harshly judged for it—not only by male observers but also, most strikingly, by female observers, some of whom are the seventeenth-century women to whom we most often refer today as the standard-bearers for women's citizenship in the republic of letters; and yet both sisters managed, through a combination of personal charm and diplomatic savvy (or rather, despite a *lack* of the latter, in Marie's case especially), to maintain themselves for decades apart from their husbands and in the face of the husbands' sustained efforts to force them to return. Their stories are quite amazing to the modern reader, and they were no less so, certainly, to their contemporaries. Their escapades were discussed with relish by any number of contemporary memorialists and *épistoliers*—Madame de Sévigné and her cousin Bussy-Rabutin, Madame de Lafayette, Madame de Motteville, Madame d'Aulnoy, the abbé de Choisy—not to mention the "gossip columnists" of the day, the writers who reported the doings of the rich and famous in the gazettes. Thus, the sisters failed miserably to avoid giving rise to gossip. They were regularly called *folles* by both female and male observers, and their behavior was referred to as *folie* or *bizarrerie.* For example, Madame de Sévigné wrote to her daughter, Madame de Grignan, on June 20, 1672, three weeks after Marie and Hortense's departure from Rome:[12]

> In the midst of our sorrows, the description you gave me of Madame de Colonna and of her sister is divine. . . . what a fine picture. The comtesse de Soissons [Olympe and Marie-Anne Mancini] are in a fury over those madwomen [*folles*] and say that they should be locked up; they have declared themselves strongly opposed to this strange folly [*folie*]. People do not believe that the king will want to displease the constable [Marie's husband], who is most certainly the greatest seigneur in Rome. In the meantime, we will see them arrive like Mademoiselle de l'Étoile; the likeness is remarkable.[13]

Furthermore, the rumors about them reflected and reinforced the conventional link between female independence and sexual wantonness. On June 26, 1672, Madame de Scudéry, sister-in-law of the famous novelist and *salonnière* Madeleine de Scudéry, wrote to Bussy-Rabutin:

---

12. Hortense reports in her memoir that when they passed through Provence, where Madame de Grignan's husband was lieutenant to the governor of the province, Madame de Grignan kindly sent them some fine shifts and said that they "were traveling like true heroines of a novel, with an abundance of jewels but no clean linen" (80).

13. Madame de Sévigné to Madame de Grignan, Paris, June 20, 1672, in *Correspondance,* 1: 536–37. Mademoiselle de l'Étoile was a character from Scarron's *Roman comique* who first appears posing as a lady of quality in Rome and later reappears in Nevers, reduced to nothing and traveling in most undignified style with the rest of her troupe of players.

Madame Colonna and Madame Mazarin have arrived in Aix; the story goes that they were found there disguised as men, and that they came to see the two brothers, the Chevalier de Lorraine and the comte de Marsan; . . . To tell you the truth, I can certainly conceive that people can fall in love, but I cannot understand how a woman of quality can resolve to give up all honor, propriety, and reputation; I hold that there should be some form of corporal punishment for ladies who have so taken leave of their senses.[14]

With their "honor" in this sorry state, then, both Hortense and Marie went further and took the outrageous step of publishing their life stories, under their own names and not only during their own lifetimes but while they were still quite young (they were twenty-nine and thirty-eight, respectively, at publication of their memoirs). This was unseemly in the extreme: noble women did not make their personal life-writing public, or if they did, that writing was of a devotional or edifying nature, and it was circulated among the elite in manuscript form. This foray into commercial publication was a gambit in both sisters' cases: it was a decidedly unfeminine means to reclaim and rehabilitate their feminine honor—both are at pains throughout their memoirs to counter the rumors of their affairs and their wanton behavior, and Marie declares that her only reason for writing is to set the record straight after the publication of the salacious pseudo-memoir under her name. They hope to salvage their feminine honor, then, by a bold act of unfeminine self-display; they endeavor to convince their readers that their outrageous escapades had only the most modest and decorous objectives; and they put into motion this operation of feminine rehabilitation with the ultimate aim of retaining and buttressing an autonomy which was unheard of for women of their time and their social status. Outlandish as their wager may have appeared to their contemporaries, and unlikely as it may seem to readers today, certain conditions would have helped to make this conduct conceivable for Marie and Hortense, and would have allowed them to imagine that they could, as women, pretend to a kind of masculine *gloire* without losing all standing in society.

LIVES "LIKE SOMETHING OUT OF A NOVEL"

There were personal, practical, and cultural factors at work. First of all, there were the personal histories of the two sisters. Early in her life, Marie

14. Madame de Scudéry to Bussy-Rabutin, Paris, June 26, 1672, in *Correspondance de Roger de Rabutin, comte de Bussy, avec sa famille et ses amis (1666–1693)*, ed. Ludovic Lalanne, 6 vols. (Paris: Charpentier, 1858–59), 2: 128.

had enjoyed the peculiar *gloire* of a reigning royal mistress: the usual requirement of feminine modesty was suspended in such cases, and the fact that
all eyes were on her was not a mark of shame; rather, royal mistresses were
allowed a measure of fame in their own right, although of course the praise
that was heaped on them only concerned their beauty, perhaps their wit,
and always the force of the king's attachment to them. Furthermore, both
Marie and Hortense had been brought up as quasi-royalty at the center of
a French courtly and salon society known across Europe for the freedom
it granted women to mix with men and to participate alongside them in
literary and philosophical pursuits. Both women remark repeatedly in their
memoirs on the great differences they found between the customs of France
and those of Italy or Spain, and they express a strong preference for France.
Marie says, for instance:

> All these reasons, together with the natural aversion I felt for the cus-
> toms of Italy and for the way of life in Rome, where dissimulation and
> hate among families reign more supreme than in other courts, made me
> hasten the execution of the plan I had formed to withdraw to France;
> for France was the country where I had been raised, where most of my
> relatives were, and finally where I felt at home in my way of thinking,
> since I loved novelty and vivacity, and talk of arms and soldierly sub-
> jects, rather than a peaceful place and a pacific government. (130)

Beyond their personal inclinations pushing them to seek their independence through radical means, there was also the belief that those means
were necessary as a last resort because legal appeals were destined to fail,
even in "feminist" France, let alone Italy, where the subjection of wife to
husband was even more absolute. Indeed, French marriage law was evolv-
ing in the 1670s toward an ever more stringent standard for proving that a
husband's conduct merited the grant of a legal separation to a petitioning
wife.[15] Hortense had been pursuing this avenue for several years prior to her
decamping with Marie, and her memoir makes it clear that she was aware of
the fact that the courts in France regarded as practically the only compel-
ling argument the one she uses, namely, that her husband's mismanagement
of the fortune bequeathed to him was jeopardizing the inheritance due to
her son.[16]

---

15. For background on French marriage law during this period, see Joan DeJean, *Tender Geographies: Women and the Origins of the Novel in France* (New York: Columbia University Press, 1991),
109–14, 144–45, 148–53, and notes to these sections.
16. DeJean, *Tender Geographies*, 152.

But finally what favored the sisters' resort to "masculine" means was the general mid-seventeenth-century intellectual and political climate. Both in representation and in reality, it was the age of the *femme forte:* in the 1640s, collections of images of classical "virile women" were published and painted in abundance, and then during the Fronde (1648–53) modern "virile women" such as the duchesses de Longueville, de Montpensier, and de Chevreuse appeared in the flesh to rally populations and ride into battle at the heads of armies.

In addition to these martial women, there were also the writing women—specifically, the writers of fictionalized memoirs, thanks to whom a sort of Moebius strip of life imitating art imitating life developed. Hortense acknowledged the phenomenon at the start of her memoir, saying, "if the events that I have to recount to you seem like something out of a novel, blame it on my unhappy fate rather than my inclination" (27). Between 1671 and 1674, Hortense's friend Madame de Villedieu published her fictional *Mémoires de la vie de Henriette-Sylvie de Molière,* in which the protagonist (whose initials happen to be H. M., as Elizabeth Goldsmith has observed),[17] repeatedly jumps the walls of convents and takes off on picaresque adventures disguised as a man, just as Hortense and Marie were doing in real life (with their progress being reported and commented upon every step of the way by the gazettes and individual letter writers). In 1675, Hortense published her memoirs in her paradoxical bid to defend her feminine honor by making her exploits a matter of public record. In 1676, the pseudo-memoir appeared under Marie's name, clearly aiming to attract a readership titillated by indecorous female behavior. Then the following year, Marie responded with her authentic memoir in defense of her honor. Meanwhile, Hortense's legal battles against her husband continued by fits and starts, with a crucial episode occurring in 1689, when he mounted his strongest attack in the courts. Their entire saga was very much in the public eye: the arguments of the lawyers for both sides were printed, along with the ruling by the court, as soon as the case was decided, and the gazettes were of course full of discussion of the couple's situation.[18] Thus, it is not surprising that when the comtesse de Murat published her fictional *Mémoires de Madame la comtesse de M**** in 1697, the story of an unhappy marriage which it told had a great many points in common with the story of Hortense and her husband.

17. Elizabeth C. Goldsmith, *Publishing Women's Life Stories in France, 1647–1720: From Voice to Print* (Aldershot, UK: Ashgate, 2001), 104.

18. An English translation appeared in London in the year of Hortense's death (1699), including an acerbic refutation by Saint-Evremond in the place of her lawyer's arguments.

SINGULARITY VERSUS UNIVERSALITY

Through the many twists and turns of their separate but intertwined lives, both Marie and Hortense Mancini persistently pursued their goal of an independent life—a modest enough goal by modern standards, but of course a very unfeminine one for their time, and a goal which also called for unladylike means in its pursuit. To what extent do their memoirs help to further the cause of women's right to self-determination in general? It is hard to say. From one point of view, the *femme forte* image is well suited to the situation of the Mancinis, whose options and whose constraints were quite different from those of most women because of their extremely high status. The image of the *femme forte* is partly founded on the principle of exceptionality—the figure is significant precisely because she is not like other women; she stands alone, she is not meant to serve as a model for women in general. From another point of view, however, they appeal to the reader's sense of fairness in making their cases, and appealing to a universal principle of justice implies that they are making a case for women in general, although neither makes such a claim. Ultimately, one could argue that the sensational and unfeminine form of *gloire* which the two sisters achieved could indeed have served as a model of sorts for other women: it certainly made them cluck their tongues at first, but then it may have made them think.

A NOTE ON TEXTS AND TRANSLATION

The French editions on which I have based my translations for this volume are, for Hortense's memoir, the Mercure de France edition by Gérard Doscot, and for Marie's memoir, the Scholars' Facsimiles and Reprints edition of *La Vérité dans son jour* by Patricia Francis Cholakian and Elizabeth C. Goldsmith.[19] In preparing his edition, Doscot followed very precisely the 1929 edition by Pierre Camo of both sisters' memoirs.[20] Both modern editions of Hortense's text include paragraph breaks, which did not exist in the original 1675 edition; I conserve the paragraph breaks as they appear in Camo and Doscot for ease of reading. The frequent use of italics throughout Hortense's memoir occurs in the original edition, and I include it in the present volume, as do Doscot and Camo in their editions.

19. Marie Mancini, *La Vérité dans son jour* (see note 7 above); *Mémoires d' Hortense et de Marie Mancini*, ed. Gérard Doscot (Paris: Mercure de France, 1965, 1987, 2003).

20. *Les Illustres Aventurières, ou Mémoires d' Hortense et de Marie Mancini*, ed. Pierre Camo (Paris: Jonquières, 1929).

As I explain above, I have translated *La Vérité dans son jour* rather than *Apologie* for this volume, in the hope of coming as close as possible to the style and tone of Marie's own expression. I have followed the edition by Cholakian and Goldsmith, which conforms to the original edition in all respects—paragraph divisions, spelling, punctuation, and capitalization.

I have tried to remain as close as possible to the French text of each memoir. In general, I have maintained the authors' syntax and their basic structure of principal and relative clauses, and I have kept the overall style of long, multiclause sentences; however, I have broken up some excessively long sentences in the interest of readability. I have also modernized (and of course, anglicized) the punctuation, so that, for example, for the authors' relatively numerous colons, I have usually substituted semicolons, commas, or periods.

As for capitalization, I have generally followed the French texts. I have left names, titles of nobility and of office, and forms of address in French, in exactly the forms that the authors use (even when the people to whom they refer are not French), except for certain offices for which the French and English words differ enough so that a reader who speaks no French would not understand without translation. Thus, I have used "Monsieur le Cardinal," "Madame la Comtesse," and "Monsieur le duc d'Ossune," but "the constable," "the bishop of Fréjus," and "the archbishop of Amasia." Finally, for place names I have used English forms for well-known cities and regions (Rome, Turin, Brittany), but for less widely known places I have used the modern form of the name in the language of the place itself. Instead of Marie's "Montalte," I have used "Montalto"; instead of "Frescati," "Frascati"; and instead of "Civita-Vecchia," "Civitavecchia."

VOLUME EDITOR'S BIBLIOGRAPHY

PRIMARY SOURCES

Editions of the Memoirs of Hortense and Marie Mancini

Cendre et poussière. Mémoires. Ed. Maurice Lever. Paris: Le Comptoir, 1997. [Reprint of *Mémoires de M.L.P.M.M. Colonne, G. Connétable du Royaume de Naples.* Cologne: Pierre Marteau, 1676.]

Mancini, Hortense. *Mémoires D.M.L.D.M.* Cologne: Pierre Du Marteau, 1675.

——. *Memoires of the Dutchess Mazarine.* London: William Cademan, 1676.

——. *Le Memorie della signora duchessa Mazarini.* Cologne: Pierre Du Marteau, 1678.

——. *The Memoires of the Dutchess Mazarine.* Trans. P. Porter. London: R. Bentley, 1690.

Mancini, Marie. *La Vérité dans son jour, ou les véritables mémoires de M. Manchini, Connétable Colonne.* N.p., n.d. [Madrid, 1677.]

——. *La Verdad en su luz, o las verdaderas memorias de Madama Maria Manchini, Condestablesa Colona.* Saragossa, 1677.

——. *Apologie, ou les Véritables mémoires de Mme Marie Mancini, connétable de Colonna, écrits par elle-même.* Ed. Sébastien Bremond. Leiden: Van Gelder, 1678.

——. *The Apology: or, The Genuine Memoires of Madam Maria Manchini, Constabless of Colonna, eldest Sister to the Duchess of Mazarin.* London: J. Magnes and R. Bentley, 1679.

——. *Apologie, ou les véritables mémoires de Marie Mancini, Princesse Colonna.* [Reprint of 1678 edition by Bremond.] Ed. Georges d'Heylli. Paris, 1881.

——. *La Vérité dans son jour.* Ed. Patricia Francis Cholakian and Elizabeth C. Goldsmith. Delmar, NY: Scholars' Facsimiles and Reprints, 1998.

Mancini, Hortense, and Marie Mancini. *Les Illustres Aventurières, ou Mémoires d'Hortense et de Marie Mancini.* Ed. Pierre Camo. Paris: Jonquières, 1929.

——. *Mémoires d'Hortense et de Marie Mancini.* Ed. Gérard Doscot. Paris: Mercure de France, 1965, 1987, 2003.

Mémoires de M.L.P.M.M. Colonne, G. Connétable du Royaume de Naples. Cologne: Pierre Marteau, 1676.

Le Memorie della S.P.M.M. Colonna. Cologne: Pierre Du Marteau, 1678. [Translation of *Mémoires de M.L.P.M.M. Colonne, G. Connétable du Royaume de Naples.*]

Other Primary Sources

Aulnoy, Marie-Catherine Jumelle de Berneville, comtesse d'. *La Cour et la ville de Madrid vers la fin du XVIIe siècle.* Ed. B. Carey. 2 vols. Paris: Plon, 1874–76.

Brienne, Louis-Henri de Loménie, comte de. *Mémoires inédits.* Ed. F. Barrière. 2 vols. Paris: Ponthieu; Leipzig: Ponthieu, Michelsen, 1828.

———. *Mémoires.* Ed. Paul Bonnefon. 3 vols. Paris: Renouard; Société de l'Histoire de France, 1916–19.

Bussy, Roger de Rabutin, comte de. *Correspondance de Roger de Rabutin, comte de Bussy, avec sa famille et ses amis (1666–1693).* Ed. Ludovic Lalanne. 6 vols. Paris: Charpentier, 1858–59.

Choisy, François-Timoléon, abbé de. *Mémoires de l'abbé de Choisy: Mémoires pour servir à l'histoire de Louis XIV. Mémoires de l'abbé de Choisy habillé en femme.* Ed. Georges Mongrédien. Paris: Mercure de France, 1966.

Colbert, Jean-Baptiste. *Lettres, instructions et mémoires de Colbert, publiés d'après les ordres de l'empereur, sur la proposition de Son Excellence M. Magne, ministre secrétaire d'état des finances.* Ed. Pierre Clément. 8 vols. Paris: Imprimerie Impériale/Imprimerie Nationale, 1861–82.

Dangeau, Philippe de Courcillon, marquis de. *Journal du marquis de Dangeau.* Ed. Eudoxe Soulié, L. Dussieux, Philippe de Chennevières, Paul Mantz, Anatole de Montaiglon. 19 vols. Paris: Firmin Didot Frères, 1854–60.

Erard, Claude, and Charles Marguetel de Saint-Denis, seigneur de Saint-Evremond. *The arguments of Monsieur Herard for Monsieur the Duke of Mazarin against Madam the Dutchess of Mazarin, his spouse: and the factum for Madam the Dutchess of Mazarin against Monsieur the Duke of Mazarin, her husband, by Monsieur de St. Evremont.* London: C. Broom, 1699.

La Fayette, Marie-Madeleine Pioche de La Vergne, comtesse de. *Vie de la princesse d'Angleterre.* Ed. Marie-Thérèse Hipp. Geneva: Droz, 1967.

Loret, Jean. *La muze historique; ou, Recueil des lettres en vers contenant les nouvelles du temps.* Ed. J. Ravenel, E. V. de La Pelouze, C.-L. Livet. 4 vols. Paris: Jannet, 1857–78.

Mazarin, Armand-Charles de La Porte, duc, and Claude Erard. *Plaidoyez touchant la demande faite par Monsieur le duc de Mazarin pour obliger Madame la duchesse de Mazarin, son epouse de revenir avec luy, après une longue absence, & de quitter l'Angleterre où elle est presentement: avec l'arrest intervenu le 29 decembre 1689 sur ces plaidoyez.* Toulouse: J.J. Boude, 1689.

Mazarin, Hortense Mancini, duchesse, and N. Sachot. *Reponse de Dame Hortence Mancini, duchesse de Mazarin, aux plaidoyez de Messire Armand Charles, duc de Mazarin, son epoux.* Toulouse: J. J. Boude, 1689.

Montpensier, Anne-Marie-Louise d'Orléans, duchesse de. *Mémoires.* 2 vols. Paris: Librairie Fontaine, 1985.

Motteville, Françoise Bertaut de. *Memoirs of Madame de Motteville on Anne of Austria and Her Court.* Introduction by C.-A. Sainte-Beuve. Trans. Katharine Prescott Wormeley. 3 vols. Boston: Hardy, Pratt, 1901.

Retz, Jean-François Paul de Gondi, cardinal de. *Mémoires. La Conjuration du comte Jean-Louis de Fiesque. Pamphlets.* Ed. Maurice Allem and Édith Thomas. Paris: Gallimard, 1956.

Saint-Evremond, Charles Marguetel de Saint-Denis, seigneur de. *Miscellaneous Essays.* London: John Everingham, 1692.

Saint-Réal, César Vichard, abbé de. *Œuvres de M. l'abbé de Saint-Réal.* 6 vols. Amsterdam : François l'Honoré, 1740.

Saint-Simon, Louis de Rouvroy, duc de. *Mémoires.* Ed. Gonzague Truc. 7 vols. Paris: Gallimard, 1947–61.

Sévigné, Marie de Rabutin-Chantal, marquise de. *Lettres de Madame de Sévigné.* Ed. Emile Gérard-Gailly. 3 vols. Paris: Gallimard, 1953–63.

———. *Correspondance.* Ed. Roger Duchêne. 3 vols. Paris: Gallimard, 1972–78.

Somaize, Antoine Baudeau de. *Le Dictionnaire des précieuses.* Ed. Charles Louis Livet. 2 vols. Paris: Jannet, 1856.

Villars, Marie Gigault de Bellefonds, marquise de. *Lettres de Madame de Villars à Madame de Coulanges (1679–1681).* Ed. Alfred de Courtois. Paris: Plon, 1868.

Villars, Pierre, marquis de. *Mémoires de la cour d'Espagne sous le règne de Charles II, 1678–1682.* Ed. Sir William Stirling Maxwell. London: Trübner, 1861.

SECONDARY SOURCES

Beasley, Faith. "Altering the Fabric of History: Women's Participation in the Classical Age." In *A History of Women's Writing in France*, ed. Sonya Stephens, 64–83. Cambridge: Cambridge University Press, 2000.

———. *Revising Memory: Women's Fiction and Memoirs in Seventeenth-Century France.* New Brunswick, NJ: Rutgers University Press, 1990.

———. *Salons, History, and the Creation of Seventeenth-Century France: Mastering Memory.* Aldershot, UK: Ashgate, 2006.

Chantelauze, R. *Louis XIV et Marie Mancini d'après de nouveaux documents.* Paris: Didier, 1880.

Cholakian, Patricia Francis. "Sex, Lies, and Autobiography: Hortense Mancini's *Mémoires.*" In *Women Writers in Pre-Revolutionary France: Strategies of Emancipation*, ed. Colette H. Winn and Donna Kuizenga, 17–30. New York: Garland, 1997.

———. *Women and the Politics of Self-Representation in Seventeenth-Century France.* Newark: University of Delaware Press; London: Associated University Presses, 2000.

DeJean, Joan E. "Notorious Women: Marriage and the Novel in Crisis in France, 1690–1710." In *Scarlet Letters: Fictions of Adultery from Antiquity to the 1990s*, ed. Nicholas White and Naomi Segal. Houndsmills, UK: Macmillan Press; New York: St. Martin's Press, 1997.

———. *Tender Geographies: Women and the Origins of the Novel in France.* New York: Columbia University Press, 1991.

Démoris, René. *Le Roman à la première personne. Du classicisme aux Lumières.* Paris: A. Colin, 1975.

Dulong, Claude. *Marie Mancini. La première passion de Louis XIV.* Paris: Perrin, 1993, 2002.

Goldsmith, Elizabeth C. "Fugitive Lives: Travel, Identity, and Runaway Women in the Age of Versailles." In *The New Biographical Criticism*, ed. George Hoffmann, 110–24. Charlottesville, VA: Rookwood, 2004.

———. "Louis XIV, Marie Mancini et la politique de l'intimité royal." In *Ordre et contestation au temps des classiques*, ed. Roger Duchêne and Pierre Ronzeaud, 1: 235–43. Paris: Papers on French Seventeenth-Century Literature, 1992.

————. "Publishing the Lives of Hortense and Marie Mancini." In *Going Public: Women and Publishing in Early Modern France*, ed. Elizabeth C. Goldsmith and Dena Goodman, 30–45. Ithaca, NY: Cornell University Press, 1995.

————. *Publishing Women's Life Stories in France, 1647–1720: From Voice to Print*. Aldershot, UK: Ashgate, 2001.

Goldsmith, Elizabeth C., and Dena Goodman, eds. *Going Public: Women and Publishing in Early Modern France*. Ithaca, NY: Cornell University Press, 1995.

Goldsmith, Elizabeth C., and Colette Winn, eds. *Lettres de femmes. Textes inédits et oubliés du XVIᵉ au XVIIIᵉ siècle*. Paris: Champion, 2005.

Goldsmith, Elizabeth C., and Abby Zanger. "The Politics and Poetics of the Mancini Romance: Visions and Revisions of Louis XIV." In *The Rhetorics of Life-Writing in Early Modern Europe: Forms of Biography from Cassandra Fedele to Louis XIV*, ed. Thomas Mayer and Daniel Woolf, 341–72. Ann Arbor: University of Michigan Press, 1995.

Goubert, Pierre. *Le Siècle de Louis XIV. Etudes*. Paris: Fallois, 1996.

————. *Splendeurs et misères du XVIIᵉ siècle*. Paris: Fayard, 2005. [This volume contains two earlier works by the author: *Mazarin* (Paris: Fayard, 1990) and *Louis XIV et vingt millions de Français* (Paris: Fayard, 1991).]

Grobe, Edwin Paul. "Gabriel and Sébastian Bremond." *Romance Notes* 4, no. 2 (1963): 132–35.

————. "Sébastian Bremond: His Life and His Works." Ph.D. diss., Indiana University, 1954.

Harth, Erica. *Cartesian Women: Versions and Subversions of Rational Discourse in the Old Regime*. Ithaca, NY: Cornell University Press, 1992.

Livet, Georges. *Le duc Mazarin, gouverneur d'Alsace (1661–1713). Lettres et documents inédits*. Strasbourg and Paris: Le Roux, 1954.

Mongrédien, Georges. *Une aventurière au Grand Siècle, la duchesse Mazarin*. Paris: Amiot-Dumont, 1952.

Mossiker, Frances. *The Affair of the Poisons: Louis XIV, Madame de Montespan, and One of History's Great Unsolved Mysteries*. New York: Knopf, 1969.

Perey, Lucien [Clara Adèle Luce Herpin]. *Une princesse romaine au XVIIᵉ siècle. Marie Mancini Colonna d'après des documents inédits*. Paris: Calmann Lévy, 1896.

————. *Le Roman du Grand Roi. Louis XIV et Marie Mancini d'après des lettres et documents inédits*. Paris: Calmann Lévy, 1894.

Ranum, Orest. *The Fronde: A French Revolution, 1648–1652*. New York: Norton, 1993.

————. *Paris in the Age of Absolutism: An Essay*. Rev. ed. University Park: Pennsylvania State University Press, 2002.

Rosvall, Toivo David. *The Mazarine Legacy: The Life of Hortense Mancini, Duchess Mazarin*. New York: Viking Press, 1969.

REFERENCE WORKS

Anselme, Père. *Histoire généalogique et chronologique de la maison royale de France, le tout dressé sur les titres originaux . . .* 3rd ed. Amsterdam: Châtelain, 1713.

Aubert de La Chesnaye-Desbois, François-Alexandre. *Dictionnaire de la noblesse, contenant les généalogies, l'histoire & la chronologie des familles nobles de la France, l'explication*

de leurs armes et l'état des grandes terres du royaume. 3rd ed. 19 vols. Paris, 1863–76;
Nendeln/Liechtenstein: Kraus Reprint, 1976.

————. *Sommaires détaillés des généalogies des familles mentionnées dans les tomes xiii, xiv et xv du Dictionnaire de la noblesse de La Chesnaye des Bois.* Paris: A. Aubry, 1863.

Barbiche, Bernard. *Les institutions de la monarchie française à l'époque moderne : XVIe–XVIIIe siècle.* Paris: Presses Universitaires de France, 1999.

Biographie universelle, ou Dictionnaire historique des hommes qui se sont fait un nom par leur génie, leurs talens, leurs vertus, leurs erreurs ou leurs crimes. New ed. Ed. F.-X. de Feller and M. Pérennès. 13 vols. Paris: Méquignon Junior et J. Leroux; Gaume Frères, 1844.

Biographie universelle ancienne et moderne, ou Histoire, par ordre alphabétique, de la vie publique et privée de tous les hommes qui se sont fait remarquer par leurs écrits, leurs actions, leurs talents, leurs vertus ou leurs crimes. 85 vols. Paris: Michaud Frères, 1811–62.

Bluch, François. *Dictionnaire du Grand Siècle.* New ed. Paris: Fayard, 2005.

Dictionnaire de biographie française. Ed. J. Balteau, M. Barroux, M. Prévost. Paris: Librairie Letouzey et Ané, 1933–.

Litta, Pompeo, et al. *Famiglie celebri italiane.* Unbound fascicles in 10 boxes. Milan: P. E. Giusti, 1819–83.

Nouvelle biographie générale depuis les temps les plus reculés jusqu'à nos jours. Ed. Jean Chrétien Ferdinand Hoefer. 46 vols. in 23. Paris: Firmin Didot Frères, 1855–66.

Robert, Paul. *Le Nouveau Petit Robert. Dictionnaire alphabétique et analogique de la langue française.* Ed. Josette Rey-Debove and Alain Rey. Paris: Dictionnaires Le Robert, 1994.

ONLINE SOURCES

ABC Genealogía. Available at http://www.abcgenealogia.com/

Bunel, Arnaud. *Héraldique européenne.* Available at http://www.heraldique-europeenne .org/. 1997–2008.

Carné, Alain de. *Site de la famille de Carné.* Available at http://a.decarne.free.fr/. 1999–2006.

The Catholic Encyclopedia. Available at http://www.newadvent.org/cathen/. 2003–7. [*Catholic Encyclopedia*, vol. 1. Robert Appleton Co., 1907.]

Cheney, David M. *The Hierarchy of the Catholic Church: Current and Historical Information about Its Bishops and Dioceses.* Available at http://www.catholic-hierarchy.org/. 1996–2007.

Miranda, Salvador. *The Cardinals of the Holy Roman Church.* http://www.fiu.edu/~mirandas/cardinals.htm. 1998–2008.

Romei, Danilo. *Banca Dati 'Giulio Rospigliosi'.* Available at http://www.nuovorinas cimento.org/rosp-2000/home.htm. 1998-2000.

Shamà, Davide. *Genealogie delle dinastie nobili italiane.* Available at http:/www.sardimpex .com. 2003–8.

Pierre Mignard (1612–95), *Hortense Mancini*, (mid-seventeenth century).

TO M.***
[THE MEMOIRS OF HORTENSE MANCINI]

Since the obligations that I have toward you[1] are such that I must spare no effort to show you my gratitude, I am quite willing to tell the story of my life as you request. Not that I am ignorant of the difficulty of speaking judiciously about oneself, and neither are you unaware of my natural reluctance to talk about my own affairs; but it is even more natural to defend ourselves against calumny, at least to those who have done us great favors. They deserve to be shown that we are not entirely unworthy to have received them. In any case, I could make no more innocent use of the leisure of my retreat. And if the events that I have to recount to you seem like something out of a novel, blame it on my unhappy fate rather than my inclination. I know that a woman's glory lies in not giving rise to gossip,[2] and those who know me know well enough that I do not care for making a public sensation; but one cannot always choose the kind of life one wishes to lead, and there is fate even in the very things that seem to depend most on conduct.

I would not mention my birth to you, however advantageous it might be, if my uncle's detractors had not been at pains to tarnish its brilliance;[3] but since their fury has extended to everything related to him, I think I am

1. The work is dedicated "To Monsieur," Charles-Emmanuel II, sovereign duke of Savoy (1634–75), son of Victor-Amédée I, duke of Savoy, and of Christine of France, who was the daughter of Henri IV and sister of Louis XIII. Charles-Emmanuel was one of Hortense's early suitors during the French court's journey to Lyon in the autumn of 1658. She dedicates this memoir to him because at the time of its composition (1675), she had been living as his guest in the château de Chambéry for three years.
2. This commonplace goes back at least as far as Thucydides' *History of the Peloponnesian War* (book 2, section 46).
3. Cardinal Mazarin had no shortage of detractors, many of whom decried his inferior social extraction and his foreign nationality. These were common themes, notably in the *mazarinades*, the mostly anonymous pamphlets which proliferated during the period of revolt known as the Fronde (1648–52).

justified in telling you that I come from one of the oldest families of Rome, and that my ancestors for more than three hundred years have held a high enough rank there so that I would have led a happy life, even if I had not been heiress to a chief minister of France. The Academy of Great Wits of that land, which began at the nuptials of a gentleman of my family,[4] is proof enough of the high regard in which the family was held already at that time; and to add to my good fortune, I am privileged to have been born of a father whose virtue and extraordinary intellect raised him above the finest of our forebears.[5]

I was brought to France at the age of six [1653], and only a few years later Monsieur Mazarin[6] refused my sister the constabless[7] and conceived

4. Indeed, Rome's Accademia degli Umoristi (Hortense calls it the Académie des Beaux-Esprits) was born in the Palazzo Mancini, at the wedding of Hortense's paternal grandparents, Paolo Mancini and Vittoria Capocci, on February 7, 1600. Many eminent Roman poets presented their verse compositions and comedies to mark the occasion; afterward the group continued to assemble regularly in the Palazzo Mancini, and by 1602 or 1603 the *"uomini di bell'umore"* were established as the Accademia degli Umoristi. Roman nobles of both sexes flocked to the gatherings of the Umoristi to listen to the most celebrated writers of the time, and the group was extremely influential throughout the first half of the seventeenth century, remaining active until 1670.

This information, as well as most of the unattributed biographical information supplied in the footnotes to both memoirs in this edition, can be found in one or more of the following biographical dictionaries: *Biographie universelle, ou Dictionnaire historique des hommes qui se sont fait un nom par leur génie, leurs talens, leurs vertus, leurs erreurs ou leurs crimes*, new ed., ed. F.-X. de Feller and M. Pérennès, 13 vols. (Paris: Méquignon Junior et J. Leroux; Gaume Frères, 1844); *Biographie universelle ancienne et moderne, ou Histoire, par ordre alphabétique, de la vie publique et privée de tous les hommes qui se sont fait remarquer par leurs écrits, leurs actions, leurs talents, leurs vertus ou leurs crimes*, 85 vols. (Paris: Michaud Frères, 1811–62); *Dictionnaire de biographie française*, ed. J. Balteau, M. Barroux, and M. Prévost (Paris: Librairie Letouzey et Ané, 1933–); and *Nouvelle biographie générale depuis les temps les plus reculés jusqu'à nos jours*, ed. Jean Chrétien Ferdinand Hoefer, 46 vols. in 23 (Paris: Firmin Didot Frères, 1855–66).

Several online references also were extremely valuable sources of biographical and genealogical information: Arnaud Bunel, *Héraldique européenne*, http://www.heraldique-europeenne .org/; Alain de Carné, *Site de la famille de Carné*, http://a.decarne.free.fr/; Salvador Miranda, *The Cardinals of the Holy Roman Church*, http://www.fiu.edu/~mirandas/cardinals.htm; and Davide Shamà, *Genealogie delle dinastie nobili italiane*, http://www.sardimpex.com/.

5. Lorenzo (or Michele Lorenzo) Mancini (1602–56), son of Paolo Mancini and Vittoria Capocci (or Capozzi). In 1634, Lorenzo married Hieronyma (or Geronima or Girolama) Mazzarino (or Mazzarini) (1614–56), a younger sister of Cardinal Mazarin; Hortense and Marie were two of their eight children who survived beyond infancy. Lorenzo's chief claim to fame was his knowledge of astrology and necromancy.

6. That is, Armand-Charles de La Porte de La Meilleraye (1632–1713), who became the Duc Mazarin as a result of his marriage to Hortense and his inheritance of the cardinal's fortune and name. His father was grand master of the artillery *(grand maître de l'artillerie)* and marshal of France *(maréchal de France)*, and he was also a first cousin of Cardinal Richelieu. Even while recounting this early period in their lives, Hortense refers to her husband, her siblings, and their spouses by the names and titles they bore in 1675 when she composed her memoir.

7. Marie Mancini, Constabless Colonna (1639–1715), who married Lorenzo Onofrio Colonna, prince and duke of Paliano, Grand Constable of the kingdom of Naples (1637–89), in 1661.

such an intense passion for me that he once said to Madame d'Aiguillon[8] *that if only he could marry me, he would not regret dying three months later.* He has had even more than he had hoped: he has married me and has not died, thank God. When Monsieur le Cardinal first heard of this passion, he seemed so far from approving of it, and so outraged by Monsieur Mazarin's refusal of my sister, that he said several times *that he would rather give me to a valet.*

He was not the only person whom I had the misfortune to please. An Italian eunuch, a musician to Monsieur le Cardinal and a man of great wit, was accused of the same thing; but in truth it was as much for my sisters as for me. People jeered that he was even in love with the beautiful statues of the Palais Mazarin; and the love of that man truly must have brought bad luck, since those poor statues have been so cruelly punished for it, just as I have, although they were no guiltier than I.[9]

If I failed to love as I was loved, it was not for lack of incitement by my sister the constabless. As she felt a sincere attachment to the king,[10] she would have liked very much to see a similar weakness in me; but my extreme

---

8. Marie-Madeleine de Vignerot, marquise de Combalet, duchesse d'Aiguillon (1604–75). Madame d'Aiguillon was a niece of Cardinal Richelieu, to whom she was deeply devoted and closely allied. At the age of eighteen she was widowed, and having no children, she expressed a strong desire to take her vows as a Carmelite nun. However, her uncle refused to allow it and instead had her named *dame d'atours* to the Queen Mother, Marie de Médicis. Madame d'Aiguillon took on the role of hostess for the cardinal's salon; she was educated, spoke Italian and Spanish, and frequented the salons of Madame de Rambouillet and Madame de Sablé. Corneille dedicated *Le Cid* to her, and she was a protectress of many other writers including, notably, Marie le Jars de Gournay. When Madame d'Aiguillon refused adamantly to remarry, her uncle bought the duchy of Aiguillon for her in southwest France (1638); at the time of his death in 1642, he left the lion's share of his fortune to her but also extracted from her a promise not to enter a convent but to remain in the world and act as guardian for her young nephews. During the last half of her life, she financed the establishment of numerous hospitals and charitable institutions in France, Italy, Canada, North Africa, and East Asia. At her death, she bequeathed her duchy, titles, and fortune to her niece, Marie-Thérèse de Vignerot (1636–1704), who had always refused to marry, who had declared her desire to follow a religious vocation from an early age, and who finally did enter a convent in Paris in 1692.

9. A reference to one of the Duc Mazarin's most outrageous episodes, which helped establish his reputation in society as utterly deranged. Motivated by ferocious religiosity and an extreme anxiety about sexuality, he attacked the priceless art collection he had inherited from Cardinal Mazarin, breaking offending body parts from statues, slathering black paint over nudes in pictures, and slashing objectionable tapestries to shreds. His obsessive concern over sexuality was such that he considered having his daughters' front teeth ground down or pulled out in order to ensure their salvation by destroying their beauty. And in the lands he governed, he decreed that women should neither milk cows nor spin wool on a wheel because the motions that these tasks required might inspire impure thoughts in them. Georges Mongrédien, *Une Aventurière au Grand Siècle, la duchesse Mazarin* (Paris: Amiot-Dumont, 1952), 33, 82–83; Toivo David Rosvall, *The Mazarine Legacy: The Life of Hortense Mancini, duchess Mazarin* (New York: Viking Press, 1969), 122–23.

10. Louis XIV (1638–1715).

youth did not allow me to become attached to anyone, and all I could do to please her was to show some particular interest in those young boys around us who amused me the most in the children's games which occupied me at the time. The presence of the king, who never budged from our quarters, often disturbed them. Although he lived among us with marvelous kindness, there has always been something so serious, so solid, and frankly so majestic in all his manners that he could not help inspiring awe in us, even without intending to. My sister the constabless was the only person who was not ill at ease with him; and you can easily understand that his attentiveness had charms for those who caused it, which it did not have for others. Since passion makes people do things which seem ridiculous to those who have never felt any, my sister's passion often laid her open to our ribbing. One time, for instance, we teased her when she, seeing from a distance a gentleman of the household who was the same size as the king and whom she only saw from behind, had run toward him with her arms open, shouting, "*Ah! My poor Sire.*"

Another thing that gave us a good laugh at that time was a joke which Monsieur le Cardinal played on Madame de Bouillon,[11] who must have been about six years old. The court was at La Fère at the time. One day when he was ribbing her about some admirer whom he said she had, he eventually got the idea of reproaching her, claiming that she was with child. The resentment she showed amused him so much that people decided to keep telling her it was so. They took in her clothes from time to time, and they made her think that it was she who had grown fatter. This continued for as long as was necessary to make her think it might be true; but she would never believe a bit of it, and always denied it very sharply, until one morning when the time had come for the delivery and she found a newborn child between her sheets. You cannot imagine her astonishment and her dismay at the sight of it. "*Well then,*" she said, "*the Virgin and I are the only ones to whom this has happened; because it didn't hurt a bit.*" The queen [12] came to console her and offered to be godmother, many people came to celebrate with the new mother, and what had begun as a private joke eventually became a public entertainment for the whole court. People pressed her hard to declare who the father of the child was, but all they could draw out of her was *that it had to be either the king or the comte de Guiche,*[13] *because those were the only two men who had*

---

11. Hortense's youngest sister, Marie-Anne Mancini (1649–1714), who married Maurice-Godefroy de La Tour d'Auvergne, duc de Bouillon (1636–1721), in 1662.

12. Anne of Austria (1601–66), mother of Louis XIV and regent from the death of Louis XIII in 1643 until 1651.

13. Armand de Gramont, comte de Guiche (1638–73). A military hero, a handsome seducer of both women and men, and a regular participant in court intrigues and scandals, he was

ever kissed her. For my part, being three years older than she, I was very proud to know the truth of the matter; and I never tired of laughing about it, just to show that I knew it.

You will doubtless find it hard to believe that at that age, when philosophical reasoning is usually the last thing on a person's mind, I had such serious thoughts as I had about every aspect of life. And yet it is true that my greatest pleasure at that time was to shut myself up alone and write down everything that came into my head. Not long ago I came across some of these writings again; and I confess to you that I was tremendously surprised to find in them ideas far beyond the capacities of a little girl. They were filled with doubts and questions which I posed to myself about all the things I found hard to understand. I never resolved them to my satisfaction, but I kept doggedly seeking the answers that I could not find; and if my conduct since then has not shown great judgment, at least I have the consolation of knowing that I once wanted very much to acquire it.

I still remember that at about this same time, when I wanted to write to one of my friends whom I loved very dearly, I eventually tired of writing *"I love you"* so many times in the same letter; so I told her that I would just start marking a cross to stand for those three words. Using this fine invention, I sometimes found myself writing letters to that girl containing nothing but lines of crosses, one after another. One of those letters later fell into the hands of some people who had an interest in penetrating the mystery, but they could never find fault with such a devout cipher.

My childhood having been spent among these various amusements, people began to discuss my marriage. Fortune, who wanted to render me the unhappiest person of my sex, started off by pretending to want to make me a queen; and she did her very best to make the match she had destined for me seem odious by comparison with those with whom she flattered me at first. However, I can testify in my own defense that those illustrious matches did not dazzle me; and Monsieur Mazarin would not dare to contend that he has ever observed in me any vanity above my station.

Everyone knows about the proposals, made several times, to marry me to the king of England;[14] and as for the duc de Savoie, you know what was said about that during the Lyon trip, and that it was broken off only because

---

banished more than once by Louis XIV. See below, notes 96 and 132. This comte de Guiche was the son of Antoine III de Gramont-Touloujon, comte de Guiche and later duc de Gramont, *maréchal de France* (1604–78), upon whom the character of the comte de Guiche in Rostand's *Cyrano de Bergerac* is based.

14. Charles II Stuart (1630–85), son of Charles I and Henriette-Marie of France. Charles was in exile in France during part of the period of the Commonwealth, which lasted from the execution of his father in 1649 until his own return to the throne in 1660.

of Monsieur le Cardinal's obstinate refusal to give up Geneva in consideration of the marriage.[15]

We were lodged at Bellecour,[16] and the windows of our rooms, which faced the square, were low enough so that someone could easily climb up to them. Madame de Venelle,[17] our governess, was so accustomed to keeping watch over us that she would get up even in her sleep to come and see what we were doing. One particular night, my sister was sleeping with her mouth open, and when Madame de Venelle came to check on her, feeling her way in the dark as usual and still asleep herself, she stuck her finger so far into my sister's mouth that my sister woke up with a start and bit down hard on it. Just imagine their astonishment at finding themselves in that situation, once they were both wide awake again. My sister flew into an extraordinary rage. The story was told to the king the next day, and the whole court was much amused by it.

Whether out of modesty or dissimulation, Monsieur le Cardinal always appeared as firmly opposed as the queen to the affection that the king had for my sister. As soon as the marriage negotiations with Spain had been concluded, his most pressing concern was to get her away from the king, for fear that she might pose some obstacle to the marriage.[18] He sent us, some time after the return from Lyon, to wait for him at Fontaine-

15. The duke of Savoy was the benefactor to whom Hortense addressed this memoir. He had proposed marriage with her to Cardinal Mazarin during the expedition that the French court made to Lyon in the autumn of 1658; the journey was ostensibly to negotiate a possible marriage contract between Louis XIV and Princess Marguerite of Savoy, the duke's sister. However, Mazarin had no intention of actually marrying the king to Marguerite; he made a show of the negotiations solely to press Philip IV of Spain to move toward a peace treaty between France and Spain and a marriage between his daughter, the Infanta Marie-Thérèse, and Louis XIV. Thus, the negotiations for Marguerite were doomed to be fruitless, and her brother the duke also rode away empty-handed—and quite bitter—because the cardinal refused to cede French control over two Savoyard fortresses as a condition of the marriage contract. See Marie's memoir, note 32.

16. In the center of Lyon; Hortense is recounting an episode from the court's sojourn there in 1658.

17. Madeleine de Gaillard Longjumeau de Ventabren, dame de Venelle (or Venel), was first placed by Mazarin as lady-in-waiting in the household of the eldest Mancini sister, Laure (1636–57), who was married in 1651 to Louis de Bourbon-Vendôme, duc de Mercoeur (1612–69). She had been governess for the cardinal's elder nieces, who were brought to France in 1648, and she played that role again for Hortense and Marie. Madame de Venelle came from a Provençal family of erudite jurists and financiers, and she herself was well enough educated to have been able to read and comment (presumably in French) on such authors as Plutarch and Philostratus with her young charges. According to Pierre Camo, Madame de Venelle was separated from her husband, who was a member of the *parlement* of Aix. *Les Illustres Aventurières*, 39. See also Dulong, *Marie Mancini*, 25–26.

18. The forced separation came in June 1659.

bleau.[19] From there he brought us to Poitiers, where he let her choose the place to which she wished to retire. She chose La Rochelle, and Monsieur le Cardinal, who wanted to send her even further away, eventually sent a proposal to her at Brouage,[20] by way of Monsieur de Fréjus,[21] to marry the constable;[22] but she refused him, not yet being attracted to Italy by that which later attracted her there.

He had resolved to bring Madame de Bouillon and me to the wedding;[23] but since my sister the constabless obstinately refused to let us go when he sent for us unless she went too, he preferred to deprive himself of the pleasure of seeing us there rather than to let her come with us. Upon their return from the border, we were summoned to Fontainebleau, where the court was. The king treated my sister rather coldly, and the change in him began to make her resolve to marry in Italy. She often implored me to speak as ill of him as I could to her. But besides the fact that it was practically impossible to speak ill of such a prince as he, who lived among us with familiarity and a charming sweetness, I was only ten at the time,[24] and my age did not allow me to really understand what she desired of me. All that I could do to help her, since I could see she was miserable and I loved her dearly, was to weep with her over her misfortune, until such time as she could help me weep over mine.

The chagrin that Monsieur le Cardinal felt over her liaison with the king had inspired in him a strong aversion to her; and since their involvement had begun before she had come out in society, one could almost say that he had never liked her.

19. The château de Fontainebleau is located forty miles southeast of Paris; the court came there regularly nearly every year during the reign of Louis XIV. See Marie's memoir, note 31.

20. After two months in La Rochelle, Marie chose to move thirty miles south to the windswept seaside fortress of Brouage; she said that the sadness and solitude of the place were in tune with her own mental state. As Hortense hints here, Marie's romance with the king was not yet clearly over during her time at Brouage; indeed, although all contact between them had by then been strictly forbidden by Mazarin and the queen (Anne of Austria), they were continuing a secret exchange of letters and tokens.

21. Zongo Ondedei, fellow Italian and confidant of Cardinal Mazarin; the cardinal made him bishop of Fréjus in 1658.

22. Lorenzo Onofrio Colonna was Grand Constable (*Grand Connétable*) of the kingdom of Naples. Thus, Hortense and Marie commonly refer to him as "Monsieur le Connétable" throughout their memoirs. The Grand Constable was a high officer of the crown—in this case, of the Spanish crown—who had supreme command of the army.

23. Louis XIV and Marie-Thérèse were married on June 9, 1660, in Saint-Jean-de-Luz on the Atlantic coast near the border with Spain.

24. Actually, since Hortense was born June 6, 1646, she would have been fourteen at the time.

My brother's[25] temperament scarcely pleased him any more, and his behavior even less, especially since he had been accused of taking part in the debauchery of Roissy;[26] for one of the subjects upon which Monsieur le Cardinal was most unhappy with us was religious devotion. You would not believe how much our lack of it pained him. There were no arguments which he failed to use in the attempt to inspire some in us. On one occasion, complaining because we did not hear mass every day, he reproached us, saying that we had neither piety nor honor. *"At least,"* he said, *"if you do not hear it for God's sake, hear it for the world's."*

Although I had as great a share as the others in his reprimands, nevertheless either because as the youngest I seemed to him to be the least culpable, or because there was something in my temperament which he liked better, for a long time he showed as much tenderness for me as aversion for them. That is what impelled him to choose me, to leave his estate and his name to the husband he would give me; and it is also what made him more concerned about my conduct than about that of the others, and ultimately also more displeased when he believed he had reason to complain of it. He was very afraid that I might commit myself to someone out of love. Madame de Venelle, who had orders to spy on me, spoke to me incessantly of all the young men with whom I kept company and whom I might love, in order to discover through my words what my feelings were for each of them; but since I had nothing in my heart, she could not find anything out, and she would still be in that difficulty if the indiscretion of my sister had not given her to believe I had a love in my heart which I did not have.

I have told you that my sister always wanted me to be in love. For several years she pressed me so insistently to tell her if there were not some man at court who pleased me more than the others that finally, overcome by her persistence, I confessed to her *that I sometimes saw in our quarters a young boy whom I found quite pleasing, but that I would be very sorry to like him as much as she liked the king.* Delighted to have drawn that confession out of my mouth, she asked me his name; but I did not know it, and however hard she tried to get me to

25. Philippe-Julien Mancini, duc de Nevers (1641–1707), who married Diane Gabrielle Damas de Thianges (ca. 1655–1715), niece of Madame de Montespan, in 1670.

26. This "debauchery" lasted several days during Holy Week in 1659 and took place at the estate of the comte de Vivonne (brother of Madame de Montespan) at Roissy, near Paris. It was alleged that the participants—who included such noted libertines as Bussy-Rabutin, the comte de Guiche, and the comte's intimate friend Manicamp—had played at holding a "black Mass" and on Good Friday had eaten a suckling pig which had been "baptized" as a carp for the occasion by the young abbé Le Camus, the king's chaplain. Cardinal Mazarin was so irked by Philippe's involvement that he had his nephew confined in his fortress of Brisach in eastern France near the border with Germany.

describe him, she went for two months teasing me about him without know-ing who he was. She eventually found out that he was an Italian gentleman who was newly come from being a page of the chamber[27] and who was still only a sublieutenant of the guards; he was killed a few years ago in Flanders with a much higher rank. She told me his name, and she also told the king, to whom she made a fuss over my supposed infatuation, and from whom she kept no secrets. Monsieur le Cardinal found out about it soon after; and thinking that it was a much more serious matter than it was, he spoke to me about it with tremendous anger. That was precisely the way to make some-thing out of nothing, and if I had been capable of forming an attachment out of spite, his reproach would have made me resolve to deserve it.

As the gentleman was a regular visitor to the house, he heard about the stir that Monsieur le Cardinal had caused, and it may have given him ideas which he had not had before. Be that as it may, he managed to make his feel-ings known to me; and if my sister had had her way, I would have responded to his passion rather than spurning it.

Meanwhile, Monsieur le Cardinal's health was deteriorating visibly. The desire to perpetuate his name won out over the indignation he had conceived against me. He opened up about it to the bishop of Fréjus and asked him his opinion on several possible matches whom he had in mind. The bishop, who had been bought off by Monsieur Mazarin with a promise of fifty thousand écus, spared no effort to earn them. And yet he never received them. He returned the bond that he had been given for them straightaway, intimating *that he would prefer the bishopric of Évreux if possible;* but the king having disposed of it otherwise, after two months of importuning Monsieur Mazarin, Monsieur de Fréjus asked for the fifty thousand écus again, and Monsieur Mazarin was no longer of a mind to give them.

As soon as the marriage negotiations were concluded, he sent me a large cabinet in which, among other objects of value, there were ten thousand pis-toles[28] in gold. I shared them liberally with my brother and my sisters, to

---

27. Page of the chamber is one of the myriad offices within the administration of the king's household. When he went from being page of the chamber to sublieutenant of the guards, this gentleman shifted from the *Maison civile* to the *Maison militaire;* these were two of the three main divisions of the king's household (the *Maison du Roi*), the third being the *Maison ecclésiastique.*

28. It is difficult to get a clear picture of the value of the sums that Hortense and Marie cite in their texts, because of the fluctuation of currencies and values both in their time and in our own. For one thing, foreign currencies continued to circulate in France, despite an effort over the course of the seventeenth century to establish French money as the exclusive means of exchange in the kingdom. The fact that Hortense received 10,000 gold pistoles (or at least, that she referred to them as such) twenty years after an important reform of the French

console them for my opulence, which my sisters could not see without envy, no matter how they hid it. They did not even need to ask me. The key always remained where it was when the cabinet was brought to me; whoever wanted to could take from it. And one day, when we had nothing better to do, we threw more than three hundred louis [29] out the windows of the Palais Mazarin, for the fun of making a crowd of valets in the courtyard fight over them.

This prodigality having come to the attention of Monsieur le Cardinal, he was so displeased by it that people believed it had hastened his death. However that may be, he died one week later [30] and left me the richest heiress and the unhappiest woman in Christendom. When we first heard the news, all that my brother and my sister did by way of grieving was to say to

---

monetary system is evidence of this: the pistole was a Spanish gold coin worth 2 escudos. The reform of 1640–41 created the louis d'or, bearing the image of Louis XIII, as the French equivalent of the pistole. The value of the various coins was expressed in livres; the livre (or livre tournois) was a money of account, that is, a conventional measure of value, which originally represented the value of one pound of silver. The values of coins as expressed in livres were fixed by monetary edicts, and they varied according to the financial needs of the kingdom throughout the seventeenth century; however, roughly speaking, they were as follows: (1) The louis d'or, created in 1640, was the principal gold coin, worth first 10 livres and later 24. There were also double louis and half louis out of gold. (2) The écu (or écu blanc), created in 1641, was the principal silver coin, worth 3 livres. (3) The franc was a gold coin worth 1 livre; 1 franc was also worth 20 sous (or sols). François Bluch, *Dictionnaire du Grand Siècle*, rev. ed. (Paris: Fayard, 2005), 884, 1049–51; *Nouveau Petit Robert* 1295. These equivalencies are rough approximations over time; it is even more difficult to estimate with any precision their value relative to today's money. Pierre Goubert has offered the following appraisal of levels of wealth in seventeenth-century France, referring to the size of various women's dowries. He estimates that a dowry of 1,000 livres would be roughly equivalent to a value of 60,000 French francs at their 1982 value. The average value of a 1982 U.S. dollar was around 6.5 French francs, which we might round down to 6 francs for simplicity's sake. Thus, a dowry of 1,000 livres might be vaguely equivalent to a value of 10,000 1982 dollars. Goubert compares this to the dowry of a prosperous merchant's daughter, which might be 10,000 livres (or 600,000 1982 francs, or 100,000 1982 dollars). In turn, he observes that Colbert's eldest daughter had a dowry of 400,000 livres (24 million francs, or 4 million dollars), and that each of Mazarin's nieces received a dowry of 600,000 livres (36 million francs, or 6 million dollars). Goubert, *Le Siècle de Louis XIV. Etudes* (Paris: Fallois, 1996), 98. But of course, Hortense received vastly more than this; estimates of the total value of her dowry and the inheritance bestowed on her and her husband range from 19 million to 28 million livres (from 190 million to 280 million dollars). Using the values proposed by Goubert, then, the 10,000 pistoles that Hortense mentions here would be equivalent to something like 1 million dollars (assuming that a pistole was worth 10 livres at the time); and the 50,000 écus promised to the bishop of Fréjus would be something like 1.5 million dollars.

29. Hortense appears to use "pistoles" and "louis" interchangeably, just as the coins themselves were still being used more or less interchangeably.

30. Cardinal Mazarin died March 9, 1661, at the château de Vincennes.

each other, *"Thank God, he's croaked!"* [31] To tell the truth, I was hardly any more afflicted; and it is a remarkable thing that a man of his merit, after having worked all his life to exalt and enrich his family, should have received nothing but expressions of aversion from them, even after his death. If you knew with what severity he treated us at all times, you would be less surprised by it. Never has a man had such gentle manners in public and such harsh ones at home; and all our temperaments and inclinations were contrary to his. Add to that the incredible subjection under which he held us, our extreme youth, and the insensitivity and carelessness about everything which excessive wealth and privilege ordinarily cause in people of that age, however good a nature they may have.

In my own particular case, fortune has been careful to punish my ingratitude, through the continuous series of misfortunes of which my life has consisted since that death. I do not know what presentiment my sister had of it, but during the first troubles that followed my marriage, the sum of her consolation for me was to say, *"Crepa, crepa, you will be even unhappier than I."* [32]

Monsieur de Lorraine, [33] who loved her passionately, had been pressing her to marry him for a long time and continued in that pursuit even after the death of Monsieur le Cardinal. The Queen Mother, who did not want her to stay in France under any circumstances, ordered Madame de Venelle to break up that courtship whatever the cost; but all their efforts would have been useless if reasons unknown to everyone had not coincided with them. And although the king had the generosity to let her choose whomever she

---

31. *"Dieu merci, il est crevé"* (Doscot, ed., *Mémoires d'Hortense et de Marie*, 42).

32. Hortense shows her sister sprinkling her speech with Italian expressions here. *"Crepa, crepa"* translates to something like "To hell with you!"

33. Prince Charles of Lorraine (1643–90) was the nephew of Charles IV, duke of Lorraine (1604–75). Both men maintained a fractious and adversarial relationship with France, while Louis XIII and Louis XIV strove to finally subdue these last feudal lords. At the uncle's death, the nephew was recognized as Charles V, duke of Lorraine, by all the powers of Europe except France. This was because in the Treaty of Montmartre (1662), Charles IV had made Louis XIV heir to his states, in exchange for a lifetime annuity and the recognition of the princes of Lorraine as princes of the blood royal. However, the treaty never took effect; the French made yet another military foray into Lorraine, and in 1663 a new treaty ceded Charles IV's last rampart, the fortress of Marsal, to France. Thus, although Hortense here ignores the political stakes involved in any proposal of marriage between the house of Lorraine and Marie Mancini, they probably weighed at least as heavily as Marie's own feelings. In fact, the first to make a play for her hand was the uncle, Charles IV, who was nearing sixty at the time; however, Mazarin rejected his overtures when their cynical motivation came to light through the interception of letters between the duke and his mistress. By many accounts, the nephew's proposal found favor with Marie, but the cardinal balked at his request to have the duchy of Bar restored to the house of Lorraine. See Marie's memoir, note 52.

wanted to marry in France if Monsieur de Lorraine did not please her, and although he showed deep displeasure at her departure, her unlucky star led her to Italy, against any number of good reasons. The constable, who did not think that there could be any innocence in the loves of kings, was so delighted to find evidence to the contrary in the person of my sister that he cared but little that he had not been the first master of her heart. Thanks to this experience, he shed the poor opinion which he, like all Italians, held of the freedom that women have in France, and he desired that she enjoy the same freedom in Rome, since she knew how to make such good use of it.

Meanwhile the eunuch, her confidant, who had lost his standing due to her absence and to the death of Monsieur le Cardinal, undertook to make himself indispensable to me; but in addition to the fact that I was inclined to avoid any kind of intrigue, Monsieur Mazarin had me watched too closely. Enraged by this obstacle, he resolved to take revenge on Monsieur Mazarin himself. The man had retained fairly free access to the king since the time when he was the confidant of my sister. And so he goes and complains loudly to him about the rigor with which Monsieur Mazarin was treating me, saying *that he was obliged to take an interest in the matter as Monsieur le Cardinal's man and my personal servant, that Monsieur Mazarin was jealous of everyone and especially of His Majesty, and that he had me watched with very special care in all the places where the king, who had no interest in me, might see me. And what's more, that he acted like a great minister, and that he had threatened to have all the Italians banished from Paris.* To all this the king replied to him simply *that if everything he said was true, the Duc Mazarin was a fool, and that he had not inherited Monsieur le Cardinal's power along with his wealth.* The part of this report which was true is that Monsieur Mazarin, when he learned something of the eunuch's scheming, had threatened to throw him out of the Palais Mazarin where he was lodged.

Not content with what he had done, he had the poor judgment to boast about it in the presence of a woman of quality from Provence named Madame de Ruz, who knew Monsieur Mazarin, I am not sure how.[34] She

---

34. In Madame de Sévigné, *Correspondance,* Roger Duchêne offers some surprising background information on this woman (2: 295 n. 1). She was Françoise de Soissan (1631–99), who married Esprit de Rafélis de Rus, in 1649. By Duchêne's account (from which Hortense differs slightly here), she took advantage of Louis XIV's passage through Avignon to attach herself to the Duchesse Mazarin and follow her to court. She was a consummate schemer, who got herself exiled from court through involvement in the Fouquet affair, then became the mistress of the comte de Suze and bilked him out of valuable properties without even losing his affection. Her most striking accomplishment came in the 1670s, when she insinuated herself into the household of the dying *intendant des galères* in Marseille, Nicolas Arnoul. (About Arnoul, see Marie's memoir, note 151.) She became the mistress of Arnoul's son Pierre, who was *intendant des galères* in Toulon, and eventually married him. Furthermore, in 1676 she arranged the

alerted him to the disservice that had been done him. He wanted to place some lady with me who, although she would not be called a governess, would perform that function; and finding this Madame de Ruz quite apt to play the role, he looked to her, in gratitude for the advice that she gave him. He told her to find a way to be introduced to me, without my knowing that he was acquainted with her. Some time later, Monsieur de Fréjus spoke of her to me as if of his own accord, and he brought her to me by a hidden stairway one day when Monsieur Mazarin was hunting. I was much taken with her; and since I believed that if it was known that I liked her, I would not be allowed to have her, I did not want anyone in the household to know her before she was established there. One day when I was alone with her, Madame de Venelle came in abruptly, bursting through a doorstop which we had put behind the door to shut ourselves in. Immediately Madame de Ruz, with a marvelous presence of mind, began rolling her eyes back in her head, crying and shouting in a voice like a true beggar's *that she was a poor gentlewoman from Lorraine, and that she implored me to have pity on her wretchedness.* Since she has a very mobile and expressive face, like most Provençal people, her grimaces worked so well and disfigured her so much that I had difficulty recognizing her myself. Madame de Venelle was very frightened of her; she promptly got as far away from her as she could, and afterward she went all about saying *that she had found the Devil in my room.*

The deceitful behavior of Monsieur Mazarin in the choice of this woman, at a time when he could not yet have had any cause to complain of me, is enough to show you his suspicious nature and the frame of mind in which he had married me. As he was fearful of having me stay in Paris, he constantly moved me around among the lands that he possessed and governed. During the first three or four years of our marriage, I made three trips to Alsace and as many to Brittany, not to mention several others to Nevers, to Maine, to Bourbon, to Sedan, and elsewhere. Having no greater delight in Paris than that of seeing him, it was not as hard for me as it would have been for another person of my age to be deprived of the pleasures of the court. Perhaps I would never have tired of that vagabond life if he had not taken excessive advantage of my accommodating nature. Several times he had me travel two hundred leagues while I was with child, and even very near to giving birth.

My relatives and my friends, who were worried on my account about

---

marriage of her twenty-six-year-old elder son, Horace, to Arnoul's widow, and in 1680, that of her younger son to Arnoul's twelve-year-old daughter, Geneviève. Duchêne quotes Saint-Simon as saying about her, "By dint of wit and manipulation [she] made people love and fear her everywhere she dwelt, so much so that most people believed her to be a witch."

the dangers to which he was exposing my health, would point them out to me when I came to Paris, in the strongest terms they could muster; but for a long time it was to no avail. What would they have said if they had known that I could not speak to a servant without his being sent away the next day, that I could not receive two visits in a row from the same man or the doors of the house would be closed to him, that if I showed any preference for one of my maids over the others, she was immediately taken away from me? If I called for my coach and he did not see fit to let me go out, he forbade with a smile that the horses be hitched up, and joked with me about that prohibition, until the time to go where I wanted to go had passed. He would have liked me to see nobody in the world but him; above all, he could not abide my seeing his relatives or mine: mine, because then they would get involved and start defending my interests, and his, because they did not approve of his conduct any more than did mine. I was lodged for a long time at the Arsenal[35] with Madame d'Oradous,[36] his cousin, without ever being permitted to see her.

The innocence of my pastimes, which would have reassured any other man of his temperament if he took my age into account at all, caused him as much distress as if those pastimes had been exceedingly criminal. Sometimes it was a sin to play blind man's buff with my servants, sometimes to go to bed too late. He could never come up with any more than those two causes for complaint, once when Monsieur Colbert[37] desired to know all the causes that he had. Often we could not go to the Cours[38] in good con-

---

35. Located at the eastern edge of Paris *intra muros*, between the Bastille and the Seine. Because of the office of grand master of the artillery, which his father had passed down to him in 1648, Monsieur Mazarin had a residence at the Arsenal.

36. In her memoirs, Mademoiselle de Montpensier mentions a costume party during the carnival season of 1659 which was held in this woman's apartment at the Arsenal; she refers to her as "Madame d'Oradoux, wife of a lieutenant of the artillery, cousin of the maréchal de La Meilleraye." Duchesse de Montpensier, *Mémoires*, 2 vols. (Paris: Librairie Fontaine, 1985), 2: 103.

37. Jean-Baptiste Colbert, marquis de Seignelay (1619–83), was Cardinal Mazarin's designated successor as trusted advisor to Louis XIV. He was responsible for discrediting Nicolas Fouquet, and he replaced him as *surintendant des finances* in 1661; he became *contrôleur général des finances* in 1665, and he eventually had control over nearly all the top functions of government in France, except the conduct of military affairs.

38. The Cours la Reine was a fashionable place for the nobility of Paris to see and be seen. Although it is in the heart of the city today, in the seventeenth century it was outside the city walls and had a pastoral feel to it. Ladies would go there in their coaches, and the gentlemen who came there to meet them would ride alongside on horseback as they conversed. Today, part of the Cours la Reine is still called the Cours de la Reine; the rest is the Cours Albert Ier. It is the avenue that runs along the right bank of the Seine from the Place de la Concorde, past the Petit Palais and the Grand Palais, to the Place de l'Alma. Orest Ranum,

science, and even less to the theater. Another time, I did not stay at prayer long enough. In short, his peevishness on my account was so great that if he had been asked how he wanted me to live, I think that he would have been unable to come to any conclusion in his own mind. He was impelled to say later on *that he did what he did because he knew my great worth, and that social intercourse was so contagious that however much he might be ridiculed for it, he wanted to keep me from being sullied because he loved me even more than his own reputation.* But if it was his love for me that compelled him to treat me in such a bizarre fashion, it would almost have been preferable for both of us that he honor me a bit with his indifference.

As soon as he knew that I was happy in some place, he would make me leave it, no matter what reasons there might be to keep me there. We were in Maine when the news of the Marsal journey [39] arrived. He received orders to take part in it, and he sent me to Brittany to keep his father company, who was at the provincial meeting of the States.[40] While he was arranging for his departure in Paris, he learned from the spies with whom I was always surrounded that I was greatly enjoying myself; this made him sick with displeasure, and he sent for me posthaste. His father, who heard at the same time that the doctors were sending Monsieur Mazarin to Bourbon,[41] was unwilling to let me leave, saying *that one must abstain from women while taking the waters.* He swooned with vexation upon receiving this response; and after several couriers, his father having finally let me leave, I went to accompany him to Bourbon, where I spent a month cooped up in a room with him watching him take his waters, without even so much as visiting Madame la Princesse,[42] who was there and to whom he has the honor of being related.

Paris in the Age of Absolutism: An Essay, rev. ed. (University Park: Pennsylvania State University Press, 2002), 17, 218.

39. In 1663; see above, note 33.

40. Like the States-General (*États généraux*), the provincial meetings of the States (*États provinciaux*) were called by the king to be held in certain provinces known as *pays d'États;* and like the States-General, they brought together representatives of the three "estates" of the population (clergy, nobility, and commoners). Their main function was to handle fiscal matters—to give formal consent to the royal taxes imposed and to fix the contributions to be made by the different entities in the province; however, the meetings also included the setting down of grievances (*doléances*) to be transmitted to the king and his councils. Whereas the political authority of the *États provinciaux* was greatly diminished in many parts of France by the seventeenth century, in Brittany they still played an important role in defending the interests of the province.

41. The fashionable spa town of Bourbon-l'Archambault, located fifteen miles west of Moulins and thirty miles south of Nevers.

42. The princesse de Condé, Claire-Clémence de Maillé-Brézé (1628–94), was married in 1641 to Louis II de Bourbon, prince de Condé (1621–86), who was known as *le Grand Condé.*

At first he had been unable to believe that it was his father who had kept me in Brittany; and no matter how much assurance of it he received subsequently, he always maintained that I had preferred to amuse myself there rather than to come and console him in his illness. It would have been easy for me to defend myself against his accusations if he had been willing to listen to me; but that is what he was most eager to avoid because he turned out to be entirely in the wrong whenever things were explained, and he never wanted to admit that he had been mistaken. Nothing pained me more about him than his aversion to letting himself be enlightened, because by turning a deaf ear he claimed the right to treat me forever as the guilty party.

Some time later, when he was obliged for the service of the king to go to Brittany, he took it so firmly into his head to have me with him, and he wrote such strange things on the subject to the abbé d'Effiat,[43] his kinsman, that I was forced to leave Paris three weeks after having given birth. Few women of my quality would have done as much; but what will we not do in order to enjoy such a precious good as peace? For the rest of my recovery, he had me stay in one of the most wretched villages in all that land, and in such a miserable house that we were obliged to stay outside in the meadows all day. He always chose these sorts of places, so that I would be sure not to find any company. Thus, there was none in the village itself—far from it—and those whom civility or business impelled to come and see him there were forced to camp for lack of an inn; and if they should displease him in any way, he would send them off again quickly on the pretext of asking them to attend to various matters of business over which he had authority in the province. Nevertheless we spent six months in that pleasant abode in the year 1666.

Another time, when he was alone in Bourbon and he had sent me to Brittany, he was again told by his spies that I was amusing myself quite well with Madame de Coaquin,[44] and that few days went by when we did not make some kind of outing on land or on sea. His anxiety takes hold of him.

She was the niece of Cardinal Richelieu and was thus part of the same family as Monsieur Mazarin, whose father was first cousin to the cardinal. The prince de Condé was the first prince of the blood and first peer of France; he had been one of the heads of the Fronde, and the princesse had also been an active *Frondeuse*, but they had come back into favor with Cardinal Mazarin and with Louis XIV before Mazarin's death.

43. Jean (or Charles-Jean) Coëffier-Ruzé, abbé d'Effiat (1622–98), was in fact the brother of Monsieur Mazarin's mother, Marie Coëffier-Ruzé. The abbé d'Effiat was known for his liaisons with the marquise de Courcelles (see below, note 65) and with Ninon de Lenclos.

44. Or Madame de Coëtquen; probably "Marguerite" Gabrielle Charlotte de Rohan-Chabot (ca. 1647–1720), who was married in 1662 to Malo de Coëtquen, governor of Saint-Malo (d. 1679). The château de Coëtquen was in Brittany, near Dinan.

He sends word that I should go and join him in Nevers, where *there were,* he said, *very good actors, among other entertainments.*

I was beginning to tire of performing such chores. I wrote to Monsieur Colbert to complain of it; but after he had advised me to go there, I was very surprised to find Monsieur Mazarin ten leagues from Nevers, on his way to Paris with my brother, who was returning from Italy. He never offered me any reason for such strange behavior, and we went with no further explanation to shut ourselves up in our cottage near Sedan, where my brother was kind enough to come with us, as he could see that I was very sad. It was there that for the first time Monsieur Mazarin, who was not pleased to have such a witness to his domestic behavior and who could think of no other way to be rid of him, decided to pretend to be jealous of him.[45] Imagine what resentment I must have felt over such a spiteful suggestion.

Now if all these insults seem hard to endure when you hear me recount them, the way in which they were delivered was something even crueler. You can judge from this sample of it. One evening when I was with the queen, I saw him coming toward me looking pleased, with a forced and affected smile on his face, to publicly pay me this compliment: *"I have good news to tell you, Madame; the king has just commanded me to go to Alsace."* Monsieur de Roquelaure,[46] who happened to be there, indignant like the rest of the company at this affectation but more candid than the others, could not keep from saying to him *that this was fine news indeed to come and announce with such delight to a woman like me;* but Monsieur Mazarin, without deigning to respond, serenely left the room, pleased as could be with his gallantry. The king, to whom the story was told, was moved to pity when he heard it. He went to the trouble of telling me himself *that my trip would last no more than three months,* and he kept his word to me, as he always has.

If I were not afraid of boring you, I could tell you of a thousand such acts of guile, which he carried out against me quite needlessly, and simply for the pleasure of tormenting me, as in that case. Just imagine continual opposition to even my most innocent desires; an implacable hatred for everyone who loved me and whom I loved; an avid effort to set before me all the people I could not abide, and to bribe those whom I trusted the most in order to discover my secrets, if I had had any; a tireless diligence in disparaging me to everyone and in putting a shameful cast on all my actions; in

45. Monsieur Mazarin accused Philippe of being in love with Hortense. Mongrédien, *Une Aventurière au Grand Siècle,* 50–53.

46. Gaston-Jean-Baptiste, marquis and then duc de Roquelaure (1617–83), was a courtier known for his perpetual good humor, his enthusiasm for court gossip, and his often rather inane *bons mots.*

short, everything that the malice of a sanctimonious cabal can dream up and implement in a household where it holds tyrannical sway, against a naïve, unsuspecting young woman, whose unguarded behavior every day offered her enemies new occasions for triumph.

I do not hesitate to use the term *sanctimonious cabal;*[47] for I do not believe that even the strictest rules of Christian charity require me to presume that the pious men by whom Monsieur Mazarin has been governed are among the genuine believers, after they have led him to squander so many millions. And this is the fatal point which has pushed my patience to its limit, and which is the true source of all my misfortunes. If Monsieur Mazarin had been content to overwhelm me with sadness and grief, to expose my health and my life to his most unreasonable whims, and in short to make me spend my best days in unparalleled servitude, then since heaven had given him to me as master, I would merely have moaned and complained of him to my friends. But when I saw that because of his unbelievable extravagance, my son,[48] who should have become the richest gentleman in France, ran the risk of winding up the poorest, I had to give in to the force of blood ties, and motherly love won out over all the moderation that I had intended to observe.

Every day I saw immense sums of money, priceless furniture, offices, governorships, and all the rich remains of my uncle's fortune disappear, the fruit of his labors and the reward for his services. I saw more than three millions' worth of it sold before I made any public protest; and there was almost nothing of value left to me but my jewels when Monsieur Mazarin took it into his head to seize them from me. He took advantage of his opportunity to lay hold of them one evening when I came home very late from the city. When I desired to know the reason before going to bed, he told me *that he feared I would give some of them away, liberal as I was, and that he had taken them only in order to add more to them.* I replied to him *that one could only wish that his liberality were as well ordered as mine, that I was satisfied with my jewels as they were, and that I would not go to bed until he returned them to me;* but seeing that no matter what I said, he replied only with bad jokes, spoken with a malicious smile and in a tone which seemed serene but was actually very bitter, finally in despera-

47. "*Cabale bigote,*" in Hortense's words (Doscot, ed., *Mémoires d'Hortense et de Marie,* 49).

48. Paul-Jules, Duc Mazarin and duc de La Meilleraye (1666–1731), who married Charlotte Félicité de Durfort (1672–1730) in 1685. Their son, Guy-Paul-Jules, Duc Mazarin and duc de La Meilleraye (1701–38), was the last in the male line of this family. Their daughter, Armande-Félicité de La Porte Mazarin (1691–1729), was the mother of four of Louis XV's mistresses.

tion I left the room and went off to my brother's wing,[49] in tears and not knowing what to do. We sent straightaway for Madame de Bouillon, and when she had heard about my new cause for complaint, she told me that I deserved it since I had borne all the others in silence.

I would have gone away with her that very instant if Madame Bellinzani,[50] for whom we had also sent, had not stopped me, urging me to wait until she had spoken with Monsieur Mazarin. He had given orders that no one should be admitted; when Madame Bellinzani nonetheless insisted on speaking with him, he did not give her the chance to say a word, and she could draw nothing out of him except *that she could not possibly have urgent enough business with him for her to disturb him at such an unreasonable hour, and that if she needed to speak to him, he was going the next morning to Saint-Germain[51] and he would meet her at the Croix de Nanterre.*[52] After Madame Bellinzani came back as indignant as we were at such outrageous mockery, it was decided that I would go and sleep at Madame de Bouillon's house.

The next day the whole family assembled there for my problem, and Madame la Comtesse[53] was chosen to speak to the king about it. He re-

---

49. Cardinal Mazarin bequeathed half his palace in Paris to the Duc and Duchesse Mazarin, his principal heirs, and the other half to Philippe Mancini, duc de Nevers, who was his only surviving male heir. In modern times, the Palais Mazarin, located near the Palais Royal on the rue de Richelieu, housed the Bibliothèque Nationale until the construction of the Bibliothèque Nationale de France in the 1990s.

50. Madame Bellinzani was the wife of François Bellinzani, who was a creature of Cardinal Mazarin, became *intendant* (estate manager) to the Duc Mazarin, and was employed by Colbert in various commercial missions. After Colbert's death (1683), Monsieur Bellinzani was accused of financial misdealings and died in prison before his trial; Madame Bellinzani fled France, and upon her return she was arrested and imprisoned for several years.

51. The château de Saint-Germain-en-Laye, located fifteen miles west of Paris, was the principal residence of the court until it relocated to Versailles in 1682. Versailles is located fifteen miles southwest of Paris, and nine miles south of Saint-Germain-en-Laye.

52. Along the pathways that crisscrossed the forest of Saint-Germain-en-Laye, to the north of the château, there were several shrines or "crosses," which often served as landmarks or meeting points; in addition to the Croix de Nanterre, there were the Croix Pucelle, the Croix Saint-Simon, the Croix de Noailles, the Croix du Maine, and so on.

53. Olympe Mancini (1639–1708), who married a prince of the blood, Eugène-Maurice de Savoie-Carignan, comte de Soissons (1633–73), in 1657. The comtesse de Soissons was an extremely prominent member of the court of Louis XIV; indeed, she held the highest post that a woman at court could have, that of superintendent of the queen's household. However, in 1680, both she and Madame de Bouillon (Marie-Anne Mancini) were implicated in the famous Affair of the Poisons. Madame de Bouillon appeared before the *Chambre Ardente*, which was convened in the Arsenal of Paris to examine the affair, and was exiled to Nérac in southwest France; she returned to court in 1682 but was exiled again from 1685 until 1690. Madame la Comtesse fled to Flanders to avoid her subpoena; a sentence of perpetual

ceived her most graciously, and Madame la Princesse Carignan[54] was given the order to come and collect me and bring me to the hôtel de Soissons. I stayed there for around two months, after which time I was forced to return to Monsieur Mazarin, although he did not even restore my jewels to me, and although I gained no other advantage than to be allowed to turn out a few women whom he had given me and who did not suit me. This was the only favor I was able to obtain. When I tried to insist on the jewels, Madame la Comtesse was the first to tell me that I was being base. I always had the court against me from that time on; everyone knows what difficulties that brings in all sorts of matters. I said to the king in this regard *that I would be consoled about seeing Monsieur Mazarin so clearly favored over me if he were equally favored in everything, and if the meager support that he found in his other interests did not reveal that he had no other friends than my enemies.*

As this peace was more like a triumph for him than a compromise, it made him too haughty for it to last. One hour before going to the Palais Mazarin, I sent a valet de chambre whom Madame la Comtesse had given me in the meantime since I had left there and who was transporting my personal effects. Monsieur Mazarin, who knew him as well as I did, asked him what he wanted and to whom he belonged, and then dismissed him without even waiting until I had arrived. This valet met me at two hundred paces from the dwelling; and although Madame la Comtesse, who was accompanying me, could clearly see that this was a new subject of dispute, she merely urged me to let it pass, left me at the foot of the stairs, and declined to see Monsieur Mazarin, because he had made every effort to have me stay at the hôtel de Conti,[55] as if I would not be so comfortable at the hôtel de Soissons.

I immediately asked for clemency on behalf of the valet who had been dismissed, and the position to which I was reduced by the authority of the

---

banishment was pronounced against her *in absentia;* and she lived out the rest of her life in exile after the fashion of her sisters, Hortense and Marie. Madame de Sévigné concluded her report on the exile of Madame de Bouillon with this observation, "Just look at the four sisters: what wandering star rules them! in Spain, in England, in the depths of Guyenne." Letter to Madame de Grignan dated February 16, 1680 (*Correspondance,* 2: 840).

54. Marie de Bourbon-Condé, comtesse de Soissons and de Clermont (1606–92), who married Thomas-François de Savoie-Carignan, prince de Carignan (1596–1656); she was the mother of Eugène-Maurice de Savoie-Carignan and thus the mother-in-law of Olympe Mancini.

55. The home of Armand de Bourbon-Condé, prince de Conti (1629–66), who was married to Anne-Marie Martinozzi (ca. 1637–72); Anne-Marie and Laure Martinozzi were Hortense's first cousins, the daughters of Cardinal Mazarin's sister Laura Margherita Mazzarino (or Mazzarini). The prince de Conti was the brother of *le Grand Condé,* and they fought side be side during the Fronde; his marriage in 1654 to one of the Cardinal's nieces was an act of reconciliation with the king and his minister.

official powers compelled me to submit in ways I would never have imagined from a person of my proud nature; but it was all in vain. I was dealing with a man who was determined to take advantage of the situation, and since all that I got from him were poor excuses and even worse jokes, I set about leaving him, in order to withdraw once again to my brother's part of the palace.

Monsieur Mazarin, who, as you will see, had taken steps to keep me from going out when I wished and to make a prison of my palace, threw himself in front of me and pushed me very roughly, in order to block my way; but my grief and vexation gave me extraordinary strength, and I broke through even though he was strong, too. And though he screamed like mad out the window *to close all the doors and especially the gate of the courtyard*, nobody, when they saw me all in tears, dared to obey him. I went around to the other side through the street, which was very crowded, in this sad state, alone, on foot, and in the middle of the day, to reach my usual refuge. This scandal was the result of the care he had taken to wall up the doors that led from my brother's palace to ours, and by which I had run away the previous time; but those who heard about this precaution judged from it that he had no intention, if I were to return to him, of treating me any better than in the past, since he was trying to ensure that kind of control for the future.

Upon arriving at my brother's, I wrote to the king to explain my actions to him; and Madame la Comtesse brought me to the hôtel de Soissons. But after five or six days, when Monsieur de Louvois[56] came to suggest to me on behalf of the king that I enter some convent, she would not consent to it; and she negotiated in such a way that Monsieur Mazarin was obliged to come and fetch me, on the condition that she would reconcile with him. My brother left immediately afterward for Italy, in part to make it clear that it would have nothing to do with him whether I stayed on good terms with

---

56. François-Michel Le Tellier, marquis de Louvois (1641–91). He was the son of Michel Le Tellier (1603–85), who was secretary of state for military affairs (*secrétaire d'État à la guerre*) and later chancellor of France (*chancelier de France*). With Mazarin's support, Le Tellier passed his office of secretary of state for military affairs to Louvois in 1656, when the latter was fifteen years old. They collaborated in the function until 1677, when Louvois assumed sole charge of the office. Both father and son were determined enemies of Protestants in France and worked for their forced conversion to Catholicism and for the revocation of the Edict of Nantes, which came in 1685. Louvois is credited with the total restructuring of the French military and the creation of the first modern army in Europe. He carried on a pitched rivalry for precedence with Colbert; near the end of the latter's life, Louvois bought the office of superintendent of buildings, arts, and manufacturing (*surintendant des bâtiments, arts et manufactures*), and in that role he oversaw the construction and transformation of Versailles. The comtesse de Soissons's objection to his suggestion, which Hortense reports here, may be due in part to a marked animosity between Louvois and her.

my husband; but the harmony was never more than superficial, and during the three or four months that we were together, not a day went by when I was not compelled to quarrel, no matter how much I needed and wished to live in peace.

At the end of this time, he desired to go to Alsace; and rather than agreeing to all my requests in order to impel me to follow him there, as I was resolved to do, he was so ill advised as to insist that I keep a woman whom I no longer wanted. This squabble over a trifle made me open my eyes, and gave me time to think better of what I was doing. My friends were charitable enough to make me see how unsafe it was for me to place myself in the hands of a man of his character, in such a distant region, where he had absolute authority; they pointed out to me:

That after what had happened, I would have to be a fool to expect to come back from there; that he had already sent my jewels ahead, and that he could only have done so in order to retire completely to that governorship, where his actions would not be open to public scrutiny as they were in Paris, and where my friends, however much I might need them, would no longer be able to do anything for me but send useless wishes.

These considerations, which were only too well founded, led me to take refuge with Madame la Comtesse the day before Monsieur Mazarin's departure, for fear that he might carry me off with him by force. I was so undone upon finding myself reduced once again to this necessity that I even forgot to bring along my small jewels, which had always remained to me for my daily use and which might well have been worth fifty thousand écus.[57] As they were the only possessions in the world which I had at my disposal, Madame la Comtesse had the presence of mind to ask me about them as soon as she saw me; and that was why I was able to send for them in time to get them. He came the next day to ask what I desired. He was told two things: that I not go to Alsace and that he return to me my large jewels, which had already left, and which had been the first cause of our disagreements. As for Alsace, he would easily have excused me from going because he no longer had any hope of bringing me there, but as for the jewels, he did not give any clear answer; and since at the time they were still in transit, as soon as he had left us, Madame la princesse de Bade[58] brought me to see

57. Or 150,000 livres; see above, note 28.

58. Louise-Christine de Savoie-Carignan (1627–89), who was married in 1653 (or 1654) to Ferdinand Maximilian Zähringen, margrave of Baden-Baden (1625–69). The margraves of Baden-Baden were sovereign German princes, and thus Louise-Christine was commonly called the princess of Baden. She was the sister-in-law of Olympe Mancini, and both she and Olympe had sons who built great military careers in battle against the French: Ludwig Wilhelm I, margrave of Baden-Baden (1655–1707), and Prince Eugène de Savoie-Carignan (1663–1736).

Monsieur Colbert to implore him to seize them. He did not think he could refuse me this favor; he commanded that they be brought back, and they have always remained in his hands since then.

All that was left then was to determine what was to become of me. Monsieur Mazarin gave me the choice of staying at the hôtel de Conti or at the abbey of Chelles,[59] the two places in the world which he knew I most hated, and for the best of reasons. The despondency into which my spirits had fallen absolutely prevented me from making a choice between two equally odious propositions. Others had to choose for me; and the arguments against the hôtel de Conti[60] were so strong that Chelles was preferred.

It was in that solitude that I reflected upon the obligation which my relatives told me I had, for the sake of my poor children, to obtain a formal separation of property in order to save what remained from being squandered by Monsieur Mazarin, and I finally resolved to do it. But as convinced as I was that I needed to do it, I had particular reasons to defer in all things to the feelings of Monsieur Colbert, and there I was stopped short; for when I sounded him out about this plan, I learned that he was not in favor of it.

After six months, Monsieur Mazarin came to see me as he passed through on his return from Alsace, and he tried to compel me to dismiss two maids whom Madame la Comtesse had given me since his departure. Since he had no other reason to demand that deference of me than his animosity toward her, I did not consider it my duty to satisfy him. His resentment over this pushed him to beseech the king to have me change convents, I know not on what pretext; but his real reason was that the abbess of Chelles, who

---

59. The royal abbey of Chelles, located fifteen miles east of Paris, was founded in the mid-seventh century and destroyed during the Revolution. It was at its peak in the late seventeenth century, when Hortense sojourned there (1667).

60. Those arguments had to do with the strict piety of the prince de Conti and his wife, Hortense's cousin Anne-Marie Martinozzi. Conti had earlier led a worldly and dissolute life—he had boasted of an incestuous relationship with his own sister; had kept numerous mistresses, including one who remained in his château for some time after his marriage; had contracted the pox during some carnival philandering soon after his marriage and had passed it on to his bride. As governor of Languedoc, the prince de Conti had protected Molière and his troupe when they passed through that province in 1652, and he had brought them along to Paris to perform at his wedding in 1654. However, in 1656, he finally made good on past promises to become devout, and he began to decry all worldly pursuits including the theater. Conti was received into the secret organization called the Compagnie du Saint-Sacrement (Company of the Blessed Sacrament) and began to defend its interests with Cardinal Mazarin, whom its members regarded as simonious and sacrilegious. The Duc Mazarin greatly admired Conti's devotion and would have been content to see his wife lodged at his house (see above, 46). Cf. Georges Livet, *Le duc Mazarin, gouverneur d'Alsace (1661–1713). Lettres et documents inédits* (Strasbourg and Paris: F.-X. Le Roux, 1954), 37–38; Rosvall, *Mazarine Legacy,* 31–32, 80–82.

was his aunt, treated me very civilly and I was happy there. He obtained all that he desired; and although the abbess was as offended by this as she ought to have been, and although she gave the most favorable reports of my conduct that he could have wished for, Monsieur le Premier[61] came to tell me *that I would please the king if I went to Sainte-Marie de la Bastille,*[62] and Madame de Toussi[63] came to fetch me with six guards to escort me.

A short time later, Monsieur Mazarin came to see me there as he was setting out for Brittany. He could not bear to see me with patches[64] on; it just so happened that I had put some on that day, and he told me right away *that he would not speak with me until I had removed them.* Never did a man ask for things with a haughtiness more apt to provoke a refusal, especially when he considered it a matter of conscience, as he did on this occasion; and that was also what made me insist on remaining as I was, to make clear to him that neither had I intended to offend God by that adornment nor did I believe that I had. He protested for over an hour about it; but when he could see that it was useless, he finally said what he had to say, my patches notwithstanding, and urged me no less uselessly to go to Brittany with him.

I was rather more inclined to sue him than to follow him. I obtained permission to go and discuss the matter with the king; Madame la princesse de Bade conducted me there, and His Majesty had the kindness to permit me to bring my case. But Monsieur Colbert, who was reluctant to consent to it for reasons which left no room for argument in all other situations, drew things out endlessly, until Madame de Courcelles[65] was placed in the

61. The *premier écuyer du Roi* (first equerry of the king) was referred to as "Monsieur le Premier"; in the administration of the king's household, he was in charge of the *petite Écurie* (small stable), which entailed overseeing the personnel attached to the horses and coaches: the equerries, pages, footmen, coachmen, postilions, saddlers, and grooms. At this time, Monsieur le Premier was Henri de Beringhen (1603–92).

62. A convent of the Order of the Visitation, located just to the west of the Bastille at 17 rue Saint-Antoine. This was the first house of the Sisters of the Visitation in Paris; its domed chapel was designed by François Mansart, and the construction was begun in 1634. Hortense and Marie had both been placed in another convent of the Visitation—this one in the rue Saint-Jacques—when they were first brought to Paris by Cardinal Mazarin. See Marie's memoir, note 18.

63. Louise de Prie, marquise de Toussy (ca. 1624–1709), who married Maréchal Philippe de La Mothe-Houdancourt in 1650 and later became *gouvernante* of the dauphin and of the king's children.

64. Patches (*mouches*) were the artificial beauty marks made of black taffeta which ladies applied to their faces, throats, and bosoms, primarily to set off the whiteness of their skin.

65. Marie-Sidonia de Lenoncourt, marquise de Courcelles (1650–85). A rich heiress who was left in the charge of her paternal aunt, an abbess, at the age of four and raised in the convent, she was brought out at the age of thirteen to be married to a brother of Colbert. However, she managed to maneuver Louis XIV into authorizing her marriage to the marquis

convent with me and at last I obtained permission to begin my suit, through the favor of the friends she had at court.

As she was very attractive and very amusing, I obliged her by taking part in some jokes she played on the nuns. People told the king a hundred ridiculous stories about it: that we put ink in the holy water font, so that those good ladies would smudge up their faces; that we went running through the dormitory as they were falling asleep with lots of little dogs, shouting tallyho;[66] and several other things of the sort, which were either completely invented or excessively exaggerated. For example, we once asked to wash our feet, and the nuns took it into their heads to find fault with the request and to refuse us what we needed, as if we were there to observe their rule. It is true that we filled two large chests which were above the dormitory with water; and because they did not hold the water, and the slats of the floor did not come together tightly, we did not notice that what was spilling was running through the bad floor and wetting the beds of the sisters. If you were at court at that time, you will recall that people there recounted that accident as if it had been a deliberate prank. It is also true that on the pretext of keeping us company, the sisters were keeping us under surveillance. The oldest nuns were chosen for the job, as they were considered the most difficult to suborn; but since we did nothing but run about all day long, we soon exhausted them all one after another, until two or three of them sprained their ankles striving to keep up with us. I would not recount to you these trivial things if the partisans of Monsieur Mazarin had not made them public; but since they have turned them into so many crimes imputed to me, I am glad that you should know all the enormity of them.

After we had been in that convent for three months, we received permission to go to Chelles, where I knew that we would be treated more reasonably, although we could not have as many visitors there; and Monsieur Mazarin arrived from Brittany the same day we were transferred there. It was a few days later that he came there with sixty horses and permission from Monsieur de Paris[67] to enter the convent and to take me away by force;

---

de Courcelles instead. She openly loathed her husband, but he was willing to commit in the marriage contract to never obliging her to leave the court. He did, however, eventually make a formal accusation of adultery against her, for which she was convicted. She fled to Geneva, and she too spent years on the run from her husband; she was widowed in 1678 but died herself only seven years later, at the age of thirty-four. Her memoirs and correspondence were published at least three times in the nineteenth century.

66. *Tayaut!* or *taïaut!* is the cry used during a hunt, to send the hounds after the quarry.

67. The archbishop of Paris, who was at that time Paul-Philippe Hardouin de Péréfixe (1605–70).

but his aunt the abbess, who was not content merely to refuse him entry herself, put all the keys into my hands to rid me of any suspicion that she might do me ill, with the sole condition that I speak with Monsieur Mazarin. I asked him loudly what he wanted, but he kept answering *that I was not the abbess;* and when I retorted *that I was the abbess for him that day, since I had all the keys of the house, and he could not enter except by my favor,* he turned his back on me and went away. A gentleman who had come to visit me on behalf of Madame la Comtesse went back and reported all this in Paris, adding that the rumor in Chelles was that Monsieur Mazarin had not withdrawn completely, and that he would come back the following night. You have doubtless heard how Madame de Bouillon, Monsieur le Comte, Monsieur de Bouillon, and all the worthiest noblemen at court mounted their horses upon hearing this report, to come to my aid. At the noise they made when they arrived, Madame de Courcelles and I took them for my enemies; but the fright did not upset us so badly that we failed to take note of an excellent makeshift hiding place. In the grille of our parlor there was a hole big enough for a large tray, through which we had never imagined before then that a person might be able to pass. And yet we both got through it; but it was such a tight fit that Monsieur Mazarin himself, if he had been in the convent, would never have suspected it and would have looked for us everywhere but in that parlor. We soon realized that it had been a false alarm, and the embarrassment that we felt over it made us resolve to go back inside the way we had gone out without telling anyone about it. Madame de Courcelles passed back through the hole first with ease: but I was stuck for more than a quarter hour, nearly in a faint between two iron bars which were pressing into me from either side, unable to move either forward or backward. But even though I was in extraordinary agony in that position, I obstinately refused to call anyone to our aid, and Madame de Courcelles kept pulling until she got me out. I went to thank all these gentlemen; and they left again after having joked for a time about the expedition that Monsieur Mazarin had undertaken in order to collect nothing at all.

In the meantime I obtained a ruling in my favor in the third chamber of the Enquêtes.[68] That chamber was composed almost entirely of very reasonable young men, and there was not a single one of them who did not strive to serve me. It was declared *that I would go to live at the Palais Mazarin, and Mon-*

---

68. The Parlement of Paris, which met in the Palais de Justice on the Île de la Cité, was divided into various chambers for its judicial proceedings. There were the chambers of inquests (*enquêtes*) and the chambers of requests (*requêtes*), all of which were run by junior judges, as Hortense observes here. Besides these, there was the Great Chamber (Grand'Chambre), where the senior judges met to examine the weightiest cases.

sieur Mazarin at the Arsenal; that he would give me a pension of twenty thousand francs;[69] and, most important, *that he would produce the documents with which I intended to prove that he had wasted my son's fortune.* Madame la princesse de Carignan came to fetch me and to settle me into my home. I found there all the palace servants that I needed, who had been chosen by Monsieur Mazarin, but I dismissed them, thanking them very civilly for their goodwill. Madame la Comtesse, who was always inciting me to misplaced generosity, persuaded me once again *that it would be unbecoming to demand the pension that the Parlement had awarded me.* Monsieur Mazarin was not a man who would willingly give it to me. Nonetheless, I had to live. She did ask me if I needed money; but she could be in no doubt of that, and had it not been for my small jewels, and my brother, my affairs would have been in very bad order. He came back from Italy ten days after my ruling; and although he was very angry about the lawsuit, for the same reasons which had made Monsieur Colbert disapprove of it, and although he had always predicted that Madame la Comtesse would get me mixed up in it and then drop me, I found every morning on my dressing table more than enough money for my needs, though I could never be certain from whom it came.

Meanwhile, Monsieur Mazarin had brought our case before the Grand'Chambre,[70] to have it reexamined; but they saw to it that the king intervened once again to reconcile us. We signed a document he set before us, which declared *that Monsieur Mazarin would come back to live at the Palais Mazarin, but that I would be free to choose all my servants as I wished, with the exception of an equerry whom I would be given by Monsieur Colbert; that we would each stay in our own apartments; that I would not be obliged to follow him on any journey; and that in the matter of the separation of property which I requested, Messieurs les Ministres would be the arbitrators, and we would inviolably observe and obey what they said.* The same day that I signed this agreement, I encountered Madame de Brissac[71] at the

---

69. Or 20,000 livres; see above, note 28.

70. Thus, he had the case brought before the senior judges; Hortense asserts below (56) that the older men were more inclined to be sympathetic to the husband's side.

71. Madame de Brissac had reason to speak so candidly to Hortense about the latter's situation: she herself had been through a similar marital ordeal, except that her husband was reputed to be an atheist rather than a *dévot.* Marie-Gabrielle-Louise de Saint-Simon (1646–84) was the daughter of Claude de Rouvroy, duc de Saint-Simon (1607–93), and in 1663, when she married Henri-Albert de Cossé, duc de Brissac (1645–98), she brought a dowry of 600,000 livres. Since Brissac had debts which amounted to two million, the dowry was rapidly used up, and after three years of marriage, Madame de Brissac sought a physical separation and a separation of property (*séparation de corps et de biens*). She obtained the physical separation, but although Brissac was ordered to repay the dowry, the duc de Saint-Simon continued to sue for the money until his death.

fair,[72] and she said to me with a laugh, *"So here you are, Madame, plastered up again for the third time."* For of course, we were not truly reconciled at all.

Monsieur Mazarin took it upon himself to vex me in everything. I could give you many examples, but I will simply recount one of the most striking and most widely known. I had had a stage erected in my apartment, in order to have a play performed there for some people of the court. Two hours before it was to be used, Monsieur Mazarin, without saying anything to me, took it into his head to have it pulled down, because *it was a feast day, and the theater is a profane entertainment.* All this did not prevent us from seeing each other quite easily in the afternoons; for we neither ate nor slept together. Monsieur Mazarin would have preferred it otherwise; but besides the fact that our agreement said nothing about it, it did not seem likely to me that things could long remain as they were, and if by chance we should find ourselves back in the Parlement, I did not want to run the risk of bringing a suit while great with child. My foresight did not prove vain. He soon thought better of what he had done; he implored the king to rip up the agreement and to release us from our promises. I consented to this only on the condition that the king would never involve himself in our affairs, either on one side or on the other. His Majesty was so kind as to make me that promise and has always kept it since. So there we were back in the Grand'Chambre, with things more embittered than ever.

Monsieur Mazarin and his allies never missed a chance from that time on to blacken my reputation in society, and especially in the mind of the king. The extravagant behavior of Courcelles,[73] among other things, offered them an admirable means to do so. I had forgotten to tell you that when I left Chelles, I managed to obtain permission for his wife to come and live with me. When she was there, those who had once taken her out of her husband's house were now quite pleased to give her back to him, and they slipped him into the Palais Mazarin, I am not sure how, while I was in town, so that he made it up with her and brought her back home with him. One day when I went to see her, she was imprudent enough to have it announced to me that she was not there, even though Cavoye's[74] carriage was at her door. In

---

72. The fair of Saint-Germain, on the Left Bank, which was held annually by the monastery of Saint-Germain-des-Prés. Officially, it lasted for three weeks in the spring, but it was often prolonged; it was one of the most important events of the year in Paris from the end of the fifteenth century through the rest of the ancien régime.

73. The marquis de Courcelles was reputed to be a coarse and disagreeable person, whose most prepossessing quality was his relation to the maréchal de Villeroi (*gouverneur* of the young Louis XIV), who was his uncle.

74. Louis Oger, marquis de Cavoye (1640–1716). He was raised with Louis XIV and remained one of the king's close confidants throughout his life; he was also a protégé of the great commander Turenne, and he obtained the military office of *grand maréchal*

my initial pique over her incivility, I unfortunately met her husband along my way, and I could not help saying something about it. This utter fool had wanted for some time to cross swords with Cavoye, but had hesitated for the sole reason that he did not want to appear to be jealous of his best friend. He wanted people to think that he was fighting for some other reason. He found no more plausible explanation than to spread the rumor that he was my lover and to pretend *that his wife had had in her possession some incriminating letters, which I had supposedly written to a court gentleman, that she had given them to Cavoye, that Cavoye was showing them to people, that he wanted to fight him to get the letters back, and that he had promised me to do so.* However ridiculous and ill conceived this whole story may seem on its face, there were people stupid enough to believe it and to spread it around on the strength of his word. And he did far worse. He was so foolish as to tell me the story to my face in the courtyard of the Palais Mazarin. I told him *that since I knew better than anyone that none of what he was saying could possibly be true, I could only conclude that it was all in jest, and that if I found out he had the slightest thought of provoking a duel on that impertinent pretext, I would at once inform Monsieur le Comte,*[75] *who was standing a stone's throw from us and who could hear part of what we were saying.* Courcelles, seeing clearly by the way I spoke to him that I was not kidding, shook his head as if to say that it was just a joke; he did not dare say it to me out loud because of Monsieur le Comte, who joined us just at that moment. Imagine my astonishment when I learned the next day, not only that he had fought the duel, but that in the agreement they had struck on the spot, he had had the effrontery to maintain his lie until the bitter end, and to admit a woman into the bond of secrecy which they swore to each other. He was so pleased with himself that he could not keep from boasting about how he had included her, to people whom he had not included. That was what divulged the matter, and what sent them both to the Conciergerie,[76] to do penance for the stupidity of the one. Of course, everyone at court called me a troublemaker and accused me of brutality toward this worthy subject, saying *that I would do my best to get plenty of others slaughtered too;* and because a valet de chambre of mine had been seriously injured at about that same time by some brawlers he knew, people were once

des logis du Roi in 1677. Cavoye was a friend of Racine and Boileau and a brilliant courtier known for his striking presence and his numerous love affairs. According to Gérard Doscot, he was involved with Hortense before his affair with Madame de Courcelles (Doscot, ed., *Mémoires d'Hortense et de Marie*, 61 n. 1; cf. Mongrédien, *Une Aventurière au Grand Siècle*, 61).

75. The comte de Soissons, Eugène-Maurice de Savoie-Carignan, who was the husband of Olympe Mancini and thus Hortense's brother-in-law.

76. The Conciergerie was then where it still is today, attached to the Palais de Justice on the Île de la Cité. Courtiers who misbehaved could expect to find themselves confined there as punishment.

again charitable enough to suggest to the king *that this boy had been entirely in my confidence and that he had abused my trust, so I had seen fit to have him killed.*

The insolence with which people were spouting this slander forced me to speak to the king about it. Madame la Comtesse, with whom I went there, said to him as we entered the room *that she was bringing him that criminal, that wicked woman, of whom so much ill was being said.* The king had the goodness to say to me *that he had never believed a word of it;* but he said it so succinctly, and in a manner so different from the openness with which he was in the habit of treating me, that anyone other than I would have seen cause to doubt whether he was speaking the truth.

You know that the court is a land of great contradictions. The pity that people may have felt for me when they knew that I was locked up in a convent turned to envy when they saw me appear in the queen's chambers and cause a much greater sensation there than I meant to. And yet I had no ambition but to come to some tolerable agreement with Monsieur Mazarin; but those by whom I was guided and who, as it later became clear, had other designs played at ruining me in the pursuit of their own aims. Taking advantage of my naïveté and of the blind deference which I showed to their feelings, they pushed me every day to take steps of which I understood neither the significance nor the motives.

In the midst of this confusion, our lawsuit continued to move forward. Monsieur Mazarin found the same favor with the old men that I had found with the young. I was informed after three months *that he was in control of the Grand'Chambre; that his cabal was all powerful there; that he would obtain whatever ruling he desired; that, even if I were awarded the separation of property which I had requested, I would not be allowed to remain in that of our persons, which I already enjoyed and which I had therefore not requested;*[77] *and finally, that the judges could not legally avoid ordering me to return to my husband, even if they had been as strongly disposed in my favor as they were in fact against me.* If this information had come to me from less certain sources, I would be at liberty to name them to you; but as they were taking a very risky step by giving it to me, they required of me the secrecy which I will observe eternally. Just imagine what treatment I could expect from Monsieur Mazarin, if I returned to him under the force of a legal ruling, with the court and the Parlement against me, and after the grounds for resentment which he believed he had.

Those were the motives for the strange and much censured decision I made to withdraw to Italy with my relatives, seeing that there was no

---

77. The two types of legal separation in question were the separation of property (*séparation de biens*) and physical separation or the right to live apart (*séparation de corps*).

longer any sanctuary or security for me in France. My brother, who was at once the nearest, the dearest, and the best informed, was also the first to approve of my decision and to offer me all the means at his disposal to support it. The Chevalier de Rohan,[78] his close friend and mine, got wind of it, I do not know how; he talked to us about it in such a knowing way that it would have been imprudent to conceal it from him, and in such an obliging way that we could not, without some sort of ingratitude, refuse his help. My plan at the time was not to go all the way to Rome, but only to see my sister the constabless in Milan, where I sent word for her to come and wait for me, and then to go afterward to Brussels in order to negotiate from nearer by some more stable and more advantageous arrangement with Monsieur Mazarin than the earlier ones. Monsieur de Rohan beseeched us to see fit that he come with my brother to join me there when I arrived, and we could not decently refuse him. I had my reasons for believing that Monsieur Mazarin would no sooner see me outside of France than he would accept all manner of conditions in order to induce me to return; the fright in which I had seen him every time I had threatened to go away left me in no doubt of it. The despair into which he threw me had often brought me to say to him *that if ever I got away, he would chase me for a long time before he could catch me;* but unfortunately for me, he never believed that I would have that courage until he saw it.

Once I had made my decision, I was so exceedingly neglectful of my lawsuit that a hundred times I marveled that those who took an interest in it did not guess my plan. Madame la Comtesse, with whom I was more on my guard than with any other, was the only person who had any suspicion of it, but she did not believe it. She came from time to time to my brother's house, where we pretended to think of nothing but amusing ourselves, the better to fool people; and she wore herself out harping at us *that we were not attending to my case, and that it was a disgrace.*

---

78. Louis, prince de Rohan (1635–74), was more commonly known as the Chevalier de Rohan. He was regarded as one of the most handsome and charming men at court, but he also reputedly lacked honor or scruples. In 1656, he assumed the office of *grand veneur de France* (head of the hunts in the king's household), which his father and grandfather had held before him, and he later was made *colonel des gardes;* however, after the affair involving the lost letter, which Hortense recounts below (63–64), he was stripped of these offices. It was the beginning of a downward spiral for him, which ended with his involvement in an ill-conceived plot to deliver parts of Normandy to the Dutch and Spanish enemies of France. He was arrested and tried and then decapitated in front of the Bastille. It was said that Louis XIV would have been prepared to pardon him, if only one of his family or friends had spoken up for him, but no one did, not even his mother the princesse de Guémené, whose darling he had been; and Hortense, content in her Savoyard refuge, had not wanted to hear of him.

A week before I left, she was there when one of my brother's gentlemen, named Parmillac, came to take his leave of us *to go,* he said, *to join his father, who was commanding some cavalry in Lorraine;* but in fact, he was going to order post horses for me along that route, which I had chosen because people would least suspect it. The sight of that man, who was about to begin my enterprise, so disconcerted me that I still do not understand how Madame la Comtesse failed to notice it. She was busy rambling on about my nonchalance in the midst of such important matters, saying *that this was no time to spend my days in dishabille in my room, playing my guitar, and that this appalling negligence almost made her believe what people were saying, that I intended to flee to Italy.* Her useless remonstrance ended with an exhortation that I go to Saint-Germain with her to pay my court at least; but since I had plenty of business to attend to, I prayed her to excuse me. It was absolutely necessary for my plan that she be there when I left; for if she had been in Paris, given her anxiety over my conduct, it would have been difficult to keep her from suspecting something.

At last Wednesday, June 13, 1668, the day chosen for my departure, had arrived, and while I was preparing my overnight things, she sent for me to go and dine with her at Saint-Germain. At first I tried to refuse. I was being urged so insistently on her behalf that I almost thought I had been found out; but as one must always assume that one has not been found out in these sorts of situations, no matter what signs one may see to the contrary, I thought it best to promise to go, for fear that she might come to fetch me herself. When dinnertime had passed and I had not appeared, she entreated me once again to be sure to come before the evening. I apologized as best I could for having broken my word; I promised even more emphatically this time than the last, but when she saw ten o'clock pass without any news from me, she climbed into her coach and came straight to Paris. She had come more than halfway when she met my brother. He had left at the same time as I, to go and inform Monsieur de Louvois of my journey. She asked him very curtly *where I was?* But he asked her in return *if she had not met me along the way.* And when she told him *that she had not,* he replied coolly, *"Then she must have taken the other road, because I saw her leave before me."*

At three o'clock in the morning, Monsieur Mazarin went to wake the king to implore him to have me pursued; but the king had the generosity to reply to him *that he wanted to keep the promise he had made no longer to involve himself in our affairs, when he had ripped up the agreement which we had placed in his hands, and that it did not seem likely that I could be caught, given the head start I had and the advance preparations I had made.* People in society gave that reply a different turn, and you have very probably heard the rhyme they made up about it, which begins,

Mazarin, sad and pale, his heart with grief beset,

and which ends with this joke about the revelation he had had during the grave illness of the queen, regarding the king and Madame de La Vallière:[79]

> My poor dear wife, alas! What has become of her?
> Of that, replied the king, can you still be unsure?
> The angel who tells all, has he not told you yet?[80]

Monsieur Mazarin, seeing that he could obtain nothing from the king, went from there to find Monsieur Colbert, who advised him to send some person of credit after me posthaste, to offer me anything I wanted if I would come back. He chose a lieutenant of the artillery named La Louvière; and you will see from the place where he caught up to me that the king was right to say it was a bit late to go after me.

While these things were going on at court, I was running a strange course; and I confess to you that if I had foreseen all that would come of it, I should have chosen to spend my life between four walls, and to end it by blade or by poison, rather than to expose my reputation to the calumny which is inevitable for any woman of my age and my quality who is estranged from her husband. Although I did not have enough experience to foresee the consequences, nor did those who were in my confidence, I still debated long and hard with myself before making up my mind; and if you could only know the difficulty I had in deciding, it would convince

---

79. In November 1664, Queen Marie-Thérèse gave birth prematurely to a girl who lived less than two months; after the birth, the queen remained so gravely ill that her life was in danger. At this time, Monsieur Mazarin came to the king to report that he had seen the angel Gabriel in a dream and that the angel had directed him to tell the king to mend his ways and to dismiss his mistress, Mademoiselle de La Vallière, for the sake of the nation. According to the story that circulated at court, the king replied that the angel had appeared to him, too, and had assured him that Monsieur Mazarin was mad. Mademoiselle de La Vallière was Françoise-Louise de La Baume Le Blanc, duchesse de La Vallière (1644–1710). She was the first of Louis XIV's celebrated favorites, from 1661 until 1667, and she gave birth to four of his children, two of whom survived beyond infancy. (One who died at birth was born clandestinely in January 1665, just at the time when the queen's premature baby died.) Even after the king shifted his favor from Mademoiselle de La Vallière to her friend, Madame de Montespan, he refused to let her retire to a convent as she wished to do, and he even forced the two women to share apartments at court. Finally in 1674, she was allowed to enter the Carmelite convent in the faubourg Saint-Jacques in Paris, where she became Sister Louise de la Miséricorde and where she died in 1710.

80. "Mazarin, triste, pâle, et le coeur interdit, / Ma pauvre femme, hélas! qu'est-elle devenue? / La chose, dit le roi, vous est-elle inconnue? / L'Ange qui vous dit tout, ne vous l'a-t-il pas dit?" Doscot, ed., *Mémoires d'Hortense et de Marie*, 66.

you much better than all I have related, just how pressing was the necessity of making the grievous choice which I made. I can assure you most emphatically that my entertainments were only for show once I had made my decision, and that Madame la Comtesse was very wrong to reproach me for my tranquility. I scarcely slept or drank or ate for a week before my departure; and I was so worried as I left that I had to come back from the Porte Saint-Antoine[81] to get the chest with my money and jewels, which I had forgotten. It is true that I did not even imagine that I could ever run short of money; but experience has taught me that it is the first thing to go, and especially for people who, because they have always had more than enough, have never come to know the importance of it, or the need to manage it carefully. However, I had left the keys to my apartment with my brother, so that he could take possession of my silver plate and several other pieces of furniture and objects of value; but he was so careless that Monsieur Mazarin got there first and took so much that he sold a hundred thousand francs' worth of it to Madame de La Vallière some time later.

My only company included one of my maids, named Nanon, who had been with me but six months and who was dressed in men's clothing as I was; one of my brother's servants, named Narcisse, whom I hardly knew; and a gentleman of Monsieur Rohan's, named Courbeville, whom I had never seen before. As my brother had asked Monsieur de Rohan not to leave me before I was outside of the city, he bade me farewell at the Porte Saint-Antoine, and I continued my journey in a coach and six until I reached a house belonging to the princesse de Guémené,[82] his mother, which is ten leagues from Paris. From there I traveled five or six leagues by *chaise roulante*;[83] but

81. Located by the Bastille.

82. Anne de Rohan (1604–85) was the wife—and also the first cousin—of Louis VII (or VIII) de Rohan, prince de Guémené, duc de Montbazon and peer of France (1598–1667). By the time that Hortense made this stop at her house, the princesse de Guémené was a sixty-four-year-old dowager, but in her earlier life she had been at the center of much court gallantry and also of the religious debates of the seventeenth century. She was the sister-in-law of the famous duchesse de Chevreuse; she was a great enemy of Richelieu and a mistress of Cardinal Retz; and she was one of the ladies of the highest French nobility who became converts to Jansenism and whom people called *"les belles amies de Port-Royal."* In fact, that past life may have given her a very specific reason to sympathize with Hortense in the latter's flight from her husband. In his memoirs, Cardinal Retz relates an episode from the 1630s when Monsieur Mazarin's father, Charles de La Porte, duc de La Meilleraye (1602–64), had pursued the princesse de Guémené without success; the father's imperiousness and bitter vindictiveness over being rebuffed seem entirely similar to the son's. Jean-François Paul de Gondi, cardinal de Retz, *Mémoires. La Conjuration du comte Jean-Louis de Fiesque. Pamphlets*, ed. Maurice Allem and Édith Thomas (Paris: Gallimard, 1956), 10–11.

83. A *chaise roulante* was a two-wheeled vehicle drawn by one or two horses in which there was room for just one or two passengers.

since those vehicles did not go fast enough to calm my fears, I mounted on horseback, and I arrived Friday at noon at Bar. From there, seeing that I was out of France,[84] I went no further than Nancy for the night. Monsieur de Lorraine,[85] who had asked to see me, had the decency not to insist when he learned that I was reluctant to see him. The Resident of France[86] in his lands made entreaties to have me arrested, in vain; and to crown all his generosity, he gave me twenty of his guards and a lieutenant, to accompany me all the way to Switzerland.

We had been recognized as women almost everywhere. Nanon was always slipping up and calling me Madame; and either for that reason or because my face gave away some hint of my sex, people watched us through the keyhole after we shut the door to our room, and they saw our long hair, which we let down as soon as we were alone, because we were very uncomfortable with it up under our men's wigs. Nanon was extremely small, and she looked so unnatural dressed in that way that I could not look at her without laughing.

The night I spent in Nancy, when we returned to wearing our women's clothing, the joy I felt at being on safe ground gave me the freedom to enjoy my usual pastimes, and as I was running after her for fun, I fell very hard on my knee. And yet I did not feel anything at first; but a few days later, I had had a bed prepared in a wretched village in Franche-Comté so that I could rest while waiting for dinner, when I was seized with such horrible pain in that knee that I could not get up. I had to keep going, though, and so I continued my journey on a litter, after I had been bled by a woman for lack of any other surgeon; and I arrived at Neuchâtel, where people took it into their heads that I was Madame de Longueville.[87]

You would not believe the joy that these people showed me. As they were not accustomed to seeing women of quality from France pass through their land, they could not understand how anyone other than Madame de Longueville might have business there. I know people who would have taken advantage of the opportunity to have a taste of sovereignty. All in

84. Although France was striving for control at this time, the duchies of Lorraine and Bar were still the possessions of Charles IV, sovereign duke of Lorraine and of Bar (1604–75). See above, note 33.

85. Charles IV, duke of Lorraine (1604–75); both he and his nephew had been unsuccessful suitors of Marie Mancini. See above, note 33; Marie's memoir, 98–99 and notes 50 and 52.

86. A resident is a diplomatic representative at a foreign court, similar to an ambassador but with inferior rank.

87. Anne-Geneviève de Bourbon-Condé (1619–79), who married Henri d'Orléans, duc de Longueville (1595–1663); she was the sister of *le Grand Condé* and also of the prince de Conti (married to Hortense's cousin Anne-Marie Martinozzi), and she had been one of the most celebrated of the *Frondeuses*.

all, the misunderstanding was to my advantage: I quite made up in quality what I lost in youth, but such social standing seemed to me too honorable for a fugitive. I received such poor care there, and my pain was getting so much worse, that I deliberated about returning to Paris; and the hope of soon being better off in Milan was all that kept me moving forward on my journey.

Just a few days later, as we were passing through a Swiss village where there was a garrison, we very nearly got ourselves killed, all of us, for ignorance of the language; and as a final stroke of luck, we learned when we arrived at Altorf[88] that we had to be quarantined there before we could enter the state of Milan. It was then that my patience began to wear thin. I found myself in a barbarous country, very dangerously ill, in great pain; and as for help, you can judge by what happened to Narcisse whether I could hope to find any in that miserable place. He asked for a surgeon in order to have himself bled because of some complaint he had. A farrier was brought to him, who set to work to draw blood with a veterinary lancet but missed; and when Narcisse threatened to kill him, this man replied to him, still cool as you please, *that it was nothing, and that he had not hit the artery.*

But what finally pushed me over the edge was that my servants had fallen into division. Narcisse could not abide that Courbeville, who had known me for only a week, should involve himself in my affairs without being asked to. For the same reason, Nanon could not bear either Narcisse or Courbeville; she claimed that they both should act only on her orders. But while she and Narcisse went on quarreling in this way, they did not serve me well at all, and they scarcely did anything except to outdo or to thwart each other. Courbeville, on the other hand, thought solely of how to ease my suffering. I am still persuaded that my leg would have had to be amputated without him; and as the pitiful state I was in made me exceedingly grateful, the esteem that I showed him made the others even bitterer, and they soon abandoned me entirely to his care.

It was during this quarantine that La Louvière caught up to me. I put off making a decision about the proposal he presented to me until I was in Milan. I arrived there just a few days later, by the favor of the duc de Seste,[89] who was governor of Milan and brother-in-law of the constable. He learned

---

88. Hortense writes "Altorf"; it is probably the town called Altdorf, located 45 miles south of Zurich and about 125 miles north of Milan.

89. Paolo Vincenzo Spínola y Doria, marquis de los Balbases, duke of San Severino and Sesto (1628–99), who in 1653 married Anna Colonna (1631–89), sister of Marie's husband, Lorenzo Onofrio Colonna, Grand Constable of Naples. The marquis de los Balbases was interim governor of Milan from 1668 to 1670.

that I was stalled at Altorf and forgave me eighteen days of my quarantine. My sister and the constable came to join me at a house four days' journey from Milan, where we remained for a few days; from there we went to Milan proper, where we received nine couriers from Paris during the six weeks that we were there.

I learned that immediately after my flight, everything had turned in my favor against Monsieur Mazarin; that Monsieur de Turenne[90] himself had spoken to the king in my favor; and that my decision had inspired both admiration and pity in all reasonable people; but that things had changed markedly thereafter, since all my relatives had joined a few days afterward in the lawsuit that Monsieur Mazarin had initiated against my brother and Monsieur de Rohan, to accuse them of having abducted me. I also discovered that he had sent an agent after me, to gather information from one stop to the next on all that I had done; and that is perhaps the one thing for which I owe him thanks, since the report of that man, which is recorded in Parlement, is an eternal testament to the innocence of my conduct during this journey, contrary to all that my enemies have spread about.

But that was still not the best trick in his bag. I had written to my brother and to Monsieur de Rohan as I left Neuchâtel: to my brother, to send him my news, and to Monsieur de Rohan, to thank him for the help he had given me at my departure. I had given Narcisse the task of sending these two letters; but whether his hate for Courbeville extended to the person who had given him to me, or whether it was by pure carelessness, he confessed at Milan that he had forgotten the letter for Monsieur Rohan

90. Henri de La Tour d'Auvergne, vicomte de Turenne (1611–75), who was regarded as the greatest French military leader of his time. He was only thirty-three years old when Mazarin made him *maréchal de France*, and in 1660 he became *maréchal général des camps et armées du Roi.* During the Fronde, he was first persuaded by his brother, the duc de Bouillon, and by the duchesse de Longueville, with whom Turenne was in love, to fight on the side of the Parlement members and the princes who were in revolt; but in 1651 he made his peace with the court and took command of the royal army. In a famous encounter, he sent the prince de Condé into retreat, pursued his forces into the faubourg Saint-Antoine, and would have chased them into Paris proper if Mademoiselle de Montpensier, another of the illustrious *Frondeuses*, had not commanded the cannon of the Bastille to fire on the royal troops. Turenne was killed by a cannon shot in July 1675; Madame de Sévigné wrote many letters about the general shock and grief over his death, and about the burial that the king accorded him in the royal necropolis of Saint-Denis. See her letters dated July 31, 1675, through September of that year (*Correspondance,* 2: 26–113). Turenne was part of an important Calvinist family, although he became Catholic in 1667; his parents were Henri de La Tour d'Auvergne, duc de Bouillon (1555–1623), and Elizabeth of Nassau (1577–1642), daughter of William the Silent ("Willem de Zwijger") of Nassau, prince of Orange (1533–84). Turenne was also the uncle of Maurice-Godefroy de La Tour d'Auvergne, duc de Bouillon, who married Marie-Anne Mancini in 1662.

on the mantelpiece of the postmaster of Neuchâtel, to whom he had entrusted it. La Louvière, who had found it there as he passed through, had
not done likewise. Monsieur Mazarin used it so successfully that it set everyone against me; and it was on the strength of this letter that he later had
the temerity to petition to have me deprived of all my rights, which is not
done except to women convicted of the most extreme turpitude.[91]

I have told you that Monsieur de Rohan had obtained my brother's
consent that they should come to Brussels together to join me when I arrived there. Our need of him having brought the matter to this resolution,
it was quite natural that I should speak to him of this plan in a letter which
was written solely to express my gratitude to him. This was enough for
Monsieur Mazarin to prove our plot, and to prove that the chevalier was in
love with me.[92] But in addition to the fact that as the whole court knew, he
was then in love with someone else, who was so highly placed that he was
exiled for it,[93] his behavior was out of keeping with any amorous connection
to me. It was indeed the act of a true friend to give me the means to go far
from him, and to entrust me to the care of loyal servants, but it was not really that of a lover; and the man hardly exists who, if he were favored with
an intimacy of that nature, would have been able to resolve to lose sight of
his mistress, given such an extraordinary opportunity. And yet everyone
believed what Monsieur Mazarin wanted them to believe.

91. As noted above (note 78), this letter ultimately led to the Chevalier de Rohan's downfall.
The king stripped him of his offices, and he found himself utterly discredited at court and
also overwhelmed with debts. It was in this state that he met a certain Latruaumont (or La
Truaumont or Latréaumont), a former military officer and a young man who was similarly
beset with debts and debauchery; Latruaumont drew Rohan into the plot for which he was ultimately executed. Given that his role in Hortense's escape was widely regarded as the cause
of the Chevalier de Rohan's ruin, her insistence that he had forced his way into her confidence
reads as a self-justification addressed not only to her readers but also to herself. Indeed, in
the popular interpretation of the matter, Madame Mazarin and the Chevalier de Rohan were
lovers, which accounts for Hortense's protestations in the paragraph following this one.

92. The idea was certainly made more plausible by the fact that Monsieur Mazarin had
intercepted compromising letters between his wife and the Chevalier de Rohan before, from
the very start of the marriage, and the king and court had been made aware of them. Lucien
Perey, *Une princesse romaine au XVIIe siècle. Marie Mancini Colonna d'après des documents inédits* (Paris:
Calmann Lévy, 1896), 72–73.

93. More than one person with whom the Chevalier de Rohan had been linked romantically
would fit this description. He had been raised with the king himself, and he frequented the
most prominent members of the court. By some accounts, he was exiled because Louis XIV
suspected him of debauching the duc d'Orléans, the king's brother; but he had also dared to
make overtures to the king's favorite, Madame de Montespan, and he had had a liaison with
the sister of Madame de Montespan, Madame de Thianges (who was the mother of Diane de
Thianges, wife of Philippe Mancini).

And as for my brother, a long time earlier, as you have seen,[94] Monsieur Mazarin had taken it into his head to make himself out to be jealous of him, in order to cast suspicion over his involvement in all my affairs, and to deprive me in that way of his support. There is nothing so innocent that it cannot be poisoned in support of such a foul accusation. They stooped to producing letters in verse, for lack of any better evidence. Posterity will find it hard to believe, if knowledge of our affairs reaches it, that a man of my brother's quality could have been questioned in a court of law about trifles of that nature; that they could have been held up as serious evidence by judges; that such odious use could have been made of the exchange of thoughts and feelings between people who are so closely related; finally, that my esteem and friendship for a brother whose merit was as well known as his, and who loved me more than his own life, could have served as a pretext for the most unjust and the cruelest of all defamations. One will find few stranger examples of the misfortunes of persons of my sex and my age. The most sacred bonds, in which they are engaged by nature and reason, become the greatest of crimes as soon as jealousy and envy call for it; but nothing is impossible for him who makes a profession of pious devotion: rather than his being in the wrong, it must be that the most honest and respectable people on earth are the most abominable of all human beings.

Perhaps I am getting carried away, and the memory of this cruel offense is plunging me into digressions for which you have no use; but it is very diffi-cult to keep an even temper while telling such a grievous tale. It was not easy to foresee that people might ever raise a scandal over a thing as well known as the tight bond which united my brother with my sister the constabless and me. Nearly everyone at court has seen a letter which he wrote from Rome some time after our marriages, in which he described to one of his friends his good fortune in having two sisters whom he loved very dearly in the two most beautiful cities of the world, and he ended with these two lines:

> *With beautiful Hortense, and also wise Marie,*
> *I go from one to next, and live most happily.*[95]

It is not unlikely that Monsieur Mazarin would have used this letter in his lawsuit if my sister, whom he wanted to please in order to set her against me, had not been mentioned in it, for it is certainly at least as incriminating

94. See above, note 45.

95. "Avec la belle Hortense, ou la sage Marie: / Ainsi, de sœur en sœur, je vais passant ma vie." Doscot, ed., *Mémoires d'Hortense et de Marie*, 73.

as the other letter of which he made use. My brother had written that other letter to me at Saint-Germain, where I was a few days after Monsieur Mazarin had had the stage taken down which I had had put up in my apartment, as I have told you. It begins thus:

> *You of the Universe sole sample of your race,*
> *Than Venus yet more fair, than Lucretia yet more chaste, etc.*

Next he continues with thanks for what I had written him, and with news of his health, all of which is neither here nor there; afterward he goes on in this way:

> *And yet you doubtless know what your dear husband's done,*
> *He's asked incessantly 'bout you of everyone.*
> *He came to me one eve with a sour-tempered air,*
> *And mocked me to my face for the Theater affair.*
> *Handsome duc de Navaille,*[96] *his face leaden and spent,*

96. Philippe de Montault de Bénac, duc de Navailles, *maréchal de France* (1619–84), remained loyal to the court throughout the Fronde and distinguished himself in numerous battles over four decades. He was raised in a Calvinist family, but he was placed as a page to Cardinal Richelieu at the age of fourteen, and under the cardinal's influence he reverted to Catholicism. Religious devotion and a strict sense of sexual mores, which he and his wife shared, would have made the duc de Navailles a kindred spirit with the Duc Mazarin, and so would the two men's common animosity toward Hortense's siblings. In 1651, the duc de Navailles married Susanne de Baudéan de Neuillant (d. 1700) who, like the duc himself, was devoted to the service of Cardinal Mazarin and the Queen Mother, Anne of Austria. In 1660, Madame de Navailles became *dame d'honneur* to the new young queen, Marie-Thérèse. In that role, she took it upon herself to shield the queen's *filles d'honneur* from the king's advances; thus, she foiled the plans of a group headed by the comtesse de Soissons (Olympe Mancini), who had hoped to draw Louis away from Mademoiselle de La Vallière and replace her with the *fille d'honneur* Mademoiselle de la Mothe-Houdancourt. The wrath of Madame la Comtesse and her cohort (Madame, i.e., Henrietta of England, duchesse d'Orléans, wife of the king's brother; the comte de Guiche; and the marquis de Vardes) soon came down on Madame de Navailles. The Affair of the Spanish Letter occurred in 1664, when the four plotters composed a letter which was made to look as if it came from someone in Spain; it was ostensibly intended for Marie-Thérèse, to inform her of the king's love for La Vallière. However, it was put in the king's hands before it reached the queen, and then Monsieur de Vardes alleged that it was the work of Madame de Navailles. The duc and duchesse de Navailles were obliged to sell all their offices and retire from the court to the provinces. However, the truth eventually came to light, the plotters were sent away in disgrace, and in 1665 the king transferred to the duc de Navailles three governorships which had belonged to Philippe Mancini, duc de Nevers (Aunis, La Rochelle, and Brouage, which he had, of course, inherited from Mazarin). Thus, the duc de Navailles had quite a charged history with the Mancinis and would have been understandably disposed toward the Duc Mazarin's cause.

Nearly swallowed me whole with endless argument.
For nearly a full hour the two of them remained,
And during all that time, against you they campaigned.
Monsieur de Mazarin ever seeks your dismay,
And sends the rumor round that he'll bear you off one day.
He says there is no king, queen, emperor, or pope
Who ever could prevent him thusly to elope.
Polastron[97] *volunteered to be the hatchet man*
Of so outrageous and perfidious a plan.
And I would counsel you, because your need's extreme,
To go implore Louis's authority supreme:
May he become your shield against this blackest fate,
That's been prepared for you by your ungrateful mate. Etc.[98]

The rest is nothing. As I was showing this letter to some women friends, the comte de Grammont[99] appeared and snatched it out of my hands, then brought it to the king. It was read aloud in his presence, and in all the court there was nobody but one of the king's surgeons, named Eliam, who was shocked by it. That man, who apparently was very zealous about his patients, when he heard the line,

Handsome duc de Navaille, his face leaden and spent,

97. Captain of the guard to the Duc Mazarin.

98. "Vous de tout l'Univers unique en votre espèce, / Plus belle que Vénus, plus chaste que Lucrèce, / . . . Vous saurez cependant, que votre cher époux / S'informe à tout le monde incessamment de vous. / Il me vint voir un soir d'un air acariâtre, / Et se moqua de moi, me parlant du Théâtre. / Le beau Duc de Navaille, au teint hâve et plombé, / Par son raisonnement m'avait presque absorbé. / Près d'une heure avec moi tous deux ils demeurèrent: / Et vous fûtes toujours le sujet qu'ils traitèrent. / Monsieur de Mazarin poursuit de vous braver, / Et fait courir le bruit qu'il veut vous enlever. / Il dit qu'il n'est ni roi, reine, empereur, ni pape, / Qui puisse l'empêcher qu'un jour il ne vous happe. / Polastron s'est offert à l'exécution / D'une si téméraire et perfide action. / Pour moi je vous conseille, en ce besoin extrême, / D'implorer de Louis l'autorité suprême: / Qu'il serve de bouclier à ce noir attentat, / Qu'a formé contre vous un époux trop ingrat." Doscot, ed., *Mémoires d'Hortense et de Marie*, 73–74.

99. The Burgundian chivalric house of Grammont took its name from a fortress located between Vesoul and Montbéliard in Franche-Comté, which was still a possession of Spain in the mid-seventeenth century when Philip IV of Spain established the *seigneurie* of Grammont as a *comté* (1656). The most prominent members of the family were its prelates: it produced at least three archbishops of Besançon during the seventeenth and early eighteenth centuries, all of whom were zealous Catholic reformers who pushed the application of Tridentine decrees throughout the large diocese of Besançon. Thus, it is not surprising that a member of this family—the comte de Grammont mentioned here—would take the side of the Duc Mazarin in his disputes with his wife.

could not help interrupting to say *that it was nothing, and that he would soon be purged.*

It was nonetheless on the strength of such convincing evidence that the Parlement issued a ruling by which Monsieur Mazarin was allowed to have me arrested, wherever I might be. At the same time, all my relatives signed a document in his hands, in order to make a joint appeal to the constable, who paid no attention to it, not to receive me. And yet they had sent these scandalous letters along with the appeal; and I received a private courier at the same time, who came to present me with apologies on behalf of Madame la Comtesse, but only by word of mouth and not in writing. I confess that my fortitude could not withstand such a harsh blow. I fell into an extraordinary melancholy, and since such aggressive actions left me no hope of an accommodation, I gave up the idea of going to Brussels.

My brother arrived at this juncture; but rather than consoling me, he soon began a new persecution of me, which was all the crueler because it was founded on very specious grounds. I was supposed to send Courbeville back when I arrived in Milan; but when he learned of the criminal proceedings which had been undertaken in Paris, and in which he was implicated, he threw himself at my feet and protested *that he could not return to his master without ending up on the gallows, and that since he had no means of support elsewhere, he would be reduced to the most extreme need if I dismissed him.* This gentleman had served me so effectively that I did not see how I could abandon him without being extremely ungrateful. I gave him my word to keep him as long as he wished; and the cruel vexations which befell me later because I kept that word have still not persuaded me that I was not obliged to give it. Nanon and Narcisse, enraged because I was keeping him, accused him of having spoken very insolently about my brother. The claims they made about what he had said were implausible; my brother believed them and desired that I dismiss him, but since I knew who had made these charitable claims, I did not believe them, and I insisted on keeping him. My resolve drove Nanon and Narcisse to despair, and they found no better expedient to force me into the action they desired than to circulate the rumor that he was in love with me. My brother, who wanted to ignore the obligations that I had toward this man and the word that I had given him, because he believed himself to have been offended by him and because he was accustomed to the blind compliance which I had always offered him, feared that there must be something extraordinary in my obstinacy; and he had no doubt of it when, after he had pointed out very haughtily to me the rumor that was going around, he saw that I was not going to give in. Such ridiculous slander annoyed me rather than shaking my confidence; and I was so hurt to see that he lent faith to it that I could no longer bear him. The constable and my sister at first took my side against him, but they later changed their minds. Before long there was just continual controversy between the four of us, where I was in the wrong and the others justified themselves at my expense. This strange way of life, full of bitterness and resentment against a brother and a sister whom I loved so dearly, and whose company alone I had always thought sufficient to make me happy, made it clear to me in the end—but too late—that one must never set one's heart on anything in this world.[100]

We went to Venice in the midst of these quarrels, where the constable, who did not like it there, perhaps because my sister liked it all too well, promised me the moon in order to draw me to Rome: *that he would obtain the pope's protection for me, and that he would spare no effort there to relieve the deep melancholy into which I had plunged.* Seeing that I was on such terrible terms with my brother, I thought I should keep in the constable's good graces by accommodating his wishes. We all went to Siena to stay with Cardinal Chigi;[101] after three weeks, my brother had fallen out with us, so he returned from there to Venice without saying good-bye, and we set out for Rome. The heat there was so extreme that we were forced to leave the city and go to stay six weeks at Marino,[102] a country house belonging to the constable. At the same time that we returned to Rome,[103] my brother arrived, and with him a gentleman sent by Monsieur de Rohan to have Courbeville killed, according to what I was told. I learned that when Courbeville had been taken very ill in Venice, he had believed himself poisoned; that in his despair he had written appalling letters to Paris against my brother and against Monsieur de Rohan, whom he believed to be in league with my brother to get him dismissed from my service; and that these letters had been intercepted

100. According to Lucien Perey (*Une princesse romaine,* 84–85) and Claude Dulong (*Marie Mancini,* 160), Hortense eventually had to reveal to Marie the fact that she was expecting a child by Courbeville. However, since it never became public knowledge and it is not known how the pregnancy ended—whether by natural or induced miscarriage or by clandestine delivery—Hortense can maintain her pose as victim of slander before her reader here.

101. Flavio Chigi (1631–93), nephew of Pope Alexander VII and faithful friend (by some accounts, lover) of Marie Mancini Colonna in Rome. The Chigi family was originally from Siena, and the cardinal owned both his ancestral palace in the city and the magnificent villa Cetinale in the surrounding countryside.

102. Marino is located twelve miles southeast of the center of Rome in the Alban hills and three miles southwest of Frascati. Wealthy Romans escaped the stifling summer heat and malarial stagnation of the marshy lowlands by resorting to the hills. Although Hortense refers to it simply as a country house (*une maison de plaisance*), the vast Colonna domain of Marino included numerous exquisitely decorated villas and hunting lodges surrounded by splendid gardens and forests. Dulong, *Marie Mancini,* 133–34.

103. They returned at the beginning of November 1668.

by Monsieur de Rohan, who had sent them back to my brother, so that he might administer the punishment that they deserved. The bad behavior of Courbeville, the unpleasant sensation which this affair was causing in society, and my desire to be at peace finally made me resolve to part with him, not doubting that he would willingly release me from the promise that I had made him. All I asked of the eldest son of the président de Champlâtreux,[104] who acted as mediator between us, was *that my brother not demand this deference of me so imperiously, and that I be allowed to go and stay with my aunt Martinozzi.*[105]

One hour before Courbeville was to leave, when my aunt was already at the house to fetch me, my sister, offended that I no longer wanted to stay with her, began to jeer at him in my presence, asking him *if he would not sway me again this time as he had in the past?* When the man, who was in despair over going away, replied curtly to her *that unless I ordered him to, he would not leave, and that he respected no one but me,* she commanded him to leave that instant and told him *that he would find someone who wanted a word with him in the courtyard.* He obeyed her in a rage. I had no doubt that they intended to attack him. I felt bound to save his life, so I went out with him and accompanied him to the house of my uncle, Cardinal Mancini.[106] I withdrew afterward to my aunt's house, where I remained for some time locked up as if I were in prison. Nevertheless, miserable though I was, I could not help laughing at the offer she made me to dance the *matassins* to the accompaniment of my guitar, in order to amuse me. I do not know if my refusal soured her toward me; but one day when I was at the window, she told me very harshly to come away from it, *that it was not the custom in Rome to stand there;* and another time, when I was there again, she sent her confessor to tell me *that I would be forcibly removed from it.* This monk performed the errand so insolently that tears came to my eyes. The equerry of Cardinal Chigi was exercising horses in front of the house, and when he heard my complaints, he came upstairs to offer me his

104. Jean-Édouard Molé, seigneur (or comte or marquis) de Champlâtreux, was *président à mortier* in the Parlement of Paris ; the *présidents à mortier* were presiding judges in the Grand'Chambre. Champlâtreux's father was Mathieu Molé (1584–1656), *premier président* of the Parlement of Paris. The *premier président* was the head of the whole Parlement; he was chosen by the king, and the office was neither venal nor transmissible. However, the offices of the other judges who composed the Parlement—*présidents* and *conseillers*—were venal and transmissible. Champlâtreux's son, whom Hortense mentions here, was a *conseiller* in the Parlement of Paris.

105. Laura Margherita Mazzarino (or Mazzarini) (1608–85), younger sister of Cardinal Mazarin, who married Girolamo Martinozzi (1610–39) in 1634. Their daughter Anne-Marie married Armand de Bourbon-Condé, prince de Conti; their daughter Laure married Alfonso d'Este, duke of Modena.

106. Francesco Maria Mancini (1606–72), younger brother of Michele Lorenzo, the father of Hortense and Marie. He was made a cardinal in 1660, by recommendation of Louis XIV and during the papacy of Alexander VII (Fabio Chigi).

service; but I no longer dared say anything when I saw him. He nonetheless went and reported to his master *that I had not eaten or drunk anything for two days.* Cardinal Chigi was moved to pity by this; and when Cardinal Mancini replied to him *that Monsieur Mazarin desired I should retreat for a fortnight to a convent where there was a sister of Cardinal Mazarin,*[107] I took him at his word.

My brother and my sister, seeing the deplorable state I was in, began to reflect upon their past conduct and could not rest until I had pardoned them. However, I did not want to see my brother; but in the end, they won over my resolve on this point, too, and although I clearly recognized that their remorse did not repair the damage they had done to my reputation, my accommodating nature prevailed once more over the most justified resentment. I know of nothing crueler in life than to have people come back to us in good faith, after they have mortally offended us. It is quite enough to have suffered the initial injury without then having to share the pain of their repentance. That thought, and several others which I had occasion to think, made me resolve to return to France at Monsieur Mazarin's mercy, with no preconditions, rather than to remain at risk of experiencing more episodes as cruel as those which had befallen me. I asked my aunt Martinozzi to write a letter to this effect to her daughter the princesse de Conti, and I prepared to leave as soon as the reply came.

Just a few days later, Courbeville managed, I do not know how, to get word to me *that after he had been kept for a few days at Cardinal Mancini's house, he had been taken to Civitavecchia,*[108] *where he had been a prisoner for six weeks and where he would remain,* according to the message he sent, *for a long time yet if I did not have the generosity to exert myself again on his behalf.* Whatever cause I might have to involve myself no further with that man, nevertheless, so as not to leave my work unfinished, I requested his freedom of Brother Vincenzo Rospigliosi, nephew of the pope,[109] who granted it to me.

107. Sources disagree on whether the name of this sister was Anna Maria (known in the convent as Suor Tita) or Cleria, but it was probably the former. She was prioress at the Benedictine convent of Santa Maria in the Campo Marzio quarter of Rome, and her dates appear to have been 1607–69 (as Hortense acknowledges below, she died of a heart attack after Hortense's escape from the convent).

108. There was a papal fortress in Civitavecchia, which is fifty miles northwest of Rome, on the Mediterranean coast. Civitavecchia was also the principal seaport for Rome.

109. Vincenzo Rospigliosi (1635–73), Knight and Commander of the Order of Malta, was the nephew of Pope Clement IX (Giulio Rospigliosi), whose papacy lasted from June 1667 until December 1669. Rosvall (*Mazarine Legacy,* 114) notes that while Courbeville may indeed have been freed, nothing more was ever heard of him, and it is possible that he met with a fate which was not unheard of for feckless young men without protectors at that time and in that place: he may have found himself in chains on a galley. The fact that Vincenzo Rospigliosi was also commander general of the pontifical galleys and a general in the war against the Turks on Crete lends some weight to this speculation.

Meanwhile, when the time that I was to spend in the convent had elapsed, Cardinal Mancini replied to the entreaties which my sister was making without my knowledge to bring me out of there *that he advised me to wait a bit, because it would be to my advantage if the reply which was expected from France found me there.* That reply was *that when I had remained there for two years, Monsieur Mazarin would consider what he should do.* Cardinal Mancini wanted me to submit to that condition, and as far as I was concerned, despondent as I was at the harshness of Monsieur Mazarin, I was prepared to resign myself to anything; but my sister insisted that I come out of the convent. She had negotiations undertaken to that end with the queen of Sweden,[110] who promised to receive me, and all that was left was to arrange my escape. My sister came to see me one afternoon. While we were together in my room, as I was arranging things in order to go away with her, and Nanon was all plumped up with the great number of garments and personal effects she had stuffed in under her clothes, we were informed that the queen's council had compelled her to take back the promise she had given in my favor. However unwelcome this news was, we resolved to carry on regardless of it. My sister proceeded to take her leave, and I, to accompany her downstairs on the pretext of seeing her out. My aunt Mazarin did all she could to make me stay in my room, because for a long time I had not been feeling very well; but I took good care not to make that mistake. My sister's children,[111] who

110. Queen Christina of Sweden (1626–89), who became queen in 1632 when her father Gustavus Adolphus was killed in battle. She was an only child, and on her father's orders she was educated as a male heir would have been. She began to reign in her own right in 1644, and she pressed for a rapid end to the Thirty Years War, which came in 1648 with the Treaty of Westphalia. She refused to marry her cousin, Karl Gustav, but settled on him as her successor to the throne. A serious student of philosophy, Christina questioned Lutheran doctrine, which was the only confession permitted in Sweden; she established secret communications with Jesuit advisors and may have considered herself a Catholic as early as 1652. She abdicated in favor of Karl Gustav in June 1654, and she immediately left Sweden and traveled south, disguised in men's clothing. She officially converted to Catholicism in Brussels in December 1654, although it was only made public in November 1655, by which time she had settled in Rome. As a royal convert, she was a prized tool for Catholic propaganda in the religious controversies of the seventeenth century, and Pope Alexander VII (Fabio Chigi), who had just been elected in April 1655, at first treated her very lavishly. However, she quickly involved herself in political intrigue—in 1656, she made a failed attempt at becoming queen of Naples and later had Monaldeschi, a member of her household, executed in front of her for having informed the Spanish viceroy of her plans. After this episode, she could not count on the unqualified support of the Vatican, and although she continued to live much as she pleased in Rome, she would probably have needed to consider carefully the consequences of harboring Hortense, given that a woman who had abandoned her husband and family was essentially a criminal. See Marie's memoir, note 31.

111. Filippo, prince and duke of Paliano, Grand Constable of the kingdom of Naples (1663–1714); Marcantonio (1664–1715); and Carlo, Cardinal Colonna (1665–1739).

did not have permission to enter the convent as she had, and whom she had brought along that day with the express purpose of entertaining my aunt in the parlor so that she would not hinder us, were waiting for her at the door when the abbess came to open it. Nanon launched herself at them immediately to fawn on them, and I after her. As no one suspected our plan, the abbess did not dare hold me back by force, and besides that, I did not give her the time to think about it. There I was in my sister's coach. She had the privilege of being allowed to bring a certain number of women in with her; out of pique, my aunt detained two ladies who had taken advantage of the privilege that day, even though they had nothing to do with our plan. And the poor old woman took this adventure so much to heart that she died from chagrin over it only a few days later.

We went first to the house of Cardinal Chigi, whom we did not find in, to ask for his protection. He came a short time later to my sister's house and seemed rather cold to us, because he feared that the pope would be against me; but His Holiness responded to the complaints of Cardinal Mancini *that if he had known* that I had been in the convent against my will, he would have gone to bring me out himself. Since I still could not reconcile myself to staying with my sister, I went to live on the Corso, in our paternal home,[112] where the Academy of Rome[113] has always been held. In a fit of pique, Cardinal Mancini made one of his sisters move out of the house, who would only have been a hindrance to me, anyway; but while I was on a trip to Marino, he took over the whole house, and I was compelled upon my return to rent another one.

It soon became necessary to put my jewels in pawn in order to have something to live on. I had only borrowed three thousand écus against them, which was nothing compared to their value, when I learned that the man who had them was not to be trusted. I tried to take them back, but Madame

112. The Palazzo Mancini (known today as the Palazzo Salviati and housing the Rome branch of the Banco di Sicilia) is located on the Via del Corso just north of the Piazza Venezia and very near the Piazza dei Santissimi Apostoli, where the Palazzo Colonna is situated. Right next to the Palazzo Mancini was the Palazzo dei Benzoni (known today as the Palazzo Odescalchi or Palazzo Bracciano), which was sold by the Colonna family to Pope Alexander VII (Fabio Chigi) in 1661 and completely reconstructed for him by Gian Lorenzo Bernini; this may have been the residence of Cardinal Chigi at the time Hortense is recounting.

113. At first glance, one is inclined to interpret what Hortense calls *l'Académie de Rome* as the French Academy in Rome, which was founded in 1666 by Colbert as a branch of the Royal Academy of Painting and Sculpture in Paris. The French Academy in Rome was indeed housed in the Palazzo Mancini for much of its history prior to the Revolution. However, it was not installed there until 1725; and in any event, it had been in existence for only ten years when Hortense wrote her memoir. Therefore, it is more likely that she is referring here to the Accademia degli Umoristi, which she mentioned at the beginning of her text and which had been in existence since 1600. See above, note 4.

Martinozzi had gotten there first; she had paid the sum and refused to give them back. The constable, pretending not to know that she had them, used his authority and his threats to force the man to get them back from her, since he should not have given them to her in the first place. Afterward, Monsieur Mazarin was contacted and asked to redeem them; and he replied *that they should be left where they were, and I should be denied any means of subsistence, so that I would be forced back to my duty.* I was compelled to allow Grillon,[114] who was the best friend of my brother and of the constable, to advance the money necessary to redeem them. I repaid him quickly, and the displeasure I felt at finding myself reduced to the necessity of being indebted to people who could take advantage of it made me resolve some time later to make a journey to France, to endeavor to obtain a pension from Monsieur Mazarin.

I set out with my brother, who was going to wed Mademoiselle de Thianges;[115] and it was to that union that I owed my journey. We spent nearly six months en route. When we were at the border, we decided that he should go ahead, and that I should wait there until he had taken the necessary precautions for me to cross over. But at the same time, our friends sent us word of the disaster of the poor statues at the Palais Mazarin[116] and said that the circumstances were favorable, so we went together as far as Nevers, where he left me to go to court with Grillon, who had joined us at Milan.

As soon as Monsieur Mazarin learned that we were under way, he sent Polastron, his captain of the guard, along our route to gather detailed information about the life we were leading; and he assembled all the sheriffs from around the region of Nevers to assist the commissioner of the Grand'Chambre who was coming to arrest me in accordance with the order of the Parlement. When my brother lodged a complaint with the king, His Majesty wanted to send for me straightaway on his authority; but as Monsieur Colbert judged that it would be in my best interest for Monsieur Mazarin to be treated as tactfully as possible, he sent word to him to sign a writ of attachment, and he did so with tears in his eyes, seeing clearly that the king would proceed on my behalf if he refused. Fortunately, that order arrived at Nevers the same day that Palluau,[117] councilor of the

114. I have not been able to identify this person.

115. Diane Gabrielle Damas de Thianges (ca. 1655–1715), niece of Madame de Montespan; her mother was Madame de Montespan's sister, Gabrielle Diane de Rochechouart de Mortemart, marquise de Thianges. The wedding took place on December 15, 1670.

116. See above, note 9.

117. There is a reference to a certain "Palluau, *conseiller de la Grand'Chambre,*" in a 1676 letter from Madame de Sévigné to her daughter, Madame de Grignan. It is likely that it is the same man to whom Hortense refers, as he is reported in that letter to have carried out a similar

Grand'Chambre, arrived there too to arrest me. I received at the same time an order to go to the Lys,[118] and my brother was married the day I entered that convent.

While I was there, Monsieur Mazarin had me presented with several proposals for accommodation, but all by miserable monks or other persons of similar substance, and all without any guarantees. He had told the king *that my brother was preventing me from agreeing to anything; that he controlled me with a tyrannical authority; and that if I did not fear him, I would be much more tractable.* In order to know the truth of the matter, the king sent for me after three months, by way of Madame Bellinzani and an exempt of the guard, in a coach belonging to Madame Colbert,[119] with whom my brother had implored the king to have me lodged, representing it as a place where no one could compel me to disguise my feelings. Two or three days later, he had me go to Madame de Montespan's[120] so that he could speak to me. I shall never forget the kindness with which he treated me. He prayed me to consider *that if he had not done better for me in the past, it was because my conduct had made it impossible for him to do so; that I should tell him frankly what I desired; that if I was absolutely resolved to return to Italy, he would grant me a pension of twenty-four thousand francs, but that he advised me to stay; that he would make my agreement as advantageous as I desired; that I would not be compelled to follow Monsieur Mazarin on any journey; that he would have no say over my servants; even that if his caresses were odious to me, I would immediately be relieved of any obligation to suffer them; and that he was giving me until the next day to think it over.* I could just as well have replied to him on the spot what I replied the following day, *that after Monsieur Mazarin had tried to ruin my reputation, and after he had refused to take me back when I had made him the offer from*

sort of mission. He had been deputized to go to Rocroi, on the border between France and present-day Belgium, to interrogate the marquise de Brinvilliers, who had been accused of poisoning her father and her two brothers, had fled to Liège, and had been captured and brought back into France. She was eventually executed for the crimes. See letter dated April 15, 1676 (*Correspondance*, 2: 271).

118. The Cistercian abbey Notre Dame du Lys was located in Dammarie-les-Lys, near Melun, forty miles southeast of Paris. It was a royal abbey which housed young girls of prominent families and women protected by the crown. Founded in 1244 by Saint Louis and his mother, Blanche de Castille, it was destroyed by fire in 1358 during the Hundred Years War, rebuilt starting in the fifteenth century, and destroyed again during the Revolution. Only ruins remain today.

119. Marie Charron de Menars (1630–87), wife of the influential minister of finance Jean-Baptiste Colbert, marquis de Seignelay (1619–83). See above, note 37.

120. Françoise-Athénaïs de Rochechouart de Mortemart, marquise de Montespan (1641–1707), favorite of Louis XIV, who replaced Mademoiselle de La Vallière in the king's affections (1667), bore him eight children, and was eventually replaced by Madame de Maintenon (beginning around 1676).

Rome with no preconditions, though he knew me to be in the direst need, I could not resolve myself to return to him; that no matter what precautions might be taken against his moody temperament, I would have to face twenty small acts of cruelty every day, about which it would not be fitting to trouble His Majesty; and that I accepted with an extreme gratitude the pension which it pleased him to grant me. After such legitimate reasons, you will be surprised to learn that everyone condemned my decision; but the judgments of courtiers are very different from those of other men.[121] Madame de Montespan and Madame Colbert, among others, did all they could to convince me to stay; and Monsieur de Lauzun [122] asked me *what I hoped to do with my twenty-four thousand francs?* He said *that I would run through them at the first inn I came to, and that then I would be compelled to come back all shamefaced to ask for more, which I would not receive.* But he did not know that I had learned to use money wisely. It is not that I was blind to the fact that I could not possibly live decently for very long with that sum; but given that in any case I could not obtain any more, and Monsieur Mazarin would not allow me to spend it in Paris unless I were with him, I calculated that it would at least give me

---

121. One observer who certainly took a dim view of Hortense's course of action was Madame de Scudéry, sister-in-law of the famous Madeleine de Scudéry; on March 6, 1671, she wrote to Bussy-Rabutin, "Madame de Mazarin has gone away again, this time even more madly and brazenly than before. When we women have our brains fall to pieces, it is truly irreparable." Elizabeth C. Goldsmith and Colette H. Winn, eds., *Lettres de femmes. Textes inédits et oubliés du XVIe au XVIIIe siècle* (Paris: Champion, 2005), 322. A slightly variant version of this letter also appears in *Correspondance de Roger de Rabutin*, 1: 387. Madame de Sévigné wrote an account of Hortense's departure which offered a glimpse of the latter's nonchalance in the face of the widespread disapprobation: "To everything that people here said to Madame Mazarin to persuade her to go back to her husband, she always replied with a laugh, like during the civil war: 'Point de Mazarin, point de Mazarin.'" Letter to Madame de Grignan dated February 27, 1671 (*Correspondance*, 1: 170).

122. Antonin-Nompar de Caumont, marquis de Puyguilhem, duc de Lauzun (1633–1723), whose fortunes rose and fell more precipitously than those of anyone else at the court of Louis XIV. A younger son from an old noble family of Agen, he was very young and had no fortune when he came to Paris. He was taken in by his uncle, the comte de Guiche, who introduced him to the society around the comtesse de Soissons (Olympe Mancini). The king quickly took a liking to him and showered him with favors; however, Lauzun's irascible and insolent temperament eventually caught up with him. In 1669, when the Duc Mazarin gave up his prestigious office of grand master of the artillery and Lauzun coveted it, the latter provoked a famous scene with the king which landed him in the Bastille. At the same time, the never-married duchesse de Montpensier (1627–93), known as *la Grande Mademoiselle*, first cousin of the king and the richest heiress in France, cast her eyes on Lauzun; in December 1670, they obtained the king's permission to marry, and she gave three of her duchies to her fiancé. However, Madame de Montespan and the princes of the blood opposed the marriage, and the king's favorite was able to persuade him to revoke his consent. This reversal had just befallen Lauzun in the spring of 1671, when he made the remark that Hortense reports here; little did he know that before the end of that year, the enmity of Madame de Montespan and the jealousy of Louvois would combine to discredit him and have him imprisoned in the fortress of Pignerol, where he found himself with the disgraced minister of finance Fouquet (who had been there since 1665), and where he would remain for ten years.

the time to take other measures. Since Monsieur Mazarin could do nothing worse to me, he decided to tell the king *that I was having a man's jerkin made for myself, in order to go off dressed in that fashion;* but His Majesty once again had the goodness to tell him *that he gave his assurance no such thing would happen.*

Madame Bellinzani received the order to conduct me to Rome with an exempt, and I also had two guards along with them as far as the border. I received such gracious and civil treatment from Monsieur le duc de Savoie [123] when I passed through Turin that I resolved at that moment to withdraw to no other place but to his states, if ever I should leave Rome. I finally arrived there after three months on the road; and Grillon arrived there, too, a short time later, to plunge me back into new troubles, although I already had plenty of others. I had intended to see no one in France. Grillon, who assumed that he would be excepted from this rule because of the favor he had done me in Rome in the matter of my jewels, came to see me at the Lys with Madame la Comtesse when I was first there; but I no longer agreed to see him after that. He reacted with such pique that it put him absolutely beside himself. While I was in Nevers, expecting the commissioner any day, my brother's steward had me stay, for greater safety, in the tower of a convent which is attached to the castle. As he had no extra servants to attend me, he put one of my brother's guards with me, who had been dismissed a short time earlier for some fairly trivial reason. This boy served me to the best of his ability, in the hope that I would obtain pardon for him, and I allowed him to follow me to the Lys in that hope. A rascal of a cook whom I had, in order to please Grillon who had bribed him, goes and tells him *that this poor wretch was making himself indispensable to me, and that he sometimes went into the convent.* Grillon, without further examination, goes and spreads this story everywhere, to such a point that when I arrived in Paris, Madame Colbert refused to allow the man in question to enter her house in my suite. Imagine my astonishment when I found out the reason for it. Imagine how promptly I dismissed this new servant; what resentment I must have felt at the spitefulness of Grillon; and how surprised I was, traveling through Lyon again, that he should dare to come back to me, on the strength of a letter from my brother, who beseeched me to forget everything. The coldness with which I treated him only inflamed him further. He learned upon arriving in Rome that Monsieur de Marsan [124] came to see me from time to time; and

123. Once again, Charles-Emmanuel II, the protector to whom Hortense addresses her memoir.

124. Charles de Lorraine-Armagnac (or Charles d'Elbeuf-Lorraine), comte de Marsan (1648–1708), younger brother of the Chevalier de Lorraine and also of Monsieur le Grand (Louis de Lorraine, comte d'Armagnac [1641–1718], who was *grand écuyer de France*—officer in charge of all of the king's stables—from 1658 to 1677).

after a thousand extravagant exchanges between them, they finally came together in the ridiculous affair you have heard about,[125] where without putting themselves in any danger, they were pleased to entertain society once again at my expense.

It was some time later that my sister resolved to withdraw to France, because of various complaints which she claimed to have against the constable. It would be pointless to relate to you the arguments with which I opposed her decision. The troubles that such an undertaking had caused me lent me an extraordinary eloquence; but the same star which had led me to Italy was pushing her to France. Since she had complete trust in me, she did not hesitate to bring me in on her plan; and because I had no interest in Rome except on her account, and I thought that I could lessen the risks she would surely run by sharing them, I did not hesitate to follow her. I only pointed out to her *that I would be obliged to leave her as soon as we were in France.* That necessity distressed her more than anything else; and nothing convinced me more of the strength of her reasons for leaving than to see that they could make her resolve to be separated from me.

The Chevalier de Lorraine[126] was under enough of an obligation to my sister so that he should have served her on this occasion. She had quarreled with all of Rome for his sake, and for his brother's. They were not received at any house but hers, and she had taken their side in some rather delicate situations against Cardinal Chigi and the constable himself. Nevertheless, she received no other help from them than grand promises to employ their credit in France in her service, which they did not do. And as far as her plan

---

125. Clearly, there must have been some public dispute between the two men. Claude Dulong asserts (*Marie Mancini*, 177) that Hortense and Marsan had become lovers and that she had even moved in with him.

126. Philippe de Lorraine-Armagnac (or Philippe d'Elbeuf-Lorraine), known as the Chevalier de Lorraine (1643–1702), arrived in Rome in the spring of 1670 accompanied by his brother the comte de Marsan, after having been first imprisoned in the fortress of Pierre-Encise (near Lyon) and the Château d'If (on a rock facing Marseille) and then released on the condition that he would go into exile. Accounts of the reasons for his exile vary. He was extremely handsome and seduced both women and men without distinction. His principal conquest was Monsieur—the king's brother, the duc d'Orléans—and by some accounts he was exiled at the behest of Madame, the duchesse d'Orléans, Henrietta of England. Following this version of events, the Chevalier de Lorraine was suspected of taking revenge on Madame by sending poison from Rome (since everyone in France knew that Italy was the land of poisoners) to cause her death; nothing was ever proven—not even that she had indeed been poisoned—but she did die suddenly and mysteriously in June 1670. Another explanation for the chevalier's exile was that one of his mistresses had also slept with Louvois and had passed on to the chevalier the secret that the duchesse d'Orléans was to be sent on a diplomatic mission to her brother, Charles II of England; the chevalier had revealed the secret to the duc d'Orléans, who was infuriated by it, and the king had imprisoned and then exiled the chevalier for his indiscretion.

was concerned, the chevalier merely told her *that if she had no one but herself to carry it out, he would be at pains to help her, but that since Madame Mazarin was in on it, she could be relied upon, because she had more than enough wit and resolve even for much more dangerous undertakings.* At the time he was not expecting to be called back to France as soon as he was.[127] If he had done his duty, we would have been there ahead of him, and people could not have said that we were following him; but my sister, who had counted on him alone, was forced to defer her departure when she found herself abandoned by him.

After he had gone to France, she opened up to another man of eminent quality, whom she believed to be her friend because he was much obliged to her; but he only told her *that the Chevalier de Lorraine should really have helped her in her need.* Then he asked me *what I intended to do with myself, and whether it was on my advice that my sister was undertaking this journey.* He can still attest to my reply *that it was not; that I knew very well I could not stay in France; that I would not even venture to land there except on the strength of a passport which the king had sent to my sister, for her and her retinue; and that my intention was to withdraw to Savoy as soon as I had seen her to a safe place.*

Finally, after having taken all the precautions on the French side that human prudence could recommend, we sent for a boat to wait for us at Civitavecchia; and one fine day in May,[128] when the constable had said at dinner *that he was going twelve miles from Rome to see one of his stud farms, and that we should not look for him that evening if it took him too long to return,* my sister insisted on leaving, even though we had nothing ready yet. We said that we were going to Frascati,[129] and we climbed into my coach with one of her women and Nanon, who were dressed in men's clothing as we were, with our women's clothing on top. We arrived at Civitavecchia at two o'clock in the morning, when everything was closed; so that we were compelled to plunge into the thick of the woods while we waited for our boat to be found. My valet de chambre, who had been the only one of all my servants with enough resolve to guide us, spent a long time in search of it to no avail, and so for a thousand écus he hired another one which he came across by chance. In the meantime, my postilion, who was getting impatient in the absence of any news, mounted one of the coach horses and was lucky enough to find our first boat in the end. It was very late when he got back; we had to go five miles on foot

127. Louis XIV gave his permission in January 1672 for the Chevalier de Lorraine to return to court.

128. May 29, 1672.

129. Frascati is just three miles from Marino, also on the edge of the Alban hills, and twelve miles southeast of Rome. Thus, by saying they were going to Frascati, the women hoped to throw any possible pursuers off their trail, since they were actually going in exactly the opposite direction—northwest to Civitavecchia.

to reach the boat, and we finally embarked at three o'clock without having eaten or drunk anything since Rome. Our greatest stroke of luck was to have fallen into the hands of a captain who was as skillful as he was honorable. Any other would have thrown us into the sea after having robbed us, for he could see from the first glance that we were no beggars. He said so himself; and his crew asked us *if we had killed the pope?* As for skill, suffice it to say that they sailed in a straight line one hundred miles off Genoa. After eight days we disembarked at La Ciotat in Provence, at eleven o'clock in the evening. From there we went on horseback to Marseille, arrived by five o'clock in the morning, and found the king's orders and the passport with the *intendant*.[130]

The constable, by the greatest stroke of luck in the world, stayed away from Rome for three days and did not suspect the truth until very late. There is no tale so horrible that it was not told about us; people went so far as to say that we had gone to Turkey, and the constable was compelled to obtain an excommunication from the pope against anyone who should speak of it. He dispatched fourteen couriers by as many different routes, one of whom made such good time that he arrived in Marseille before we did. A short time later, one of his men arrived there too, of the sort of fellows that they call *bravi* in Italy. My valet de chambre had gone somewhere—I am not sure where—to get ready to leave for court, where my sister was sending him, and we four women were all alone in the very inn where this man came to stay. Nanon, who was the first to see him, recognized him straightaway. She raised the alarm very quickly. We sent a request to the *intendant* for some guards; he sent us some immediately. My valet de chambre came back from town; and the *bravo*, after having spoken to us most civilly to exhort us to return to Rome, left immediately to go back there himself, with a beautiful letter from my sister for his master.

That episode led us to go and stay with the *intendant*; and a few days later we went to Aix, where we remained for a month, and where Madame de Grignan had the charity to send us some shifts, saying *that we were traveling like true heroines of a novel, with an abundance of jewels but no clean linen.*[131] After

130. The *intendants* were royal agents assigned to one or several provinces. They were representatives of the king, and as such they were invested with a number of powers and duties, including the maintenance of public order, the collection of royal taxes, and the sale of licenses and royal offices. However, as Marie's more detailed account of this episode makes clear, the royal official in question here was actually the *intendant des galères*, who was in charge of the royal fleet of galleys headquartered in Marseille. See Marie's memoir, 134 and note 151.

131. "*disant* que nous voyagions en vraies héroïnes de roman, avec force pierreries, et point de linge blanc." Françoise-Marguerite de Sévigné, comtesse de Grignan (1646–1705), was the daughter to whom Madame de Sévigné addressed the bulk of her voluminous correspondence; she was also the wife of the lieutenant general to the governor of Provence, François Adhémar de Monteil, comte de Grignan (1632–1714). Madame de Grignan must have writ-

that we went to Mirabeau, then to Montpellier, where my sister wanted to visit Monsieur de Vardes,[132] and to Montfrin, where I learned that Polastron was on his way, on the pretext of coming to pay compliments to my sister in Monsieur Mazarin's name; but in fact, it was to have me arrested with his wretched order. I withdrew alone to the fishponds to let him pass by. He did not stay any time at all with my sister when he failed to find me there; he kept right on going, thinking that he would catch up to me and that I had turned back; but he was getting further away from me rather than nearer.

Meanwhile, I went to Arles by way of the Rhône; and from there to Martigues by land, and by sea to Nice; then to Turin and to Montmélian, from where my sister called me back to Grenoble to be with her, after having taken the necessary measures for my security with Monsieur de Lesdiguières.[133] My brother came to join us there; he stayed with us for a week. We left there a week after he did for Lyon, and when my sister set out toward Paris, I headed for Chambéry, where I have finally found the peace I had been seeking fruitlessly for so long, and where I have remained ever since, with much more tranquility than a woman as unfortunate as I should have![134]

---

ten to her mother about the Mancini sisters, in terms similar to those that Hortense cites here, as Madame de Sévigné replied to her, "Your description of Madame Colonna and of her sister is divine. . . . The comtesse de Soissons and Madame de Bouillon are in a fury over those madwomen and say that they should be locked up; they've declared themselves to be strongly opposed to this strange folly. People do not think that the king will want to vex the constable, who is assuredly the greatest seigneur in Rome. In the meantime, we will see them arrive like Mademoiselle de l'Étoile; the comparison is wonderful." Letter dated June 20, 1672 (*Correspondance*, 1: 536–37). Mademoiselle de l'Étoile was indeed a "heroine of a novel" and one whose story blended elements of Hortense's and Marie's lives. She was a character in the *roman comique* by Scarron (who was, incidentally, the first husband of Louis XIV's last mistress, Madame de Maintenon), an actress who first appears as a well-born young woman in Rome but who later turns up ruined in Nevers, a burlesque and threadbare vagabond.

132. François-René du Bec-Crespin, comte de Moret and marquis de Vardes (ca. 1621–88). He had been sent away from the court in disgrace following his involvement in the Affair of the Spanish Letter, in which the comtesse de Soissons, the comte de Guiche, and Madame were also involved; Monsieur de Vardes was not allowed to return to court until 1683. See above, note 96.

133. François de Bonne de Créquy, duc de Lesdiguières (ca. 1596–1677), lieutenant general of the province of Dauphiné, of which Grenoble was the chief city.

The itinerary that Hortense cites in these last two paragraphs traces a zigzagging path all over the area of southern France broadly surrounding the mouth of the Rhone river, between Marseille and Montpellier. Her account of their peregrinations is somewhat different from Marie's; see Marie's memoir, 134–38.

134. Unfortunately for Hortense, that tranquility was soon to end. Charles-Emmanuel II died suddenly in 1675, the same year in which Hortense's memoir was published, and she was no longer a welcome guest in the duchy. She elected to accept the hospitality of another of her early suitors, Charles II of England, and she lived nearly the last half of her life in England, dying in Chelsea in 1699.

Pierre Mignard (1612–95), *Marie Mancini* (mid-seventeenth century).

THE TRUTH IN ITS OWN LIGHT; OR,
THE GENUINE MEMOIRS OF M. MANCINI,
CONSTABLESS COLONNA

As there are no actions upon which the light of public scrutiny shines more harshly than upon those of people in high places, there are also none that are more exposed to censure, nor more easily the target of malicious gossip, and especially in France, where the lampoons meant to libel and to blacken the reputations of those of our sex sell very well and pass for works of court gallantry. But although I was not unaware that there is nothing in the world so sacred that these sorts of works will not attack it, I believed I was beyond the reach of their blows, both by virtue of time and through the propriety of my actions, until I received word from France that there was in circulation a book about my life under my name.[1] This news, along with certain circumstances of which I had been informed, made me curious to see it, and the sight of it has since changed the pique and indig-

---

1. In 1676, the spurious *Mémoires de M.L.P.M.M. Colonne, G. connétable du royaume de Naples* (*Memoirs of Madame la Princesse Marie Mancini Colonna, Grand Constabless of the Kingdom of Naples*) appeared under the fictitious imprint of "Pierre Marteau, Cologne." This was the same imprint under which Hortense's authentic memoirs had been published in 1675; presumably, the great commercial success of Hortense's book was an impetus for someone to seek similar profits by purporting to offer Marie's story in her own words. Marie angrily disavows the book, both here and in letters she wrote to her husband, and her 1677 publication of *La Vérité dans son jour* (*The Truth in Its Own Light*) represents her effort to set the record straight and to rehabilitate her reputation, which she considered to have been impugned by the apocryphal book. As she recognizes here, there was enough intimate factual detail in *Mémoires de M.L.P.M.M. Colonne* so that it must have been written or commissioned by someone very close to the Colonna household. In the introduction to their 1998 edition of *La Vérité dans son jour*, Patricia Cholakian and Elizabeth Goldsmith observe that one speculative attribution favored by some critics is to the marquis de Los Balbases, who was the husband of Anna Colonna, elder sister of Marie's husband. The apocryphal memoir was recently republished with a preface by Maurice Lever as *Cendre et poussière: mémoires* (Geneva and Paris: Le Comptoir, 1997), although copies of this edition are relatively rare. For more information, see Cholakian and Goldsmith, eds., *La Vérité dans son jour*, 9–15.

nation that I had felt about it into the greatest contempt in the world for its author; for I needn't say here, for those who know me, that there is not a single adventure in it which is not made up and as far from my character as it is from the truth. People who are familiar with my conduct and with my ways will see clearly that this alleged history is a work entirely invented by its author, and that even if there are in it some of the incidents of my life, it is so distorted by the circumstances it invents that it is unrecognizable. I will not even mention the baseness of the author's style; and it is practically impossible that his mean expression not reflect the quality of his mind. But since there are people who, because they don't know me, might be susceptible to these sorts of impressions, I felt obliged to preempt the harm they could do me, by publishing myself a sincere and genuine account of everything that has happened to me since my tenderest youth; and I was urged to do so by the earnest entreaties of various people who take an interest in all that concerns me, either out of duty or out of inclination.

Rome saw my birth[2] to a family that was illustrious enough to be esteemed for its own brilliance,[3] and even if the fortune of Monsieur le Cardinal Mazarin had not heightened that brilliance, the family would still have held quite a high rank in that first city of the world. When I was seven years old,[4] my mother,[5] who considered me less beautiful than my sister Hortense, now Duchesse Mazarin,[6] put me in the Campo Marzio, a convent of the Order of Saint Benedict,[7] with the idea of raising me there as a nun, to which she expected that my aunt,[8] with whom she had placed me,

2. On August 28, 1639.

3. See Hortense's memoir, 27–28 and notes 4–5.

4. Presumably in 1646 or 1647, as she was born in August 1639; however, Marie seems to project onto this moment what must have been her mother's later preference for Hortense, based on the younger sister's beauty, since Hortense was only born in June 1646.

5. Hieronyma (or Geronima or Girolama) Mazzarino (or Mazzarini) (1614–56), a younger sister of Cardinal Mazarin, who married Lorenzo (or Michele Lorenzo) Mancini (1602–56) in 1634.

6. Hortense Mancini (1646–99), who married Armand-Charles de La Porte de La Meilleraye (1632–1713) in 1661, just before the death of Cardinal Mazarin. The couple became the Duc and Duchesse Mazarin, and in addition to the name, the duke also inherited the cardinal's vast fortune. In her memoir, Marie actually refers to her sister as "duchesse *de* Mazarin," but the correct form without the particle is substituted here and throughout this translation. Hortense herself always writes "Monsieur Mazarin" rather than "Monsieur *de* Mazarin," for example, but others among the sisters' contemporaries add the particle when referring to Hortense or her husband, as Marie most often does.

7. The convent was located in the Campo Marzio quarter of Rome.

8. A younger sister of Cardinal Mazarin, named either Anna Maria or Cleria, who was prioress at the Benedictine convent of Santa Maria in Campo Marzio, and who probably lived from 1607 to 1669. See Hortense's memoir, 71–73 and note 107.

would contribute considerably. After two years, even though my mother had much less liking for me than for my sister, she could not help being touched by my poor health, and attributing my indisposition to the strict enclosure to which I was subjected, and to the bad air I breathed in the convent, which was indeed very unhealthy, she withdrew me and brought me back to live with her.

I had been out of the cloister for about two years when the fortunes of my uncle the cardinal, which were already near their peak, were to increase still further, just as wealth does, by the sharing of them.[9] That is what brought him to call to his side my mother and my aunt Martinozzi,[10] with the order to each of them to bring along her eldest daughter;[11] that particular seemed to exclude my sister, as a younger daughter, but her beauty had given her the birthright in the affections of my mother. Nevertheless, my mother did declare to me my uncle's wishes, though she would doubtless have been delighted if I had refused to obey him; it was not difficult for me to guess this by the choice she gave me to go to France or to stay in Rome with my aunt and to dedicate myself to God in a cloister, asking me very carefully if I had not made some vow which might bind me, and thinking of everything that could possibly oblige me to return to the convent. Whereupon I remember that I replied to her that there were convents everywhere, and that if it should please heaven to inspire such pious impulses in me, it would be as easy to follow them in Paris as in Rome; besides which I was not yet of an age to make a choice of such importance.

That response disabused my mother of the misguided hopes she had harbored until then and made her resolve to take me along. And to spare herself the resentment that the preference of me over my sister might have caused her, she took us both.

So we boarded a galley from Genoa,[12] which that republic had sent

9. By Marie's account, it is almost as if the Fronde never happened; her only reference to it is her mention below of "the time when His Eminence was obliged to withdraw from the court" (86).

10. Laura Margherita Mazzarino (or Mazzarini) (1608–85), younger sister of Cardinal Mazarin, who married Girolamo Martinozzi (1610–39) in 1634. Their daughter Anne-Marie married Armand de Bourbon-Condé, prince de Conti; their daughter Laure married Alfonso d'Este, duke of Modena.

11. That is, each was to bring along the eldest daughter left in Rome. A first group of Mazarin nieces and nephews had already been sent to France in September 1648. It included Laure Mancini (1636–57); Paul Mancini (1636–52), for whom the cardinal had high hopes, but who was killed in the battle of the faubourg Saint-Antoine during the Fronde; Olympe Mancini (1639–1708); and Anne-Marie Martinozzi (ca. 1637–72).

12. In the spring of 1653. The party included Madame Mancini with Marie (1639–1715) and Hortense (1646–99) and also Philippe (1641–1707), and Madame Martinozzi with her second daughter, Laure (ca. 1640–87).

to us out of special consideration for Monsieur le Cardinal. I will not stop here to describe that movable house. It would take up too much time to portray all its beauty, its order, its riches, and its magnificence. Suffice it to say that we were treated like queens there throughout our voyage, and that the tables of sovereigns are not served with more pomp and brilliance than was ours four times a day.

We finally landed in Marseille, where my rather too scrupulous aunt refused for a long time to receive the official emissaries of the city, who wanted to pay us their respects, because she could not reconcile herself to the French way of greeting people.[13] We finally overcame her sensitivity with great difficulty, and it was a subject of hilarity for many people, who were understandably surprised that she should make such a fuss over an accepted practice, authorized by so longstanding a custom.

We proceeded from Marseille to Aix, where we were received by the governor of the province, who at that time was the duc de Mercoeur, the first of the seigneurs of France to have entered into a marriage alliance with Monsieur le Cardinal up until then, and who had wed Victoire Mancini, my eldest sister, after having gone himself to Cologne to ask the cardinal for her, during the time when His Eminence was obliged to withdraw from the court.[14] We stayed eight months in that city, where my brother-in-law the duc treated us with the greatest magnificence in the world, and where my

13. Madame Martinozzi was shocked to learn that in France, the customary welcome included a kiss on the lips. When she finally consented to receive this greeting, the women also received as a welcome gift twenty jars of preserved fruits, five dozen candles, and twelve bottles of red wine and claret. Dulong, *Marie Mancini*, 16.

14. Louis de Bourbon-Vendôme, duc de Mercoeur (1612–69), was the son of César de Bourbon, duc de Vendôme (1594–1665), legitimized son of Henri IV of France with his mistress Gabrielle d'Estrées. Before Cardinal Mazarin was forced into exile by the Fronde, he had negotiated the marriage of his eldest niece, Laure-Victoire Mancini (to whom Marie refers as Victoire but who was usually called Laure) (1636–57), to the duc de Mercoeur. When the rumor of this marriage reached the ears of *le Grand Condé* (Louis II de Bourbon, prince de Condé), he was outraged that this upstart foreign interloper should have the audacity to forge marriage alliances with French princes of the blood; he famously accosted Mazarin at the Louvre and publicly slapped him. *Le Grand Condé* soon became a leader of the Fronde as did the duc de Mercoeur's brother the duc de Beaufort; the cardinal went into exile with his family; and the duc de Mercoeur might have been expected to break off his marriage to Laure Mancini. On the contrary, he followed her into exile and then married her in 1651 in Paris. As the Fronde ended, it was clear that the duc de Mercoeur had backed the right horse, and *le Grand Condé* went into exile while Condé's brother, the prince de Conti, applied to the cardinal for the right to marry a niece, any niece. He was given Anne-Marie Martinozzi. In contrast to the prince de Conti, the duc de Mercoeur was apparently motivated by sincere affection for his wife; after she died at the age of twenty-one, while giving birth to their third son, the duc de Mercoeur took orders and entered a Capuchin convent. He was made a cardinal in 1667.

sister his wife came to join us two months after our arrival and did all she could to amuse us and to make our stay most pleasant.

When this time had passed, which was the period set by my uncle to tame us (as he said), we received the order to set out for Paris, and my sister, who was expecting her first child at the time, insisted on accompanying us there, despite the rigors of winter. Because of the danger to which she was exposing herself, and because we wanted to please the duc her husband, we would have much preferred to spare her this expression of kindness, but her affection proved stronger than all our admonitions and won out over all other considerations. Anyone who will have known her will easily believe this, and will agree that heaven has never joined so beautiful a soul with such a beautiful body, nor such perfectly virtuous sentiments with so entire a beauty.

After one month's journey, during which there was not a single mishap, we finally arrived in Paris,[15] where my uncle saw us in private and received us with such tenderness that it is impossible to express it; I can only give some idea of it by citing the comparison he made between our meeting and that of Joseph with his brothers, which he accompanied with all the outward signs of great affection.

Although my sister Hortense was not supposed to make the journey with us, as I have already said, her beauty caused my uncle to approve the decision my mother had made to bring her, and he was plainly delighted to see her.

Having recovered a bit from the fatigue of the journey, we went to see Their Majesties,[16] who received us with gestures of exceptional kindness. I did not enjoy this happiness for long, for these pleasures were soon interrupted by a mortification, the cause of which I will explain.

The fatigue of the road, from which I was not yet fully recovered, a continual agitation brought on by my cheerful and high-strung nature, and my poor eating habits—I ate as readily the foods that disagreed with me as those that might do me good—had reduced me to a pitiful state; for that reason, Monsieur le Cardinal resolved to put me in a convent, to see, as he said, if it would fatten me up a bit.

In addition to that reason for putting me in the convent, he considered me very young and unpolished, as indeed I was;[17] and I did not know the

15. Sometime early in 1654; they were present at the wedding of Anne-Marie Martinozzi and the prince de Conti on February 22, 1654.

16. King Louis XIV (1638–1715) and his mother, Queen Anne of Austria (1601–66).

17. Marie would have been fourteen years old in early 1654.

language, which seemed to him to be a great obstacle to my appearing in so brilliant a court. And although my sister, by all appearances, should have had the same fate as I, for the same reasons, her youth made her more excusable and her great beauty spoke well enough for her. So I was put in the Convent of the Visitation, in the Faubourg Saint-Jacques,[18] where two months later my sister Hortense came to keep me company by order of His Eminence. For he found her too young and childish to be at court, where her great beauty had made a place for her, and where everyone was so delighted to see her that even Monsieur,[19] though only a child, could not live without her. His Eminence added that she was a bit too obstinate, which he blamed in large part on the freedom she had been afforded in that society.

So there we both were in a convent, under the supervision of Sister Marie-Elisabeth de Lamoignon, sister of the *premier président* of the Parlement of Paris,[20] who had the task of instructing us and teaching us the language and everything that she judged necessary for girls of our age and our station, a task which she carried out extremely well. I had been in the convent for eighteen months when my uncle sent for me by way of Madame de Venelle,[21] lady-in-waiting to my sister the duchesse de Mercoeur, whom he ordered to bring me to La Fère in Picardy,[22] where the court was at the time.

Before this journey, His Eminence, wanting to form a marriage alliance

---

18. In the seventeenth century, the faubourg Saint-Jacques—south of the Sorbonne and east of the Jardin du Luxembourg—was home to nearly a dozen convents and monasteries. Sainte-Marie de la Visitation in the faubourg Saint-Jacques was the second convent of the Sisters of the Visitation to be established in Paris, after one in the rue Saint-Antoine, which was built in the 1630s by François Mansart. See Hortense's memoir, note 62. The convent of the Visitation in the faubourg Saint-Jacques no longer exists; the place where it stood along the rue Saint-Jacques is occupied today by the Institut de Géographie and the Institut d'Océanographie. The Order of the Visitation, which was founded in 1610 by Jeanne de Chantal (1572–1641) under the direction of François de Sales (1567–1622), played an important role in the instruction of girls in seventeenth-century France, and Marie acknowledges in this passage the quality of the education she received from the Visitandines. Jeanne de Chantal was the paternal grandmother of Madame de Sévigné, and the latter made frequent visits to the convent in the faubourg Saint-Jacques.

19. The younger brother of Louis XIV, Philippe, duc d'Orléans (1640–1701).

20. The *premier président* of the Parlement of Paris was Guillaume de Lamoignon (1617–77). The *premier président* was the head of the whole *parlement*; he was chosen by the king, and the office was neither venal nor transmissible.

21. Madeleine de Gaillard Longjumeau de Ventabren, dame de Venelle (or Venel); see Hortense's memoir, note 17.

22. La Fère is located one hundred miles northeast of Paris and sixty miles northwest of Reims.

with Monsieur le maréchal de La Meilleraye, had proposed to give me in marriage to his son Monsieur le Grand Maître,[23] thinking it proper that I be provided for first, as I was the elder; but since love and reason follow separate laws, it mattered little that His Eminence had intended the Grand Maître for me, if the Grand Maître had other ideas, and if he had devoted himself to my sister Hortense from the first moment he saw her, with such focused intentions that he declared point-blank he would cast himself into a cloister if he could not marry her.

And so I arrived at La Fère knowing nothing of the proposals that had been made regarding my marriage, having heard nothing but vague references to them from secondhand sources. A few days after my arrival, the agreement was called off, because of the Grand Maître's reply and the affection he professed for my sister. From then on, I remained with the court wherever it went. And since I had by then become fairly enlightened with age and through the instruction I had received, I found there certain charms that I had not discovered before; not that I partook freely of the pleasures of the court, for my mother, who knew how vivacious I was and who, as I have said, had less affection for me than for my sisters, held me back as much as she could and maintained such a close watch over me that I never went out except with her, and in fact most of the time she left me at home.

That mortification was great, but as bad or good fortune is amplified in our minds through comparison, my misfortune increased greatly with the comparison I made between the constraint under which I lived and the freedom that was given to my sister Olympe, since become comtesse de Soissons,[24] and which was also enjoyed to some extent by my sister Hortense, who had come out of the convent two months after I. I confess that I never contemplated the entertainments they had at court, of which I was deprived, except with bitterness and tremendous resentment. The grief I felt became so intense one day that, reproaching my mother for the way she treated me, I said to her in a very sharp tone that even if she loved only my sister Hortense, because she was beautiful, she should still remember

---

23. The maréchal de La Meilleraye was Charles de La Porte, marquis and then duc de La Meilleraye, peer of France (*pair de France*) and marshal of France (*maréchal de France*) (1602–64). He was a first cousin of Cardinal Richelieu, whose protection he enjoyed; during the Fronde, he remained loyal to Mazarin. The maréchal de La Meilleraye was one of the important military leaders of the seventeenth century, and he passed his office of grand master of the artillery (*grand maître de l' artillerie*) to his son, Armand-Charles de La Porte de La Meilleraye (1632–1713), in 1648. Monsieur le Grand Maître did marry Hortense in 1661, of course, and he became Duc Mazarin.

24. Olympe Mancini (1639–1708), who married a prince of the blood, Eugène-Maurice de Savoie-Carignan, comte de Soissons (1633–73), in 1657. See Hortense's memoir, note 53.

that I was the elder. This little fit of anger so irritated my mother that she told His Eminence she could no longer live with me, and that it would be much better to make me a nun than to leave me in the world, where she foresaw that I would be very unhappy, having no docility, nor deference for those toward whom I should have the most.[25]

After my mother's complaints, my uncle reprimanded me in such acid tones and such cutting terms that any other girl than I would have been sick with remorse, but since I did not take things to heart at all, everything he said to me made a clear impression on my memory and made none at all on my spirit.[26]

It is fairly common to have presentiments of joy or sadness on the eve and at the approach of happy or unhappy events: the melancholy into which my mother fell a few days before her death served as an example of this for me. She had taken on such a nasty disposition that she was unbearable. And since I was the least loved, and the only one exposed to her ill-humor, my sister Olympe being in a separate apartment, and my sister Hortense being with Madame de Mercoeur, under the supervision of Madame de Venelle, who was raising her with great kindness and affection, I confess that I was having a very hard time of it, and that nothing could equal my displeasure. To add to my troubles, my only retreat was the worst room of all, and my only company an old *femme de chambre* named Rose, who raised us; and moreover I believed that I was on the verge of returning to a convent.

My personal affairs were in this state when my mother fell ill. At the beginning her condition was not dangerous; nevertheless, His Majesty did her the honor of coming to visit her every evening, and since he noticed in me a great deal of passion, vivacity, and cheerfulness, he always said something to me in passing, which was more than a little relief from the misery my mother put me through, but which strangely increased her suffering, so that she refused to let me enter her room when she had company.

She finally recovered from her illness, only to fall back into a more dangerous one, which only ended with her death, the emetic that she was

25. Madame Mancini lent credence to the astrological predictions of her husband, Lorenzo Mancini, who said that their daughter Marie was destined to bring trouble down on the whole family.

26. Marie's description of her own character here does not contradict what Madame de La Fayette said about her: "Mademoiselle Mancini had no beauty, there was no charm in her physical person and very little in her way of thinking, although she was infinitely intelligent. Her spirit was bold, resolute, quick-tempered, libertine, and far removed from any sort of civility and courtesy." Comtesse de La Fayette, *Vie de la princesse d'Angleterre*, ed. Marie-Thérèse Hipp (Geneva: Droz, 1967), 16–17.

given as a last resort in the most acute cases having carried her off in just a few days.[27]

Good breeding is the richest gift that parents can give children after having given them life; but it is very important that it be administered with loving care: too much severity often serves only to strip them of affection, since love and fear are almost always incompatible.

I can attest to this from my own experience; for my mother had been dead for more than two years, and yet my imagination, obsessed by a lingering apprehension, made me dream that she was still alive, and even when I was awake, I would think I saw her, and just the thought of it caused me incredible distress.

Some time later Madame de Mercoeur died suddenly, after having given birth to a boy, and left in everyone's heart the sadness that the loss of such a beautiful and virtuous person can cause.[28]

After my mother's death, Madame de Venelle was made governess for us all, namely, for my sister Hortense and my sister Marianne, who had come some time after us with my brother Alphonse, who died very young and very unfortunately from a blow to the head which he received when he was being tossed in a blanket by some other schoolboys at the Collège de Clermont, where he was boarded.[29]

The death of my mother and the marriage of my sister Olympe[30] had

---

27. Madame Mancini died in the Palais du Louvre on December 29, 1656, at the age of forty-two.

28. Laure Mancini, duchesse de Mercoeur, died in childbirth on February 8, 1657, at the age of only twenty-one; some said that she let herself die because of the extreme grief she felt over her mother's death barely a month earlier. The duc de Mercoeur was himself so grief-stricken at the loss of his wife that he took orders and became a Capuchin monk. Doscot, ed., *Mémoires d'Hortense et de Marie*, 106 n. 1. The couple had three sons: Louis-Joseph, duc de Penthièvre and later duc de Vendôme et de Mercoeur (1654–1712); Philippe, *grand prieur de France* (1655–1727); and Jules-César (1657–60).

29. These two youngest Mancini children came to France in 1655. Marie-Anne Mancini (1649–1714) was the youngest of all the siblings; she married Maurice-Godefroy de La Tour d'Auvergne, duc de Bouillon (1636–1721), in 1662. As Marie states here, Alphonse Mancini (1644–58) died after an accident at school, which happened during the Christmas holidays of 1657–58. Although tossing in a blanket was often a form of hazing, Lucien Perey contends that in this case, it was simply a game. *Le Roman du Grand Roi. Louis XIV et Marie Mancini d'après des lettres et documents inédits* (Paris: Calmann Lévy, 1894), 83–84. Surgeons performed a trepanation in an attempt to save Alphonse's life, but he died on January 16, 1658. The school—the Collège de Clermont in Paris—was a Jesuit institution which counted among its students the sons of all the most powerful houses of France; it is known today as the Lycée Louis-le-Grand and is still located at 123 rue Saint-Jacques, just east of the Sorbonne.

30. Olympe was married on February 21, 1657, less than two weeks after her sister Laure's death and less than two months after her mother's.

left me freer, and when I enjoyed all the privileges attached to the status of elder sister, which I then possessed, I led quite an undisturbed life and began to savor its pleasures. The satisfaction of the mind is almost entirely responsible for the health of the body. My condition at that time was quite convincing proof of this for me. I was like a new person; and I can say that my good fortune had had as positive an effect on my mind as on my body, and had greatly increased my wit and gaiety.

The kindness of the king was so great that we lived on familiar terms with him and with Monsieur. And since that familiarity allowed me to say what I thought fairly freely, perhaps I said it with a certain charm. I continued to behave the same way during a trip that the court made to Fontainebleau[31] (for we followed it everywhere), and on the way back I noticed that the king did not dislike me; for I had gained enough insight to understand that eloquent silence, which often is more persuasive than any rhetoric. And it may also be that the fondness and the inclination that I had for His Majesty, in whom I had recognized more merit than in anyone of his kingdom, made me more discerning in this matter than I would otherwise have been.

However, the testimony of my eyes did not suffice to make me believe something of such consequence; but the courtiers, who are so many eyes watching over the actions of kings, having noticed His Majesty's inclination just as I had, soon confirmed me in the opinion I had formed, through their respect and their extraordinary deference. And the attentiveness of the king, the magnificent presents I received from him, his care, his zealousness, and the indulgence with which he treated me in everything soon managed to convince me completely of it.

A storm, which quickly passed over, came to disturb the serenity of those happy days. There was talk of marrying the king with Princess Marguerite of Savoy, the daughter of Madame Royale, who later became duchess of Parma, and whose rare intellect added even greater brilliance to the

---

31. The château de Fontainebleau is located forty miles southeast of Paris. Louis XIV brought the court there nearly every year, usually in the late summer or early autumn. The trip to which Marie refers here occurred in August and September 1658, shortly after the king had been taken dangerously ill during a military campaign. He had been touched to learn afterward that Marie had cried openly and bitterly at court, while most other people busied themselves with paying court to Louis's brother Philippe, on the assumption that he would soon be king. The previous year (on November 10, 1657), Fontainebleau had been the scene of what the French court judged a barbarous act by Queen Christina of Sweden: convinced that her *grand écuyer* and favorite, named Monaldeschi, had betrayed her, she had him murdered in her presence in the château de Fontainebleau. See Hortense's memoir, note 110.

nobility of her blood; and this prospect obliged the court to make the journey to Lyon.[32]

Just mentioning the opening of these negotiations was enough to alarm me, and anyone with a discerning mind will see clearly how painful is the fear of losing a person for whom one has a great fondness, and especially when that fondness is based on boundless merit and on nobility, and when reason is on the side of the heart and justifies all its impulses.

As my pain was intense, it lasted no longer than such things do. The marriage of the king having been broken off almost as soon as it was proposed, by the coming of Pimentel[33] who arrived just as the agreement was about to be concluded, and by the proposal of a peace treaty for which he had drawn up the plan, Their Highnesses turned back toward Savoy, and my mind toward its usual calm.

Short-lived reversals, especially when they are followed by prosperity,

32. The court made this journey in the autumn of 1658; the reason for moving the entire French court to Lyon for the marriage talks was to make a great show of it, in order to urge Philip IV of Spain to negotiate seriously toward peace with France and a marriage between Louis XIV and the Infanta of Spain, Marie-Thérèse. Madame Royale was Christine of France (1606–63), daughter of Henri IV and Marie de Médicis, and thus sister of Louis XIII and aunt of Louis XIV; Princess Marguerite was therefore a first cousin of Louis XIV (as was the Infanta of Spain—doubly—since her father was the brother of Anne of Austria, and her mother was another sister of Louis XIII, Elisabeth of France). After the death of her husband, Victor-Amédée I, duke of Savoy (1587–1637), Madame Royale became regent first for her son François-Hyacinthe I (1632–38) and then for her son Charles-Emmanuel II (1634–75). Although Charles-Emmanuel II was emancipated in 1648, his mother continued to have strong influence over him until her death in 1663, and it was she who took charge of negotiating her daughter's marriage. Princess Marguerite was Marguerite-Yolande (or Marguerite-Violente) (1635–63), who married Ranuccio II, duke of Parma (1630–94), in 1660. During the journey to Lyon, the king and the other young people of the court enjoyed themselves immensely, riding on horseback rather than in coaches and dancing late into the night at each town where they stopped. Louis seemed devoted to Marie during the journey, although Mademoiselle de Montpensier relates in her memoirs that when he first saw Princess Marguerite, he was quite pleased with her; Marie's reaction was to ask the king if he was not ashamed that people wanted to give him such an ugly wife (Montpensier, *Mémoires*, 2: 77–78). See Hortense's memoir, note 15.

33. Don Antonio Alonzo Pimentel de Prado (1604–71) was the Spanish envoy who came to Lyon to pursue negotiations with Mazarin for the Peace of the Pyrenees and the marriage of Louis XIV and the Infanta Marie-Thérèse. He reached Lyon just before the arrival of the Savoy court from Chambéry on November 28, 1658, and he remained in France—in semisecrecy as he and Mazarin continued their negotiations—until early June 1659, when the preliminary agreement for the peace was signed and Mazarin prepared to travel to the Spanish border to complete the talks. Pimentel had distinguished himself some years earlier in a diplomatic mission to Sweden. He had come to the court of Queen Christina in 1652, had become the queen's confidant and perhaps her lover, had helped her establish contacts with Jesuit priests, and had facilitated the support of the Spanish crown for her conversion to Catholicism and her abdication in 1654.

do not stifle the appetite for pleasure, they whet it. Thus, I took even greater joy in the renewed gestures of kindness I received from the king, once I had gotten over all my fears. And I had all the more reason to be happy, since the Queen Mother often showed a special regard for me, and since my uncle made gestures of goodwill toward me that he had never made before.

In the midst of so many blessings, I was not satisfied, precisely because I had too much satisfaction. I complained that I had nothing left to desire. And I would have liked some slight misfortune, in order to appreciate by contrast the good fortune I enjoyed. Fate proved all too compliant with that wish a short time later, as I will soon relate.

Upon our return to Paris, our sole concern was to amuse ourselves. There was not a single day, or rather a single moment, that was not devoted to pleasure, and I can say that never was time spent more enjoyably than it was by us. His Majesty, wishing to assure our continual entertainment, commanded all the men in our cabal to treat us by turns. So there were feasts and balls, one after another. And although they were all held in rustic settings, still they could not have been more magnificent. And as proof, one need only consider that these entertainments were given by people of the highest rank, and that Love, who is ingenious, and who breathes life into everything he touches, arranged them with care. For indeed, there was not a gentleman who would have failed to take his turn. The Grand Maître did his utmost to please my sister Hortense. The marquis de Richelieu[34] put forth

---

34. Jean-Baptiste-Amador de Vignerot du Plessis, marquis de Richelieu (1632–62), was a great-nephew of Cardinal Richelieu. Before his death in 1642, the cardinal named as guardian of this great-nephew and his four siblings Marie-Madeleine de Vignerot, marquise de Combalet, duchesse d'Aiguillon (1604–75), who was the cardinal's niece and the aunt of the children. (See Hortense's memoir, note 8.) The duchesse d'Aiguillon was chagrined in 1652 when the marquis de Richelieu married Mademoiselle de Beauvais, daughter of one of Anne of Austria's *femmes de chambre*, whose reputation was not sterling and whom Madame d'Aiguillon considered to be far beneath her nephew. (Clearly, the marquis's marriage did not keep him from courting ladies other than his wife.) The eldest child of that marriage, Louis-Armand de Vignerot du Plessis, marquis de Richelieu, duc d'Aiguillon (1654–1730), would later create a sensation when he eloped in 1682 with Hortense's eldest daughter, Marie-Charlotte Mazarin (1662–1729), who climbed the convent wall of Sainte-Marie de Chaillot and ran off with her suitor to Antwerp, where they were married. In a sense, the close friendship between the elder marquis de Richelieu and the grand master (Marie-Charlotte's father, the Duc Mazarin), which Marie mentions here, was the reason for the elopement. Monsieur Mazarin had been reluctant to agree to the marriage out of fear over incest, and he had put his daughter in the convent while he traveled all over Europe to consult theologians on the question. The young couple were indeed distant cousins, but that was not the basis for his concern; as Hortense's biographer Rosvall puts it, "Mazarin was afraid that since he himself as a young lad had been such an intimate friend of the father of this young Richelieu that they had enjoyed each other in a way boys can but ought not, the marriage of their children might bear the taint of incest" (*Mazarine Legacy*, 212). Madame de Sévigné's com-

the same efforts for Mademoiselle de la Motte-Argencourt,[35] the marquis d'Alluye[36] for Mademoiselle La Fouilloux,[37] whom he has since married, in whom His Majesty and I placed great confidence, and several others who had similar attachments and about whom I will not take the time to speak here.

The gallant episodes that accompanied our meals and our outings would take up an entire volume. Thus, I will pass them all over in silence and will recount just one of them, which will make clear how delicately and gallantly the king courted, and how he did not miss the chance to show it along one tree-lined *allée* (it was, if my memory does not fail me, at Bois-le-Vicomte).[38] As I was hurrying along, His Majesty tried to give me his hand, and when mine hit, although quite lightly, against the pommel of his sword, he drew it out of the baldric and threw it away. I will not undertake to describe the look on his face when he did it—there are no words to express it.

These pleasures had already gone on for some time when, as I had wished earlier for some small obstacle to make me savor them even more, Fortune went beyond my wishes and gave me a bigger one than I had asked for—one she had been working on during the time when I least expected it.

The Spanish, weary of a long war, had sent Pimentel to France to pitch the peace plan. He met with considerable success, his arrival in Lyon having caused the marriage negotiations with Princess Marguerite of Savoy, which were nearly concluded, to be broken off, as I have said above. People turned their attention to the Infanta of Spain,[39] who was seen as the

---

ment on Monsieur Mazarin in the midst of this affair was, "How does one keep from losing patience with such a madman?" Letter to Bussy-Rabutin dated December 23, 1682 (*Correspondance*, 3: 91).

35. Mademoiselle de la Motte-Argencourt was a *fille d'honneur* to Anne of Austria. In early 1658, the king favored her with his attentions for a brief time, but his mother frowned on the liaison ; she eventually removed Mademoiselle de la Motte-Argencourt from court and placed her in the convent of Sainte-Marie de Chaillot.

36. Paul d'Escoubleau, marquis d'Alluye (d. 1690), governor of Orléans.

37. Bénigne de Meaux du Fouilloux (d. 1720). Mademoiselle de Fouilloux first appeared at court as a young beauty in 1652 and later became a *fille d'honneur* to the queen; she married the marquis d'Alluye in 1667. She was part of the comtesse de Soissons's inner circle of court intriguers, and the two of them were caught up together in the Affair of the Poisons in 1680, as was the marquis d'Alluye. The latter was exiled to Amboise; the two women took flight together toward Flanders, although the marquise d'Alluye soon returned to court.

38. The château Bois-le-Vicomte was located twenty miles northeast of Paris; today nothing but ruins remain at the site of the château, which is just south of the Roissy-Charles de Gaulle airport.

39. Marie-Thérèse of Austria (1638–83), daughter of Philip IV of Spain and Elisabeth of France.

only guarantee of peace between these two crowns and of the repose of all Christendom, and France began from then on to desire her ardently for its queen.

Since love is ordinarily born of communication, it would seem that the king could not yet have been stirred by that passion for a princess whom he knew only by reputation; but her portrait, which had been sent to France, did all on its own what a long acquaintance might have done and revealed enough charms to appeal to the monarch's heart, even if the insinuations of the queen and of His Eminence, and the advantages for his crown that he hoped to gain from it, had not been enough to impel him to desire this alliance.

Before the court was ready for this journey, which was to return calm to these two powerful states, His Eminence set out, and he was determined to take us away in order to remove me from the king's sight, judging perhaps that my presence would be an obstacle to the step that he was about to take.[40]

This would be an apt place in which to speak of the sentiments that people said His Majesty had in my favor, if modesty did not prevent me. And for the same reason, I will not elaborate on the palpable sadness that this prince felt when he saw me leave,[41] after which he withdrew for a week to Chantilly and did nothing but send couriers to me, the first of whom was a musketeer bearing five letters of several pages each. But I cannot conceal the pain that this separation caused me; nothing has hurt me so deeply in my

40. Mazarin and Pimentel signed the preliminary agreement for the peace treaty on June 4, 1659, in Paris; then it was necessary for the cardinal to head toward the Spanish border to meet with the chief minister of Spain and hammer out the final agreement. He obliged Marie and her sisters Hortense and Marie-Anne to depart with him on June 22; they traveled together as far as Poitiers, and then he continued toward Bordeaux while the sisters and Madame de Venelle went to La Rochelle.

41. Every account of the love between Marie and Louis includes the famous scene of their parting on June 22, 1659. It had been preceded closely by a desperate interview between the king and the cardinal, during which the king had begged on bended knee to be allowed to marry Marie, and Mazarin had positively refused; and on the evening of June 21, the king had had a long tête-à-tête with his mother in the bath chamber of the queen's apartments, from which he had emerged red-eyed but resigned. Thus, on the morning of June 22, he accompanied Marie to her coach, crying openly; Marie's famous line, as reported by Madame de Motteville, was "You weep, and yet you are the master!" Françoise Bertaut de Motteville, *Memoirs of Madame de Motteville on Anne of Austria and Her Court*, intro. C.-A. Sainte-Beuve, trans. Katharine Prescott Wormeley, 3 vols. (Boston: Hardy, Pratt, 1901), 3: 178. According to the abbé de Choisy, the line was, "Ah! Sire, you are king, and I am leaving!" (Ah! Sire, vous êtes roi, et je pars!). François-Timoléon, abbé de Choisy, *Mémoires de l' abbé de Choisy: Mémoires pour servir à l' histoire de Louis XIV. Mémoires de l' abbé de Choisy habillé en femme*, ed. Georges Mongrédien (Paris: Mercure de France, 1966), 85.

life. All possible suffering seemed to me as nothing in comparison with this absence. There was not a moment when I did not wish for death, as the only cure for my ills. In short, I was in a state which cannot possibly be expressed either by what I have just said or by any stronger terms.

There is scarcely a wretch who does not harbor some hope of relief for his pain. I did not refuse this remedy for mine; and considering that the peace had not yet been made, and that there were great obstacles to be overcome, I sometimes dared to tell myself that no agreement would be reached, and that I would recover through the failure of these negotiations what I had just lost. But all the difficulties were surmounted, and only my misfortune proved invincible.

My uncle had gone to Bordeaux to await Don Louis de Haro,[42] chief minister of Spain, and the court arrived there soon after; meanwhile, he sent us to La Rochelle, allowing me to go anywhere in the region of Aunis. But since solitude was most apt to fuel my reveries, I chose the château de Brouage,[43] as a place where my sisters and our servants could not amuse themselves, nor go every day to the theater, as they did in La Rochelle. For it seemed to me that everyone ought to take part in my affliction, and that I would have been blameworthy for any entertainments that the others might have enjoyed.

And so I was in that fortress, from which all pleasures seemed to be banished, and where I had none but those I received from the letters that the courier brought me from time to time, and from the kindness of my sister Hortense, who often declined to go off with my sister Marianne, in order to keep me company. During that time, the bishop of Fréjus[44] came on

42. Luis Méndez de Haro, Mariano y Guzmán (1598–1661). Don Luis had also negotiated for Spain in the Treaty of Westphalia in 1648. While the French court waited in Bordeaux, the two ministers pursued arduous negotiations on the Île des Faisans, a tiny island near the mouth of the River Bidassoa, which forms the border between Hendaye, France, and Irún, Spain. The Peace of the Pyrenees was finally signed on November 7, 1659.

43. Brouage is thirty miles south of La Rochelle along the Atlantic coast; although the sea has receded today, it lapped at the rocks beneath the château de Brouage in the seventeenth century. (See Hortense's memoir, note 20.) Marie claims here that it was the solitude of the place that attracted her, but she also had an "accomplice" there who was willing to help her and the king continue their correspondence despite the strict interdiction imposed by Mazarin and Anne of Austria. His name was Colbert de Terron, and he was a cousin of Jean-Baptiste Colbert, through whose assistance he had acquired the position of intendant to Mazarin in Brouage and La Rochelle, of which the cardinal was governor. When Colbert de Terron's role in the secret correspondence was discovered, Colbert felt so deeply disgraced that he offered Mazarin his resignation, which the latter refused. Dulong, *Marie Mancini*, 65–68.

44. Zongo Ondedei, fellow Italian and confidant of Cardinal Mazarin; the cardinal made him bishop of Fréjus in 1658.

behalf of His Eminence to present me with the proposal of the constable.[45] The latter had sent the Marquis Angelelli, a Bolognese gentleman, to ask my uncle for me when he was at the conference; and this compelled my uncle to request of Don Louis de Haro that the constable, as a subject of the Spanish crown, be permitted to marry me.[46]

Not only did the bishop point out to me that this was one of the best matches in Rome, thanks to his family and also his fortune, but he also added that he had preferred me over the others, and had pressed his request most zealously.[47]

Any other woman would instantly have heeded these arguments, but my unhappiness had given me such a great distaste for all worldly concerns that I replied angrily to the pressing entreaties of the bishop. I said that he might as well excuse himself, since he had nothing to propose to me but that I leave France; that I could not be forced into any marriage; and that this was the promise my uncle had made me when he had obliged me to leave the court and follow him.

The bishop brought this response to Monsieur le Cardinal, who, wishing vehemently to see my sisters, was about to summon them; but my entreaties and those of Madame de Venelle prevented the execution of that plan. After the conclusion of negotiations for the marriage and the peace,[48] Madame de Venelle received an order from Monsieur le Cardinal to bring us to Paris. We arrived there a short time before the court left Bordeaux,[49] and Prince Charles[50] began to show me attentions which were not disagreeable to me, and of which Madame de Venelle did not disapprove, aware as she was that the goal of all his pursuits was marriage.

45. Lorenzo Onofrio Colonna (1637–89), Grand Constable (*Grand Connétable*) of the kingdom of Naples, prince and duke of Paliano, prince of Castiglione, duke of Tagliacozzo, duke of Marino, etc. Marie was married to him in 1661. Thus, Marie was commonly called either "Madame la Connétable" or "Madame la Princesse." Likewise, Marie refers to her husband as "Monsieur le Connétable" throughout her memoir, which is translated here as "the constable."

46. The kingdom of Naples was under Spanish rule at this time.

47. A nice touch on the part of the constable (or perhaps of his envoy), particularly in comparison with the attitude of suitors such as the prince de Conti, who had made it clear to Mazarin that any of the cardinal's nieces would be as good as another, as far as he was concerned.

48. The treaty was signed on November 7, 1659.

49. By the time the negotiations were finally complete, it was so late in the year that the royal wedding had to be put off until the following spring; it was eventually celebrated in Saint-Jean-de-Luz on June 9, 1660. In the meantime, the court was obliged to follow the king to Provence, where he went to calm a brewing rebellion.

50. Prince Charles of Lorraine (1643–90) was the nephew of Charles IV, duke of Lorraine (1604–75). See Hortense's memoir, note 33.

My sisters were not as pleased as I with the attentions of this prince, and because they very often found themselves obliged to follow me to the Tuileries, they tired of my frequent outings. Since people are not very indulgent toward those who have some small failing, especially when they have no affection for them, this suitor was often the target of their petty mockery, and they even harassed me over the kindness I showed him, even though he was infinitely worthy.

When the duc de Lorraine became aware of his nephew's intentions, he feared that through this marriage the nephew would draw the favor of His Eminence, and that as the rightful successor to the duc, the nephew might receive from the Cardinal certain offices which perhaps would not be to the uncle's liking. And so the uncle took it into his head to absolutely forbid him to woo me, and he took the nephew's place, without considering that at his age he could not play the role fittingly, and that his efforts to pursue me at the Cours[51] and the Tuileries could not meet with the same success as the attentions of his nephew.[52]

51. The Cours la Reine was a fashionable meeting place for Parisian society. See Hortense's memoir, note 38.

52. The duke was known as an unabashed opportunist, both in political or military matters and in marriage dealings. Over his life he compiled a remarkable record of cynical matrimonial maneuvers. In 1621, he married Nicole, elder daughter of Charles's uncle Henri II, duke of Lorraine (1563–1624), known as Henri le Bon; Henri had added a clause to the marriage contract which stipulated that unless he were to have a male child before his death (he had only two daughters), the duchy would pass to Nicole. It did indeed pass to her upon Henri's death in 1624, and she and Charles's father and Henri's brother—François, comte de Vaudémont—claimed that, according to the will of his great-grandfather René II, he was the rightful heir to the duchy. Charles supported his father's claim, and François enjoyed a four-day reign, during which time he had coins minted with his image, ennobled a great many people, and issued letters of pardon for others, and he paid all his debts out of the coffers of the state; then he abdicated in favor of his son, and Charles ruled alone from that time on. To be doubly sure that the duchy could not pass into foreign hands, Charles arranged for his brother, Nicolas-François de Vaudémont, to marry Henri II's other daughter, Claude de Lorraine, in 1634; these were the parents of Prince Charles. Nicolas-François was a cardinal and bishop of Toul, although he had not taken priestly orders; he did not hesitate to marry, and what is more, he granted himself the necessary dispensation to marry his first cousin, since his position as diocesan bishop afforded him that power. (Charles briefly resigned his estates in favor of his brother in 1634.) In 1637, Charles claimed that his marriage to Nicole was null and void, and he publicly married Béatrice de Cusance, princesse de Cantecroix. The pope excommunicated him, and a court of law declared his marriage to Nicole legitimate, but he continued to live with Béatrice; however, by the time of Nicole's death in 1657, he had tired of Béatrice, and he refused to legitimize their union until just hours before her death. At the time when he was courting Marie, Béatrice was still alive (she died in 1663); soon after her death, he sought to marry Marianne Pajot, the daughter of an apothecary, but when the duchesse d'Orléans opposed the marriage and had Marianne put into a convent, Charles instead married the thirteen-year-old Marie Louise d'Aspremont. He was sixty-one.

During the time when this suitor was wasting his efforts and his attentions in my pursuit, the court arrived at Fontainebleau,[53] and from there the
cardinal sent for us in Paris, to come and curtsey before the queen. Because
of a presentiment that this honor would cost me dear, I cannot deny that I
prepared to receive it with considerable displeasure. I saw only too well that
the presence of the king was going to reopen a wound that was not yet fully
healed, and that his absence would have been better suited to curing me.
And since I had not counted on the coldness and indifference with which
His Majesty treated me, I confess that it caused me such surprise and grief
that it made me wish the whole time that I could return to Paris.

It is the defect of our sex that we do not much care to hear the praises
even of those women whose merit we know; but if those praises come from
the mouth of a person whom we love, and have as their subject the woman
who stole his heart from us, nothing is more painful, nothing is crueler.
The king often put me to the test in this way, and I was to be pitied all the
more because I could not reproach him or disapprove of his conduct. For
after all, he had reason on his side, and the orders of my uncle, who had
forbidden me to speak of my feelings, prevented me from condemning him.
Nevertheless, the impulses of my heart got the better of both my reason and
my uncle's orders and compelled me to speak my mind two or three times
to His Majesty, who reacted so harshly to my complaints that I resolved to
make no more of them to him.

I needed a cure for my pain, though, so I put all my efforts toward finding one. Thus I practiced a part of what Ovid teaches for countering love.[54] I
removed from my sight all the objects that might keep my passion alive, and
in search of a specious pretext for banishing it from my heart, I beseeched
my sister, in whom I had the greatest confidence, to speak ill of the king
to me. It was a difficult assignment, and one in which even someone much
cleverer than she could not have succeeded. I even stayed away from the
court as much as possible and went there only very rarely. At that time it
was at Vincennes,[55] where Monsieur le Cardinal was already unwell. As his
illness grew worse every day, I resolved to marry the constable, who still
persisted in asking for me most vehemently. When His Eminence saw me
thus resolved, he wrote of it to the Marquis Angelelli, who was in Brussels
at the time and who, as I have said, had handled my marriage negotiations

---

53. In August 1660.

54. A reference to *Remedia amoris;* this and many other works by Ovid were well known in
seventeenth-century literary circles.

55. The château de Vincennes is seven miles east of the Louvre, on the edge of the Bois de
Vincennes.

with my uncle during the time of the conference. The marquis did not fail to come straightaway. And as he combined a perfect grace and elegance with very ingratiating manners, he was able to put the constable and the customs of Italy in such a favorable light that I had Monsieur de Fréjus press my uncle to conclude the deal as soon as possible.

A few days before the conclusion of the marriage contract for my sister Hortense with Monsieur le Duc Mazarin, the articles of mine were signed in Paris by His Eminence, who died very soon afterward, and whose death was honored by His Majesty with all the marks of an exceptional esteem.[56] After we had accorded our emotion over the loss of His Eminence that which duty and inclination required, far from our perceiving any change in the kindness of the king, it seemed that it had increased. For indeed, not a day passed when he did not come to our house, followed by all the most illustrious members of the court. Never has a handsomer or a more select company been seen, and never has there been such brilliant, high-stakes gaming as there was at that time in our house.

Meanwhile, however, despite all these entertainments, I could not help but feel anxious because the articles that the constable was to sign and send from Rome had not yet arrived.[57] And as this delay led everyone to suppose that doubtless he had changed his mind after the death of His Eminence, the king was kind enough to offer me some of the leading seigneurs of the court; but since I was already committed, as much out of spite as out of honor I replied to His Majesty's kind offers that I would enter a convent for the rest of my days if the constable refused me.

Not many days after that proposition, the courier brought the articles that we were awaiting, and then my wedding ceremonies were celebrated at the Louvre in the king's chapel;[58] the archbishop of Amasia,[59] now Patriarch

---

56. The marriage contract for Marie was signed by Mazarin on February 21, 1661; the contract for Hortense was finalized on February 28, and her marriage was celebrated on March 1; and the cardinal died at the château de Vincennes, of which he was governor, on March 9.

57. On March 25, 1661, the papal nuncio in France, Monseigneur Celio Piccolomini, wrote to the French secretary of state in Rome, "The queen feels great jealousy when she sees the king making new demonstrations of love to Mademoiselle Marie Mancini, for whom His Majesty had formerly shown a great passion. The queen would like very much for this lady to leave as quickly as possible to wed the constable; he tells me to endeavor to hasten the response from Prince Colonna, as the queen is very much pained to hear no news of it." Doscot, ed., *Mémoires d'Hortense et de Marie,* 117 n. 2.

58. On April 15, 1661. The privilege of being married in the king's chapel of the Louvre was normally reserved exclusively for princes and princesses of the blood.

59. Don Carlo Colonna (1607–86) was an uncle of Marie's husband Lorenzo Onofrio Colonna. He was a Benedictine monk known by the name of Friar Egidio. He was an irascible drinker and brawler, who had entered holy orders only to escape punishment after having

of Jerusalem, who gave me a very beautiful gift, said the mass, and Monsieur le Marquis Angelelli married me in the name of the constable. Once that ceremony had been performed, I was treated as a foreign princess, and as such I received the *tabouret* in the queen's chambers.[60]

I had done only half the work; I had to travel in order to finish it, and so from then on I worked to hasten my departure, and I could not rest until I was ready to set out on the road.[61] For once I have made a decision, whether advantageous for me or not, I have to carry it out, since I am not the type to back down. Thus I took my leave of Their Majesties, and the king bade me farewell, assuring me that he would always remember me and that he would protect me everywhere. I left accompanied by the archbishop of Amasia, by the Marquis Angelelli, and by Madame de Venelle, and followed by one hundred guards, to whom His Eminence before his death had given the order to escort me all the way to Milan, where the constable was to come and receive me.

Until my arrival nothing worthy of mention happened, and thus I will not take the time to talk about the journey.[62] We boarded a very handsome *bucentore*[63] on the Canal, where the constable and Monsieur le Marquis

---

killed one of his friends—Don Gregorio Gaetani—in a duel over a ridiculous incident of "road rage" which occurred on the feast of Saint Egidio, September 1, 1634. During Marie's journey toward Rome, the archbishop of Amasia amused himself by telling her horror stories about her new husband and about the customary ill treatment of their wives by the Colonna men (poisoning, imprisonment). Dulong, *Marie Mancini*, 113–14; Perey, *Une princesse romaine*, 5–8, 10–12.

60. According to protocol, a foreign princess had the right to receive a stool (*tabouret*) and to sit in the queen's presence.

61. Indeed, the whole large convoy of coaches and guards which was to convey Marie to Milan prepared and departed within a week of the marriage ceremony.

62. They arrived in Milan on May 20, 1661. Marie glosses over quite a lot here. According to the reports sent back to the French court by the abbé Elpidio Benedetti, a diplomatic attaché to the pontifical court who was part of Marie's traveling party, several men fell to their deaths during the passage through the Alps, others were killed or injured when a balcony collapsed at one of their stops; torrential rains and flooding made their travel even more hazardous than it would otherwise have been; and the relentless rain dogged them all the way to Milan, ruining the splendor of the ceremonial entry which was planned for them. Dulong, *Marie Mancini*, 112–13; Doscot, ed., *Mémoires d'Hortense et de Marie*, 119 n. 1; Perey, *Une princesse romaine*, 13–15.

63. The *bucintoro* (or *bucentoro* or *bucentauro*) was the name for the magnificent ceremonial vessel used for certain occasions in Venice, and particularly for the annual ceremony in which the doge "wedded" the sea by throwing a ring into the water. The mythological bucentaur was a centaur whose body was that of a bull; presumably, this name was used for the boat because the carved stern may have represented the mythological beast at one time. Clearly, Marie is using the word here as a generic term for an ornate ceremonial boat, since the events she describes took place in Milan rather than in Venice.

Spinola,[64] his brother-in-law, came to meet me. The latter stepped forward to greet me, pretending to be the constable, who had hung back in order to see what kind of a reception I would give him; since the marquis (whom I believed to be who he claimed he was) did not seem to me either as young or as good-looking as I had imagined the constable, I received his compliments with a coldness equal to my surprise, and turning fairly abruptly to one of my maids, called Hortense,[65] I said to her that if this was the husband who had been chosen for me, I did not want him and he could make himself another match.[66] Hortense, who had seen the constable's portrait, spotted him just then, and seeing that he was hiding behind the marquis, she set me straight and pointed him out to me. And then, to help me over my surprise, he himself came forward, and after having greeted me, he gave me his hand to lead me to a small country house around six leagues from Milan, where a magnificent dinner had been prepared for us. After the meal, we set out in order to arrive that evening in Milan, where we were received with such preparations that it would take too long to describe them. The Marquise Spinola[67] took me in her coach, and Monsieur le duc de Gaetano,[68] who was then governor of that state, came out to meet us and accompanied the constable, who was determined to consummate the marriage on the very night we arrived, despite all the scrupulous objections of Madame de Venelle, who could not consent to it unless and until we had heard mass.

The fatigue of the journey, the displeasure of being away from my family, and especially the sorrow at having left France—a sorrow that was made worse by the difference I found between its customs and those of Italy, which I had only noticed in Milan—put me in the worst humor in the world. This kept the constable quite busy, as he put all his efforts to

64. Don Paolo Vincenzo Spínola y Doria, marquis de los Balbases, duke of San Severino and Sesto (1628–99), who married Lorenzo's sister Anna Colonna (1631–89) in 1653.

65. She will reappear later in the memoir as the Comtesse Stella (see below, 118, 122); although she was one of Marie's closest confidantes, she eventually bore three illegitimate children by Lorenzo.

66. The marquis de los Balbases was ten years older than the constable and described by contemporaries as ugly and ungainly; Marie's impetuous remark turned her brother-in-law into her enemy from the moment of her arrival in Italy. Dulong, *Marie Mancini*, 115.

67. Donna Anna Colonna, Marie's sister-in-law.

68. Don Francesco Caetani (or Gaetani or Gaetano), duke of Sermoneta and San Marco, Marquis of Cisterna, Seigneur of Bassiano, Ninfa, Norma, and San Donato, gentleman of the king's chamber to Philip IV of Spain, and knight of the Order of the Golden Fleece (1594–1683), was viceroy and governor of the duchy of Milan from May 1660 until June 1662. Incidentally, he was also the brother of Don Gregorio Gaetani, who was killed in a duel by the archbishop of Amasia, uncle of Lorenzo Onofrio Colonna. See above, note 59.

amusing me, going so far as to put on a carousel[69] which he himself entered, and in which I can say dispassionately that he excelled, since the skill with which he carries out all those exercises leads him to perform admirably in such encounters.

One after another, all the ladies of the highest rank in the city hosted magnificent entertainments for me in their homes, and among others the marquise de la Fuente acquitted herself with great pomp. But the melancholy I felt, and the low spirits into which I had been cast by a fever that seized me regularly every day, took away my taste for all pleasures. This lasted ten days, at the end of which we had to leave for Rome, my illness notwithstanding, because the constable wanted to enter the city ahead of the hot weather. Madame de Venelle and the guards took leave of us then and turned back toward Paris, and we embarked in a very beautiful *bucentore* and arrived in Bologna, where the Marquis Angelelli received us and treated us in his home with great magnificence. People also gave balls for us in that city, but my ever-increasing affliction prevented me from enjoying these entertainments. After having remained there three days, we continued our journey by way of Loreto,[70] to avoid being held up by compliments in Florence, which is the place in Europe where people do the most of that sort of thing. In Pesaro my illness became so much worse that the constable was obliged to engage a doctor to accompany us on the journey and to observe carefully all the ups and downs of my sickness. Since we were proceeding by relay, we reached Loreto in two days, but I was no longer in condition to go any further. The constable's distress over my illness was inconceivable, and his grief was all the greater because my indisposition was causing me to miss seeing the cavalcade that they have every year in Rome for Saint Peter's Day, on account of which he had hastened our departure and pressed so hard along the way.[71]

Meanwhile my affliction left almost no hope for my survival, and seeing nothing but fatal signs, the constable sent for the best doctors from the surrounding cities; but unfortunately for me, out of the ten or twelve

---

69. A carousel is a tournament of horsemanship in which riders execute various formations.

70. An important pilgrimage town near the Adriatic coast, ninety miles southeast of Rimini; Pesaro is located between Rimini and Loreto. Going straight south from Bologna by way of Florence would indeed have been the more direct route to Rome.

71. Saint Peter's day is June 29. The cavalcade in question was called the *chinea*, in which the riders paraded across Rome in great pomp in order to convey the tribute money of the kingdom of Naples (which was ruled by the Spanish viceroy) to the pope. This was an important annual opportunity for the constable to reassert his protocolary precedence over other Roman princes with feudal allegiances to Spain by leading the cavalcade; unfortunately for him, he was forced to be absent from the *chinea* of 1661.

who came to treat my illness, not one was skillful enough to do so. They all judged my sickness to be life-threatening, but none knew what to do or what to suggest to deliver me from such a dangerous pass; not a day went by when they did not assemble two or three times, but all their conferences brought me no relief, as they always came out of their assemblies as unresolved as when they'd gone in. This ignorance, which was extremely dangerous given my condition, obliged the constable to send to Rome to summon in haste two of the most skilled physicians of the city. As he had by the same messenger notified my uncle Cardinal Mancini[72] of the critical condition I was in, the latter set out and arrived almost as soon as the doctors; the distress he expressed over seeing me in that state was unspeakable, and he did everything possible to console me.

The violence of such an affliction and the despair and grief it causes scarcely allow a sick person to have any regard for anyone else; thus I had very little for the constable, and I must confess that he was made to suffer furiously by my bad temper. Meanwhile, however, the cardinal did his very best to mollify me and to reduce my bitterness. I should have liked him to endeavor likewise to moderate the humor of the archbishop of Amasia, whose ingenuity and indiscreet zeal plagued me frightfully; for he never entered my room but to tell me that I could no longer hope to live and that I needed to prepare for death. While I was none too set on that eternal departure, I did nevertheless make preparations for it and gave the order to find me a friar who knew French. Fortunately, one was found, from the Society of Jesus, a very gifted man, and one who took the trouble over three or four sittings to have me make my entire general confession. During this time, the constable, who was more upset by my sickness than I was myself, inquired constantly of the doctors whom he had summoned whether there was any hope; and when they replied that there was, so long as my affliction did not grow worse on the thirteenth, which was the day I was to be purged, he came into my room with a merry look on his face and informed me of this good news, beseeching me not to be distressed by the sinister predictions of the archbishop. The outcome confirmed the doctors' expectations, and after I had been purged, my affliction diminished markedly and I was entirely out of danger. Soon afterward, I went to offer thanks to Our Lady, and I took communion in the chapel, where the constable, in order to fulfill the vow he had made for the recovery of my health, later sent one of the

---

72. Francesco Maria Mancini (1606–72), younger brother of Michele Lorenzo, the father of Marie and Hortense. He was made a cardinal in 1660, by recommendation of Louis XIV and during the papacy of Alexander VII (Fabio Chigi).

richest and most magnificent lamps ever. Then, since it was thought that the bad air and the heat of Loreto could harm my convalescence, I was moved to Recanati,[73] which is one day's travel away. I stayed there six days, during which time the intensive care that I was given and the good air of that abode caused me to regain enough strength to continue my journey and to satisfy the constable's eagerness to bring me to Rome. It is forbidden to enter the city after the feast of Saint Peter because of the excessively hot weather there and the obvious danger to which those who enter expose themselves. Nevertheless, we got around all these prohibitions and considerations and got off with merely taking a prophylactic for the change of air.

The weakness and the exhaustion that had lingered from my illness obliged me to keep to my bed most of the time, where I received from Monsieur le Cardinal Colonna[74] gifts of very beautiful jewels and a purse with two thousand pistoles.[75] After a few days, when my health was a bit restored despite the meager diet I had kept, I began to go out on walks and anywhere else where there was some entertainment. I went there in proper dress, that is, dressed in the Italian style, having wanted to adopt that fashion because of its novelty for me. Around that time, the constable proposed that I go and visit the nieces of the pope (who was then Alexander Chigi)[76] to ask them to bring me to kiss the feet of His Holiness. As I had been raised amid grandeur and was accustomed to seeing a great king at our home all the time, I asked him rather naïvely whether the Holy Father would not come to visit me first, upon which the constable and everyone present laughed and told me that that was not the custom, and that supreme pontiffs did not do anyone that honor.

Although the customs of Italy scarcely agreed with my temperament, the liking that I was beginning to feel for the constable made them easier for me to bear, for indeed, he did everything he could to please me in any way. He dressed well, with elegance and grace, he showed inexpressible care, attentiveness, and kindness, and in the end I can say that although he does not have an extremely tender disposition, I am the one person whom he has loved the most and the longest.

---

73. Another small town, three miles further inland from Loreto.

74. Girolamo Colonna (1604–66) was an uncle of Lorenzo. He became a cardinal in 1627 during the papacy of Urban VIII (Maffeo Barberini), two months before his sister Anna married Taddeo Barberini, the Pope's nephew. In 1664, he was called to Madrid by Philip IV, who made him counselor of state and military affairs; he died in 1666 while accompanying Philip's daughter, the Infanta Margarita Teresa, to Vienna, where she was to wed Emperor Leopold I.

75. The word *pistole* was used for gold coins minted both in Spain and in Italy in the seventeenth century. For more on the variation of currencies and values, see Hortense's memoir, note 28.

76. Fabio Chigi (1599–1667) became Pope Alexander VII in 1655.

There was nothing he desired with more passion than to have children. My pregnancy made him hope that I would soon fulfill his desires, and it gave him incredible joy, but it lasted only two months because I was injured at that time.[77] The accident was followed by a fever that lasted forty days, which made people all over Rome say that the constable had married an incurable woman, that I would have greater need of doctors than of midwives, and that I would never have children; the archbishop of Amasia asserted this more definitively and proclaimed it more loudly than anyone. My indisposition, which lasted all winter, seemed to justify these rumors; but when my health began to return in the spring and I became pregnant for the second time in the summer, everyone changed their tune. Because of the accident I had had during my first pregnancy, I was kept under a closer watch during the second, and I was no longer allowed to go out except in a sedan chair. I was already in my sixth month when my brother the duc de Nevers came to Rome to spend the carnival season.[78] It gave me great joy to see him after so long an absence, and his arrival gave me all the more pleasure because I was not expecting it.[79] The constable showed no less satisfaction than I at his arrival, and seeking every imaginable opportunity to make his stay enjoyable and to entertain me, he proposed a hunt at Cisterna. The place belonged to the prince de Caserte, but his exile prevented him from being there at that time, and in his stead we found monsignor de Gaetan, who showed us all imaginable kindness and hospitality and treated us most splendidly.[80]

We stayed there a fortnight, during which we spent a good part of the time hunting. Since pleasure is not the only goal of these innocent wars, and

---

77. Marie miscarried in late October 1661.

78. This would be the carnival season of 1663. The duc de Nevers was Marie's younger brother, Philippe Mancini (1641–1707), who had come to France from Rome at the same time that she and Hortense had, in 1653.

79. One of Hortense's biographers writes about the duc de Nevers: "[H]e lived his carefree life, shirking all duties and refusing all responsibilities, just as his uncle had feared he would do. When Philippe came out of his palace in Paris of a morning and stepped into his coach, the coachman never knew whether His Grace would want to do the day's marketing, as he often did, even though he had a hundred and fifty servants to do his bidding, or whether he would casually give the order to take the road to Rome. And as soon as he was in Rome he could be just as unpredictable, come out of his palace on the Corso, lean back in his coach, and order an immediate return to Paris." Rosvall, *Mazarine Legacy*, 91–92.

80. The prince of Caserta was Don Filippo Caetani (1620 or 1626–87), son of Don Francesco, whom Marie mentioned above (103) as the duc de Gaetano, governor of Milan; Don Francesco was also marquis of Cisterna. Caserta is twenty miles north of Naples and one hundred fifty miles southeast of Rome, and there are a number of places called Cisterna between Caserta and Rome. "Monsignor de Gaetan" may have been a prelate member of the prince's family, but it was more probably Don Francesco himself, who was viceroy of the kingdom of Sicily at this time.

the glory of the spoils and the satisfaction of presenting one's friends with them are the most important, the constable made sure to bring with him some persons of quality from among his friends in addition to those of his household, so that they could return to Rome laden with game; and thus it seemed that we must have emptied the forests of boars, and we took enough of them to treat half the city.

Even though my pregnancy did not permit me to ride a horse, I still was able to enjoy all the entertainment, because the hunters made the hunt pass fairly often by some covered wagons of a sort which they make for such purposes. I was safe there, since even the most furious boars could not tip them over because of their weight, and my brother quite often kept me company, as he was not naturally a friend of fatigue or of pleasures that required too much effort.

Upon our return to Rome, from which Pope Alexander, because of his aversion to all forms of entertainment, had banished everything including plays, the constable continued his care and attention and endeavored to make up for this dearth of pleasures by inventing a masquerade whose subject was the fable of Castor and Pollux.[81] He and my brother played the roles of Castor and Pollux, followed by a great many horsemen; they were preceded by a man in the costume of a swan which was so skillfully made that it might have been mistaken for the real thing if nature produced animals of that species as big as he was. He was throwing the ladies the following madrigal, which was composed by a man of talent, whom I have since chosen for the education of my children and who is applying himself to the task with exceptional care.

> Questi d'amor, e fe' dui divini lampi,
> Figli d'Etereo cigno,
> Van con genio benigno
> Seminando di gioia i Latii campi;
> Son la gemina luce
> Di Castor e Polluce,

---

81. Castor and Pollux were the twin sons born from the union of Leda and Jupiter, who had taken the form of a swan. They were valiant heroes bound to each other by ties of great affection. They are associated with the stars and the heavens in a couple of different stories. In one story, they take part in the voyages of the Argonaut; during a storm at sea, Orpheus stills the water by praying to the gods and playing his harp, and afterward stars appear on the heads of Castor and Pollux. Because of this story, the twins came to be seen as patrons of seafarers and voyagers. In another story, Castor is killed in battle and Pollux appeals to Jupiter to allow Pollux to give his own life for his brother's; depending on the version of this story, Jupiter either allows them to enjoy life alternately, each of them living one day on earth and the next in the heavens, or allows them to be united in the heavens as Gemini.

Che con accese voglie,
Ascosi in queste spoglie,
Lascian d'Etra i luminosi chiostri,
Sol per arder o belle à gli occhi vostri.[82]

Pleasures and displeasures may occur close together, but they follow each other in such rapid succession that the end of the one is commonly the beginning of the other; thus all these carnival entertainments were followed by the departure of my brother, which I felt keenly although he promised to come back for my confinement, and then by the news of the death of the Marquis Angelelli. Having insisted on returning to Bologna, against the wishes of the constable and of all his friends, the marquis was murdered in an ambush by a gentleman called Bovio, who, after the fashion of that land, vented his anger on the marquis because he was the closest friend and also the brother-in-law of a person whom Bovio could not do in. I was extremely shaken by this calamity, both because of the gratitude I owed the marquis for the service he had always tried to render me during his life, and because of the esteem I felt for his merit and for his rare qualities.

A few days after this sad experience, as I had wished ardently for a boy during the whole time of my pregnancy, heaven gave me one on the seventh of April, the day of Pope Alexander's coronation.[83] And in fulfilling my wishes, it also filled with joy the constable, the archbishop of Amasia, and the whole family, who desired with no less passion than I that I should give birth to a boy. Although there was not much hope that he would survive because of his weakness and because of the pitiful state in which he was born, the festivities were nonetheless very grand, and magnificent gifts were given to those who brought the first news of his birth. Monsieur le Cardinal Colonna, who considered me the principal cause of this universal joy in the family, came to demonstrate that he shared in it and presented me with some jewels and a purse containing one thousand pistoles. After forty days, when I got up from my lying-in, I had to prepare to receive the compliments of the Sacred College, the princesses, and the ladies of the city; and

---

82. These two divine beacons of love and faith, / Sons of the celestial swan, / With a kind and gracious spirit go / Scattering jewels across the Milky Way; / They are the twin light / Of Castor and Pollux, / Who, led by ardent desire, / Hidden in these garments, / Leave the bright cloisters of the heavens, / Solely to shine, O beauties, for your eyes.

83. Don Filippo Colonna was born April 7, 1663 (d. 1714). Actually, April 7 was the anniversary of Pope Alexander's election, not his coronation. After a famously long (eighty days) conclave fraught with national and factional rivalries, Cardinal Fabio Chigi was unanimously elected pope on April 7, 1655. He chose the name Alexander VII, and his coronation took place on April 18, 1655.

so to receive their visits with the appropriate formality, I set myself up in a bed which had been prepared for me for my first confinement and which was used only this one time. The novelty as well as the magnificence of this bed filled everyone with admiration: it was a sort of seashell which seemed to float in the middle of an artfully represented sea, which served as a base for it. It rested on the hindquarters of four seahorses mounted by mermaids; the whole thing was admirably sculpted, and the brilliance of the gold had disguised so well the material underneath that it seemed to be entirely made of that precious metal. Ten or twelve little cherubs served as attachments for curtains of a very rich gold brocade, which they allowed to hang casually and which served more as ornaments than as veils, since they hid nothing from view of all that deserved to be seen in these sumptuous trappings.

My son, who was already in better health, and my condition at that time, which gave the constable hope of a second successor, so greatly increased his joy that he never seemed more satisfied in his life; and since he believed that all he lacked in order to be perfectly content was to see me happy, there was nothing that he would not do to please me. Seeing him in such a kind and obliging state of mind, I decided to take advantage of it, and since I wished to spend the carnival season in Venice, I proposed that he take me there, which he promised to do, provided that Monsieur le Cardinal, his uncle, consented to it. So I spoke of it with His Eminence, who raised some objections to allowing it; I overcame them finally by assuring him that I was not with child, which was the sole obstacle that he saw to this plan. Thus we set out in late autumn, and we had quite a pleasant journey, apart from the anxiety I caused the constable by showing so little concern for myself, for I rode sometimes in a coach, sometimes on horseback, and often at full gallop. His indulgence extended even to this situation, for far from complaining about all my excesses, he merely told me not to reveal my condition to anyone, for fear that his uncle might find out. In the end, what had not happened to me during the whole journey did happen at our approach to Venice, and having hurt myself, I delayed for a few days the hopes of the constable; but since I was less ill from this accident than from the first, I spent only a fortnight in bed, where I repaired the mistake that I had just made.

In all of my pregnancies I was lucky enough to feel quite well, and since I was only in the first days at that time, I spent the carnival season very merrily, at the opera, at dinners, at balls, and at other gatherings, as well as playing *la bassette*, which I adored; and Monsieur le prince de Brunswick[84]

---

84. Ernst August (1629–98), prince-bishop of Osnabrück in 1661 and later duke of Bruns- wick-Lüneberg-Calenberg (Hanover) and first elector of Brunswick-Lüneburg (Hanover),

and Monsieur le duc de Mantoue,[85] whose desire to amuse themselves had brought them to Venice, came to play it at our house, along with a number of other persons of quality.

All these pleasures and pastimes were causing me to dread leaving that place and returning to Rome, when the constable told me that I absolutely had to resign myself to going, and that as I was already fairly well along in my pregnancy, he did not want to have the same thing happen to me that had happened at our approach to Venice. I confess that this order stung me considerably, even though I should have expected it, and in exchange for obeying it, I drew from him the promise that we would come back to spend another carnival in that pleasant abode. Thereafter we departed and took leave of all our friends, particularly the prince de Brunswick, who was so pleased with our company and with the affability and generosity that the constable had shown him during our stay in Venice that he promised to make a trip to Rome just to see us, saying that he would also bring his wife the princess.[86]

I made the entire journey lying in a litter, and since we were putting in short days on the road, we only arrived in Rome at the beginning of the summer. There, after having suffered through the excessive heat, which my pregnancy made even more unbearable for me, I finally gave birth to my second son at the beginning of November, the evening before the departure of Monsieur le Cardinal Colonna, who was to travel to Spain in order to conduct the Infanta from there to the emperor.[87] His joy at seeing this further reinforcement of the family was unimaginable; and not content to express it to me in words alone, he added presents to them which were

---

became a close friend of both Marie and her husband. He was one of many men with whom Marie was rumored to have had affairs, and his wife cordially detested Marie, but it is just as likely that he was simply her confidant and that his wife's animosity stemmed from the fact that the prince did indeed have numerous affairs. When a revised edition of Marie's memoir was published by Sébastien Bremond in 1678, a year after the publication of *La Vérité dans son jour*, Bremond included a dedicatory notice to the prince of Brunswick.

85. Carlo Gonzaga, duke of Mantua and of Monferrato (1629–65). In 1659, the duke of Mantua sold the duchy of Nevers to Cardinal Mazarin, who bestowed it immediately on his nephew, Philippe Mancini.

86. Sophie of the Palatinate (1630–1714), who was a granddaughter of James I of England through her mother, Elizabeth Stuart. Leibniz, who was court librarian and privy counselor to Duke Ernst August, recognized Sophie as the intellectual and cultural hub of the court in Hanover. According to the Act of Settlement (1701), the English crown was to pass to Sophie after Queen Anne; but since Sophie died just two months before Anne, Prince Georg Ludwig, eldest son of Ernst August and Sophie, became George I of England.

87. Marcantonio Colonna (1664–1715), born either October 21 or November 17, neither of which dates corresponds clearly with what Marie reports here. In fact, although the cardinal did go to Spain at this time, he did not undertake the journey with the Infanta until 1666; in the meantime, he acted as counselor of state and military affairs to Philip IV, who died in September 1665.

every bit as magnificent as the first ones, and then he set off to carry out his task.

His absence left the constable in complete charge of all of his own property, whereas he had relied upon the guidance of His Eminence when the latter was in Rome. Just a few days later we went to Cisterna, where Monsieur le prince de Brunswick, who had come to Rome with his wife the princess, came to join us and kept us company for three days. We expressed, the constable and I, all the gratitude that we owed for such extraordinarily noble and honorable conduct; and I myself had the greatest esteem for his conscientiousness in keeping his word to us. I need not even mention the kindness, the generosity, and the liberality of this prince, for those qualities are as well known everywhere as his name.

Upon our arrival in Rome, I saw his wife the princess, or rather I should say that I saw in her style of life, in her temperament, in the cast of her mind, and even in her elegant way of dressing the distillation of all that was most perfect and most refined in France.

Around that time, my brother, who had made a trip to Venice, wrote to ask us eagerly to go and join him there for the carnival; but since we were not able to do it then, we deferred our departure until the spring. In the spring we set out, so that we arrived in Venice at Ascension and saw that famous festival and the fair that is so renowned, which attracts curious visitors from all parts of Europe; I will not stop to describe it because it would take too long to tell about it all.[88] Although I was with child, I met with no accidents during the journey or during our stay, as I took greater care to look after myself than the first time. After having seen all the magnificence of that festival, we left for Milan at the start of the summer, which we spent quite happily until the beginning of September, when the constable was obliged to make a trip to Spain. I felt incredible unhappiness at his departure, which his sister the Marquise Spinola and her husband and my brother, who had been kind enough to accompany us, endeavored to relieve with a thousand different pastimes and entertainments.

At the same time when my mind was being battered by that storm, the constable suffered a terrible one at sea, in which he ran the risk of shipwreck on a galley of the squadron of Sicily on which he had embarked. He got off with just a fright, though, and having landed fairly felicitously, although in a place devoid of everything he needed for his journey, he took the first

---

88. It was at the feast of the Ascension in May that the doge embarked in the splendid ceremonial *bucintoro*, accompanied by swarms of festooned boats, and performed the *Sposalizio del Mar* (the "Wedding with the Sea"). See above, note 63. After Ascension, there was a fair which lasted a fortnight and which featured artists and artisans selling sculpture, paintings, lace, glass, and other fine wares.

mount he found; when he reached a better equipped place, he continued on his way by land and finally arrived in Madrid three days after the death of Philip IV.[89] As the loss of this prince had caused some changes in the business world, it likewise caused some in the constable's plans; it made him decide to turn around after having stayed only a fortnight at the court. He found the way of life there too withdrawn, and besides, his impatience to see me again did not permit him to stay longer. To satisfy this desire, then, and to keep the promise that he had made me to be there for my lying-in, he traveled by way of France and arrived in Milan at the end of November;[90] I went out to meet him with his sister, and I was as glad to see him again as I had been pained by his absence. The very evening he arrived, I gave him a third successor, but since this gift cost me much dearer than the first two, and even threatened my life, I took the view that I should give him no more of these gifts which might expose me to such perils. However, it was not enough for me to have made this resolution, if he did not confirm it with his consent. It was toward that goal that I worked, and I was quite successful, as he has since kept his word to me very scrupulously in all the time that we have been together.[91] After this agreement, I thought of nothing but recovering my health, in order to be in condition to go to Venice for a second carnival. So we set out as soon as my strength permitted it, and as we had left the newborn with the Marquise Spinola and the second had stayed in Rome, we brought only the eldest with us. We spent the carnival season quite happily, apart from my episodes of jealousy, for the constable did not fail to recover elsewhere what he had lost through our agreement, and I confess I was angry that he should keep his word to me at that price.

They put on wonderful operas in Venice, among them the *Titus*, to

---

89. Philip IV died on September 17, 1665.

90. It seems that Marie must have meant to write "the beginning of November," since Carlo Colonna was born on November 4, 1665.

91. Various commentators have found this insistence by Marie on a *separazione di letto* to be quite puzzling, coming as it did at a time when she seems to have been sincerely in love with her husband. Lucien Perey (*Une princesse romaine*, 61–64) observes that the explanation Marie offered to intimates such as her sister-in-law—and the explanation alleged in the gazettes of the time—was that an astrologer had warned her she would surely die if she had a fourth child. However, Perey views this excuse as nothing more than a plausible cover for the real reason—plausible because Marie's father had been an astrologer, and she herself had written a couple of texts on occult sciences which have since been lost. The real reason, according to Perey, was that soon after the birth of Marie's third son, she received an anonymous message informing her that one month earlier, a girl child had been born to a woman of quality, and that Lorenzo was the father. Perey's source (Pompeo Litta et al., *Famiglie celebri italiane*, unbound fascicles in 10 boxes [Milan: P. E. Giusti, 1819–83]) specifies that this illegitimate daughter was named Maria, that she was raised as a girl of noble birth in a Roman convent, and that she died there at the age of eighty-five on March 4, 1750.

which I went often.[92] I was no less attracted by the sweetness of the voices and by the acting of the players—particularly that of a musician of His Royal Highness[93] called Cavagnino, and of one of my maids who performed admirably—than by the beauty of the work, which earned the applause of everyone and which was assuredly among the most beautiful that have ever been seen.

After the carnival, the constable made a short trip to Rome, along with my brother, for some business that he had there, and came back after three weeks. Upon his return he began to talk about going to Milan, where he wanted to be when the Infanta arrived there. It was harder for me to leave Venice this time than the first or the second, because I knew it better and because it did not seem to me that there was a city in the world where one could have a better time; but my resistance only increased the constable's eagerness to leave, so that we had to depart at the height of the summer. I tried nonetheless to amuse myself in Milan as much as possible, to which Madame la Marquise Spinola and her husband and some other ladies of the city contributed not a little. There was no shortage of outings during the day, or of magnificent luncheons and teas, and the evening was devoted to the concerts that we held in the *place marine*,[94] which is a place always filled with an elegant crowd, where people ordinarily go to be seen. Our fine company was later increased by those who came to join us from Venice and from Turin, from where His late Royal Highness[95] had sent one of the leading seigneurs of his court along with several gentlemen who were friends of his, to present their compliments to the empress, who arrived in late autumn. I went to greet her in Spanish dress, and in deepest mourning over the death of Monsieur le Cardinal Colonna, who had died at *il Finale* of

92. According to the false memoir published under Marie's name (*Mémoires de M.L.P.M.M. Colonne*, 1676), the opera *Titus* was dedicated to Marie. The memoir says that she attended five performances of it in a row at the theater Grimani, and that five years later (so in 1671), she desired that it be performed in Rome at the Teatro Tor di Nona. *Cendre et poussière*, 89; see also note 138, below.

93. The doge of Venice from 1659 to 1674 was Domenico Contarini.

94. The false memoir provides more details about this spot: "No doubt you know, Monsieur, that there is in Milan one of the most beautiful promenades in Italy. This place, which is called *la Marine*, is situated near the ramparts, about a thousand paces away, and it is broad enough for ten coaches to drive abreast. On each side, a stream lined with marvelously tall linden trees makes the place the most pleasant in the world. That is where all the nobles, taking care to have it watered every day so as to put down the dust and keep the place cool, go to take their entertainment in the evening, and where I went too." *Cendre et poussière*, 83.

95. Charles-Emmanuel II, duke of Savoy (1634–75), the benefactor who extended his protection to Hortense and to whom she dedicated her memoir.

an illness which had overtaken him suddenly while he was accompanying that princess.[96] Her Majesty received me with extraordinary kindness and told me that I looked and acted very Spanish, meaning thereby to raise me above other nations, for there is not a single nation whose people do not believe that what is customary for them is the most perfect and the most highly evolved. After having stayed for a month in Milan, she continued her journey toward Vienna, where the constable declined to accompany her. I will not say that it was to avoid the expense, for that would not do justice to his generosity; I will simply say that his affection for me having diminished a bit, it did not inspire in him that indulgence. So I proposed that we spend another carnival in Venice, where I was quite sure that he would not refuse to go, since he had some little entanglements there which pushed him to it more than I. But even though I found in that city the same entertainments as before, since I did not find myself in the same situation there, I enjoyed them only imperfectly; for my jealousy, in which I was confirmed by the little stories that people told me about him, and my grief at seeing others take advantage of my politic sterility, made for some very bad times for me, and had already reduced me to a pitiful state.

During that time, as if I should not have had enough things to worry about from the outside, a new one arrived inside the household, in the person of the Marquise Paleotti, married to a Bolognese gentleman by that name and daughter of the duc de Northumberland, a gentleman who was quite well known in England.[97] As this lady was then in her prime, she drew everyone's attention. The constable was not immune to her charms, and even if I had tried not to take his surreptitious glances as signs of the passion

96. Cardinal Colonna died September 4, 1666, at a place called *il Finale* in the region of Savona and Genoa; the place which was known then as *il Finale* corresponds with either the present-day Finale Ligure or Finale Marina. The cause of his death was cited as "malignant fever" (*maligna febbre*).

97. The Marquise Paleotti was a Dudley, named either Elizabeth or Catherine. According to Dulong (*Marie Mancini*, 160), her father was Sir Robert Dudley, and he was a member of Queen Christina's household; however, it seems unlikely that Marie's identification of him as the duke of Northumberland could be accurate, since although the title duke of Northumberland was indeed created in 1551 for John Dudley, it was forfeited and was not passed down to his heirs when he was executed for high treason in 1553. There was no duke of Northumberland in the 1660s, the period that Marie is recounting here; the title was next bestowed in 1674 on George Fitzroy, illegitimate son of Charles II with Barbara Villiers, countess of Castlemaine. Although Marie expresses some distress here over the presence of the Marquise Paleotti, the two women eventually became close friends, after the constable's interest in the marquise had run its course. In fact, when Marie's second son Marcantonio married the marquise's legitimate daughter, named either Cristina or Diana, in 1697, Marie supported the marriage over the strident objections of her eldest son Filippo.

he felt for that beauty, his overzealous attentions and his assiduity toward her would have left me no room for doubt, and I confess that I harbored a secret resentment over it. But the Président Donneville, whom my brother had brought along to Rome, was much more vexed by it than I, because he considered the constable's pursuits to be a great obstacle to the progress of his own passion for the marquise. The Quaranta Lupuli[98] was no smaller a burden to him because he was no less dangerous a rival, combining as he did a passionate love with the advantages he had received from nature and from his birth. Finally, after the carnival and the winter had ended, we headed back to Rome, going by way of Bologna, where the Cardinal Legate[99] received us and treated us most magnificently in his home. The young marquise, who was part of the group, saw the number of her suitors increase; but of all her worshipers, the one who loved her the most sincerely, and who made a sacrifice for her which is seldom made in these times, was the Quaranta Lupuli. He took it very much to heart that this beauty cared so little about his passion; and having gotten it into his head that other lovers were more favorably treated by her, he was seized by such intense grief and such violent jealousy that one day away from Bologna, where he had followed us with the intention of coming all the way to Rome, he fell ill with a fever which carried him off soon afterward.

We continued our journey and learned of his death upon our arrival. The marquise shed a few tears, which were promptly dried, since her suitors scarcely left her time to cry. She was staying with us, where her husband kept her company but a few months, as he was obliged to go to Ancona, where he was called by the position of standard-bearer which he had received; and after seven or eight months, she left our home and went to stay in a house which she rented.

The gambling and the feasting that were always going on in ours were pleasures too meager for carnival; thus, in order to pass the time less gloomily, and to silence those who were grumbling about the liberties they saw me taking, I conceived of a masquerade in which I played Clorinda.[100] Followed by thirty or forty horsemen dressed as soldiers, I went around tossing a madrigal about in the way that maskers do; my brother and a friend

98 I have not been able to trace the meaning of this title.

99. Bologna was part of the papal states, in which the pope was the temporal ruler; the leader of the city, in whom the papal authority was vested, was the cardinal legate.

100. Clorinda was a Persian warrior maiden, a character from Torquato Tasso's verse epic *La Gerusalemme liberata* (*Jerusalem Delivered*, 1581), which was very widely known in the seventeenth century and which provided popular themes for works of art in all genres. Thus, Marie's

of his, a gentleman called Marescoti, had composed it based on that idea, and here are the words:

> D'obliato decoro
> Questo amante guerrier non dia sospetto,
> Che s'ho viril aspetto,
> Intatto d'onestà serbo il tesoro.
> Quante in ogni confine
> Son Penelope al volto, al cor son Frine![101]

Once carnival was over, the marquise talked about returning to Bologna, and the constable showed no displeasure at that resolution, since for some time already they had not been on such good terms as before. A few days later, we set out for Milan, with the intention of going to meet my sister the Duchesse Mazarin, who I learned had withdrawn from Paris because of some disputes she had had with her husband the duc.[102] The affection that I have always had for her led me to undertake this journey with tremendous

---

answer to the criticism that her freedom was unseemly for a woman was to embrace the image of the *femme forte*—the virile woman—which was also a widespread figure in literary and artistic works. The virile woman figure was commonly a warrior maiden, a being who embodied both kinds of valor—masculine (military prowess) and feminine (sexual purity). By staging herself as Clorinda, Marie was effectively arguing that she could "act like a man" and freely mix with men without damaging the basis for her feminine honor, i.e., her chastity. The Clorinda performance took place during carnival 1668, the same carnival during which the opera *La Baltasara* was performed several times; the libretto was by Giulio Rospigliosi, who was at that time Pope Clement IX, and it featured the Clorinda story as a play within the play. For notices of the 1668 productions, see http://www.nuovorinascimento.org/rosp-2000/ documenti/ar-1668-02-08.htm; http://www.nuovorinascimento.org/rosp-2000/documenti/ ar-1668-carnevale.htm; http://www.nuovorinascimento.org/rosp-2000/documenti/ar-1668- 01-28.htm. *La Baltasara* is still performed occasionally; see http://www.nuovorinascimento .org/rosp-2000/bibliografia/stampe/libretti/comica-1992.htm. Marie does not mention any of the mythological themes employed by the Colonna household in carnival 1669, perhaps because they showed her in a less favorable light. In one of the most splendid spectacles of that year, Lorenzo appeared as Ulysses leading dogs on leashes, to represent his comrades who had been transformed into beasts by the enchantress Circe. In this rebus, Marie was understood to be Circe, and Lorenzo came off as the master of the situation, mocking the reputed lovers of his wife. Meanwhile, the constable himself was engaged in an affair with the Princess Chigi, Marie's bitter rival. Perey, *Une princesse romaine*, 82–83.

101. "Do not suspect this warrior lover / Of any lapse in decorum, / For even if I've a virile air, / I keep intact the treasure of my honor. / How many women in the world / Are Penelope outwardly, but at heart, Phryne!" Penelope was the faithful wife of Ulysses; Phryne was an Athenian courtesan in the fourth century BCE. In the seventeenth century, these two figures were commonly used to represent two types of women.

102. As Hortense reports in her memoir (58), she left Paris on June 13, 1668.

satisfaction, and I did everything I could think of to get the constable to agree to it; for his part, he did all he could to dissuade me, objecting that the heat was excessive and moreover that I did not need to go so far. The courier that Monsieur le Marquis Spinola, interim governor of Milan following the death of the late Don Louis Ponce de Leon,[103] dispatched to us in order to notify us that my sister was at Elstof[104] and to urge the constable to go there finally prevailed upon him. And so, after he had consented in the way that one does to things which one is extremely loath to do, we left, the Marquise Paleotti and I in a *chaise roulante*[105] in which we traveled at top speed, and the constable in another with the Comtesse Stella, whom I mentioned under the name of Hortense in the beginning of this history.[106] The only train we had was composed of three or four of the most necessary servants that one takes for a journey in which one wishes to travel light. And thus we reached Milan in six days; I was extremely fatigued when we arrived, not by the length of the trip but by the constant quarrels that I had with the constable, who was delighted that everything was a mess on this journey, because he had undertaken it against his will and during the harshest season of the year. Three days after our arrival, the Marquis Spinola received word that Madame Mazarin was one day's journey away, and so we went at once to greet her and found her in a country house, more beautiful than ever despite a fairly bad injury to her knee which she had gotten in a fall from a horse, and which even obliged her to keep to her bed.[107] Since she was coming straight from France, her head full of beautiful fashions, she brought with her the very spirit of that nation, which judges only on appearances and esteems people only according to how well they dress. Unfortunately for us, since neither the marquise nor I was dressed fashionably, we were received very coldly by her, and the way we were fitted out was ridiculed as it deserved to be. After this cold reception, we set out for Milan, where we arrived that same evening, by water, having deemed that means of transportation most

103. Don Luis de Guzmán, Ponce de Leon, gentleman of the king's chamber and captain of the Spanish guard, was governor of Milan from June 1662 until his death in March 1668. Marie's brother-in-law the Marquis Spinola was interim governor from April 14, 1668, to September 10, 1668, and again from March 1669 to May 21, 1670.

104. Hortense wrote "Altorf"; it was probably the town called Altdorf, located 45 miles south of Zurich and about 125 miles north of Milan. See Hortense's memoir, 62.

105. A *chaise roulante* was a two-wheeled vehicle drawn by one or two horses in which there was room for just one or two passengers.

106. See above, 103.

107. According to Hortense, she had sustained the injury to her knee by falling on it while she was playfully running after her maid Nanon. See Hortense's memoir, 61.

comfortable for my sister; and a few days later the marquise returned to Bologna. People's eagerness to see Madame Mazarin was incredible. Most things do not really live up to one's expectations of them, or else when one gets in the habit of seeing them, their luster tends to wear off. This was not the case with my sister's beauty. It seemed even greater than people had imagined it to be, and they discovered new charms each time they saw her, which did not happen as often as they wished. For in Milan she became so withdrawn and solitary that she had no contact with anyone except her servants; she was almost always shut away in the apartment that we had given her, and most often she stayed in bed with bandages on her injury. Or if she did go out with us, which rarely happened, it was always in dishabille; but she was ever more charming, her accident having served by some uncommon effect to make her more beautiful, and her simple, casual clothing making her no less dazzling than the most magnificent. After a few weeks my brother came to join us and was extremely glad to see my sister. But one of her servants,[108] whom she had allowed through an excess of kindness to hold too much sway over her mind, soon destroyed the harmony in which they were living through his impudence; I renewed their good relations for a few days, but a second disagreement later succeeded the first, as I will relate elsewhere.

I was then so morose from such a long stay in Milan that I pressed the constable to allow me to go to Venice with my sister and my brother, but he replied to my very humble request that he could not leave so soon, nor would he consent to my going without him. This refusal and the manner in which he made it so greatly irritated me—for resistance makes me bitter, particularly when I know that someone is taking pleasure in contradicting me—that I would have left his house right then if the Marquise Spinola had not overcome my resentment through the strength of her arguments and had not intervened to patch things up between us.

The constable had stayed for so long in Milan only because he was waiting for Monsieur le marquis de Mortara, whom Spain was sending to be governor of that state;[109] seeing that the latter was taking longer to arrive than he had imagined, he resolved to leave. My sister and my brother asked

108. Courbeville, the gentleman belonging to the Chevalier de Rohan, whom the latter had assigned to accompany Hortense to Italy. See Hortense's memoir, 60, 62–63, 68–71. Although Marie identifies him here as one of her sister's "servants" (*domestiques*), the term could apply at this time to anyone belonging to her household, including a gentleman of the minor nobility.

109. Don Francisco de Orozco, marquis of Olias, Mortara, and San Reale and gentleman of the king's chamber, was governor of Milan only from September 10 to December 28, 1668.

of him what I had been unable to obtain, and since he could not refrain from
granting it to them and going by way of Venice, he at least refrained from
making a long stay there (knowing that I was happier there than anywhere
else); he used as his excuse the promise that he had made to Monsieur le
Cardinal Chigi[110] to go to Siena for a hunt they had planned.

So there was no way around it: we had to leave that city, where I left my
brother whom I had reconciled with my sister for the second time, and who
promised to come and join us again before we left Siena. As Cardinal Chigi
was not yet there, we went to wait in Bologna until he arrived. The constable stayed with one of his servants in order to avoid certain ceremonies
to which other accommodations would have obliged him. The Marquise
l'Alcotti whom we found then in Bologna kept very good company with
us, but although we were treated several times to entertainments in the
country, my sister's unhappiness and the resentment I felt over her ill humor
prevented us from taking pleasure in anything at all. However, we went to
Siena as soon as we learned that Monsieur le Cardinal Chigi had arrived
there, and our woe was diminished a bit by the reception that His Eminence
gave us and by the magnificent meals that he offered us over the fortnight
we stayed there; moreover, the pleasures of the hunt which we enjoyed
every day made the time pass quite agreeably for us, and particularly for
my sister, who was extremely fond of that activity, since the blows struck
by her hands were as inevitable as those by her eyes. This fine time did not
go off, however, without one small mortification which was caused by the
dispute that my brother (who had come to join us as he had promised to do)
renewed with my sister for the third time; and then after this quarrel he went
back to Venice. After my brother's departure, we went to Marino, which
is a duchy belonging to the constable, located some twelve leagues from
Rome;[111] and after having remained there until All Saints' Day, we returned
to Rome, where Madame Mazarin continued to make a solitary refuge of

110. Flavio Chigi (1631–93), nephew of Pope Alexander VII, was perhaps the most powerful
person in Rome after the pope himself. He was an intimate friend of the Colonna household,
and he and Marie were particularly frequent companions. Marie's great rival for protocolary
precedence, the Princess Chigi (Maria Virginia Borghese), is often identified as Cardinal
Chigi's sister-in-law, but she was in fact the wife of his cousin, Agostino Chigi. She was also a
mistress of Lorenzo, and it was rumored that Marie had become the lover of Cardinal Chigi
in revenge. In any case, Marie's feelings toward the princess were bitter; this may explain why
she makes no mention of her in this memoir, while she does mention the Marquise Paleotti
and the Comtesse Stella, both of whom were Lorenzo's mistresses but who were also friends
of Marie.

111. Marino is located twelve miles southeast of the center of Rome in the Alban hills, and
three miles southwest of Frascati. See Hortense's memoir, note 102.

our house as she had done in Milan, only very rarely letting us enjoy the sight of her and the pleasure of her conversation, and refusing to receive visits from anyone. I felt considerable displeasure over her retreat, and my brother, who came to Rome a few days later, was both surprised and vexed by it. We all attributed her humor to the insinuations of certain servants of hers, in whom she placed too much confidence, and after I myself had made every effort to inspire other feelings in her, a justifiable anger at not being able to do so impelled me to speak my mind to a gentleman in her service called Courbeville, who, truth be told, was a decent fellow, but who put on too much of a show of it. This rather quick-tempered gentleman, far from excusing himself, responded quite impertinently to me, and as he had spoken of my brother in disobliging and disrespectful terms, I told him to leave the room that instant and to go downstairs, where he would find people who could teach him how to behave and how to show the proper reverence for people of my brother's quality. So he obeyed, but very angrily, and my sister, who took the incident to heart, left our house that instant and went to stay with my aunt Madame Martinozzi.[112] Courbeville went to the home of my uncle Cardinal Mancini, which he left a few days later and went to Civitavecchia,[113] where he was arrested and held in a fortress in order to tone down his haughty temper a bit; but not long after, he escaped thanks to the favor of the nephews of Pope Rospigliosi,[114] whom his kind mistress induced to take an interest in his liberty.

My sister, who was still at my aunt's house, could no longer bear the constraints under which she lived and resolved to withdraw to the Campo Marzio, with my aunt the nun,[115] whom I have already mentioned at the beginning of this history, and who was extraordinarily glad to have her company. The extreme affection that I had for my sister obliged me to visit her fairly often, but since she received my visits with great indifference at that time, I was unable to discover either her state of mind or what plans she had.

112. The aunt who had traveled to France along with Marie, Hortense, Philippe, their mother, and their cousin Laure Martinozzi, in 1653. See above, 85–86.

113. There was a papal fortress in Civitavecchia, which is fifty miles northwest of Rome, along the Mediterranean coast. Civitavecchia was also the principal seaport for Rome.

114. The pope in question was Clement IX (Giulio Rospigliosi, 1600–1669), who reigned from June 1667 to December 1669. Although Hortense (71) specified that it was Vincenzo Rospigliosi (1635–73) who was responsible for Courbeville's putative liberation, Marie also gives credit to his brothers, two of whom were or would soon become cardinals—Giacomo (1628–84) and Felice (1639–88)—and another of whom, Giovanni Battista (1646–1722), was reputedly an admirer of Marie's.

115. See above, 84 and note 8; see also Hortense's memoir, 71–73 and note 107.

During that time[116] I asked permission of the constable to make a small trip to Naples, and I obtained it without difficulty, because it was only for a few days, and moreover because the place was not as entertaining as Venice. Our party was composed of the constable's brother who was called at that time the abbé Colonna,[117] his uncle the archbishop of Amasia, my brother, the Sieur Marescoti,[118] and the Sieur Acciaioli—the first Bolognese and the second Sienese, and both great friends of the family. The Comtesse Stella, whom I have already mentioned, accompanied me on this journey, along with a *femme de chambre* in her service, called Constance, to whom my brother was not indifferent.

This little outing entirely devoted to pleasure was unexpectedly disrupted by a disagreement that the archbishop had in Naples with the constable's brother, and over which they nearly came to blows. Following their reconciliation, and after we had stayed a fortnight in that city, we departed for Rome, where I found my sister in a profound melancholy, which proceeded from her choice of retreat.[119] I can say without exaggeration that

116. Autumn of 1669.

117. Filippo Colonna (1642–86), who eventually abandoned his ecclesiastical benefices and married in 1671; Marie refers to him later as the prince de Sonnino.

118. Presumably the same person as the coauthor of the madrigal mentioned above (117). He may have been either Antonio Giuseppe Marescotti (1644–1711) or Ranieri Marescotti (1640–90), both of whom were Bolognese patricians, members of the Magistrato degli Anziani, and eventually senators. Of these two, the former seems more likely to have been a friend of Philippe Mancini's with a similarly carefree approach to life, given that he did not enter the Magistrato degli Anziani until 1675 (well after the period Marie recounts here), whereas Ranieri was in it as of 1660.

119. According to the accounts of this episode given by Perey (*Une princesse romaine,* 84–85) and Dulong (*Marie Mancini,* 160), Hortense revealed that she was expecting a child by Courbeville when Marie returned from Naples. If this is so, then Hortense's melancholy may have been caused by her choice of retreat, but only indirectly; it would have been the effect of her worry that she needed to be gone from the convent before the nuns noticed her pregnancy, despite her husband's injunction that she stay there at least two years. This would explain Marie's insistence on bringing her sister out without delay, and Perey contends further that Hortense's condition was the reason for the queen of Sweden's sudden change of heart.

However, both Perey and Dulong seem to overlook the obvious discrepancies in chronology. If, as Perey contends (82), Hortense was in the convent during carnival 1669, and given that there is no indication she ever saw Courbeville again after they both left the Palazzo Colonna some time before her entry into the convent, then how could she be only in the early or middle stages of a pregnancy by him in the autumn of 1669 (Marie writes to Colbert to offer excuses for "springing" Hortense from the convent in October 1669)? A Frenchman named Jacques de Belbeuf, who had come to Rome during the conclave following the death of Clement IX in December 1669, wrote to his mother in a letter dated December 31: "Although one does not see a great many women here, we spend our time very pleasantly with the Constabless Colonna and Madame de Mazarin, who seems extremely happy despite a

I felt as sad as if not sadder than she to see her in that state. For I am by nature extremely sensitive to the afflictions and sorrows of those who are close to me, and through a generosity of spirit which is uncommon in these times, there is nothing I will not do to bring them some relief, even though they are not the least bit grateful to me for it. Thus, guided only by the impulses of this noble nature, and overlooking the indifference that my sister showed toward me, I proposed to get her out of the convent and told her that she could count on the protection of the queen of Sweden,[120] and that I had been given to believe that she would be allowed to withdraw to Her Majesty's residence.[121] This proposal pleased my sister, and once she had accepted that course of action, I went to work immediately on the execution of the plan; but when I believed I had assured its success, the very day on which I had resolved to go and fetch my sister, I learned from those with whom I had arranged this plan that the queen could not commit to receiving her in her residence, or to offering her protection, as they had led me to expect. This reversal did not discourage me, and persuading myself that we would not lack for support and favor once she was on the outside, I went to the convent; and I brought my children along with the intention of distracting my aunt and the other nuns while we put into action what we had premeditated. Thus, after having conversed a bit with my aunt, I took my leave, telling her not to come out for fear that the air would not be good for her, as she was unwell. At the same time, I signaled to my sister to follow me, and when she made as if to show me out, we made our move. Pretending to speak to each other in private, so that that impression would keep others from following us, we moved very gradually and imperceptibly toward the door while my aunt and the other nuns were busy cooing over my children. By distracting the portress, I gave my sister the chance to get out with one of her maids called Nanon, and without taking leave of the group I ran after her. We climbed into the coach that was waiting for us and went directly to the residence of Monsieur le Cardinal Chigi to ask for his protection, or to beseech him at least to aid us with his counsel. When we did not find

---

small indisposition, which is that she is five or six months with child. . . . She is still the most beautiful in the world, and she goes right on hopping and dancing as if it were nothing!" (Perey, 89–90). Thus, it seems likely that Hortense did indeed become pregnant in 1669, although it must have happened in the spring or summer of that year, in which case it is hard to see how Courbeville could have been the father, unless she had remained in contact with him and had met him during some excursion outside of the convent walls. The whole episode is mysterious, as is the question of what came of this pregnancy, since no trace remains of any child's birth.

120. Queen Christina of Sweden (1626–89); see Hortense's memoir, note 110.

121. Christina lived in the Palazzo Riario, which is known today as the Palazzo Corsini.

him in his palace, we went to my brother's house, where we were all born and where we were raised;[122] we found it empty, one of my aunts having been moved out some time earlier.[123] While we were there, it occurred to me to send word immediately to Don Jean Baptiste Rospigliosi, nephew of Pope Clement IX,[124] who came straightaway to join us; and when we had informed him of all the circumstances of the departure, we beseeched him, my sister and I, to predispose the Cardinal Nephew[125] and the pope in her favor, for fear that our uncle Cardinal Mancini might have some violence done to her. He carried out that assignment with all the scrupulous care and all the success that we could have desired. For indeed, His Eminence was never able to inspire in His Holiness any unfavorable feelings toward my sister, and never drew from him any other response than that since Madame Mazarin had come to take refuge in his states, it would be neither right nor decent to cause her any harm. And thus she remained in that house, where she was safe, and where I saw her every day.

Some time later we made a short trip to the country, the constable and I, and upon our return we persuaded her to come and live with us, where she stayed but a few days because of a small difference of opinion that the two of us had. Toward the beginning of the spring, we saw Monsieur le Chevalier de Lorraine, whom the king had exiled because of some overly harsh words he had had (so it was said) with Monsieur Colbert,[126] on the subject of an abbey which this prince had claimed to be entirely unprofitable.[127] After having spent a few weeks in Genoa, he was curious to see Rome, where he

122. Known at the time as the Palazzo Mancini; see Hortense's memoir, note 112.

123. By Hortense's account, their aunt was made to leave by their uncle, Cardinal Mancini, when Hortense came to live there. See Hortense's memoir, 73.

124. Again, Giovanni Battista Rospigliosi (1646–1722), one of Marie's male admirers.

125. From the mid-sixteenth century through the end of the seventeenth, papal nepotism was institutionalized through the post of Cardinal Nephew, a powerful personal secretary to the pope who was responsible for the administration of the Vatican. Marie's close friend Flavio Chigi had been Cardinal Nephew during the reign of his uncle, Pope Alexander VII; at the time she recounts here—October 1669—the Cardinal Nephew to Pope Clement IX was Giacomo Rospigliosi, brother of Giovanni Battista and also former master of the chamber (*maestro di camera*) in the court of Cardinal Chigi.

126. Jean-Baptiste Colbert, marquis de Seignelay (1619–83), was Cardinal Mazarin's designated successor as trusted advisor to Louis XIV. He was responsible for discrediting Nicolas Fouquet, and he replaced him as *surintendant des finances* in 1661; he became *contrôleur général des finances* in 1665, and he eventually had control over nearly all the top functions of government in France, except the conduct of military affairs.

127. Philippe de Lorraine-Armagnac (or Philippe d'Elbeuf-Lorraine), known as the Chevalier de Lorraine (1643–1702), arrived in Rome in the spring of 1670. This is not the most widespread explanation for his exile. See Hortense's memoir, note 126.

came accompanied by his brother, Monsieur le comte de Marsan,[128] who has quite an ingratiating manner and is very pleasant in conversation, and by two of their friends, one of whom was called Monsieur de Gersé and the other Morelli;[129] the first was a man of wit and learning, sincere and faithful, and the second, adroit and witty, but cunning. That celebrated city pleased the chevalier immensely; however, what impelled him even more to remain there during the space of two years that his exile lasted was the throng of elegant society who frequented our house, which teemed with delights as if it were the very center of pleasure. For indeed, I can say without exceeding the truth in the least that the plays, the conversation, the brilliant gaming, the music, the magnificent meals—in short all the entertainments that one can imagine—followed one after another, without anyone's ever tiring of them, since their variety always served as a seasoning. At the beginning of his visits, the chevalier undertook to make a good impression on Madame Mazarin, but when his efforts did not meet with the success for which he had hoped, he lost patience and abandoned his pursuit. Some time after that, I had the idea of putting on a serenade for the queen of Sweden, in order to oblige that princess, and moreover to satisfy my natural desire for activity, since it is vital for me to keep busy, and I enjoy giving others something to do. My brother and my sister were on the best of terms at that time, and when I noticed that they both were a bit cool toward me, far from showing the slightest grief over it, since I am not a dissembling sort, I told them straight out that their efforts to avoid my company were a matter of utter indifference to me. We did not leave it at that: when my serenade, which had been applauded by everyone, was rather harshly ridiculed by my brother, who went so far as to say that the music and the lyrics were the most pitiful thing in the world and that the symphony was worse than the rest, and when I noticed that my sister was giving looks and gestures of approval for that disobliging censure, I became so angry that we fell out for good. I refused to serve as a figure of fun for them any longer, nor did I want my brother, who enjoyed making me angry and contradicting me, to continue to have that satisfaction. Following this falling out, they secretly

128. Charles de Lorraine-Armagnac (or Charles d'Elbeuf-Lorraine), comte de Marsan (1648–1708), younger brother of the Chevalier de Lorraine and also of Monsieur le Grand (Louis de Lorraine, comte d'Armagnac [1641–1718], who was *grand écuyer de France*—officer in charge of all of the king's stables—from 1658 to 1677).

129. According to Pierre Camo in his 1929 edition of the sisters' memoirs (*Les Illustres Aventurières*, 158), Morelli was a confidant of the Chevalier de Lorraine who was suspected of having poisoned Madame, the duchesse d'Orléans, Henrietta of England (wife of the king's brother), using a glass of chicory water.

formed the plan to go off to France; they did not open up to me about it until three days after having made that resolution, and then they left without saying good-bye.[130] As we are extremely sensitive to the slights we receive from people whom we love fervently, I must confess that this departure took me by surprise and cut me to the quick. When I sought to discover the cause of it, I received a letter from each of them in which they told me point-blank that they did honestly have matters in France which had obliged them to go, but that my ill temper alone had caused them to hasten their departure. They said, however, that they would not fail to come back if I wished to see them, and Madame Mazarin positively assured me of it, so that by satisfying my curiosity, I received on the one hand the mortification of reading their petty sentiments and on the other the hope of seeing them again.

A few days after my brother had arrived in Paris, he married the daughter of Madame de Thianges, niece of Madame de Montespan,[131] and because of the youth and the beauty of this damsel, and the insinuations of the king, he found himself bound to take on a yoke for which he had never had any inclination. Meanwhile, Madame Mazarin did not feel safe in Nevers, where she had remained, and fearing that her husband the duc might undertake to deprive her of her freedom and might exercise his rights to the fullest,[132] she withdrew to the convent du Lys, which is a royal abbey situated some ten leagues from Paris.[133] She stayed there until the king sent for her in order to learn what she desired, and when she replied to His Majesty that all she asked was a pension so that she could live in Italy, she obtained it with great ease. During her absence, the Chevalier de Lorraine came with us to some of the constable's country houses, where we went hunting every day; and after having enjoyed those pastoral pleasures for a time, we returned to Rome, where the outings, the frequent luncheons and teas, and the sumptuous meals that we had, now at the vineyards of Borghese, now

---

130. Hortense and Philippe set out for Paris in the summer of 1670, and by Hortense's account (74), they spent nearly six months on the journey.

131. Philippe married Diane Gabrielle Damas de Thianges (ca. 1655–1715), niece of Madame de Montespan; her mother was Madame de Montespan's sister, Gabrielle Diane de Rochecouart de Mortemart, marquise de Thianges. The wedding took place on December 15, 1670.

132. Indeed, he tried. He sent his captain of the guard, Polastron, to arrest Hortense in Nevers, on the strength of a warrant issued by the Grand'Chambre of the Parlement of Paris. The city council of Nevers met to decide on a course of action in response to this challenge to its authority, and the citizens might actually have done battle against Polastron's small army of infantry and archers if an order of protection for Hortense had not arrived from the king. Rosvall, *Mazarine Legacy,* 121–22.

133. The Cistercian abbey Notre Dame du Lys was located in Dammarie-les-Lys, near Melun, forty miles southeast of Paris. See Hortense's memoir, note 118.

at Montalto and in other pleasant abodes, contributed more than a little to our amusement.[134] I even proposed during that time that we treat each other by turns every Sunday, and of those in our cabal, Cardinal Chigi, Prince Savelli,[135] the Chevalier de Lorraine, Duc Sforza,[136] and Duc Bassanello,[137] brother-in-law of the constable, acquitted themselves of the duty among the best. That carnival season also went off more merrily than the others, Pippo Acciaioli having obtained permission from the pope to stage operas.[138]

Toward the end of the spring,[139] Madame Mazarin kept the word she had given me in her letter to come back to Rome, and after an absence

134. The rich Roman families had hilltop villas all around Rome and the outlying country-side; the Villa Borghese was a frequent destination for Colonna outings. These estates were frequently called *vigne* (vineyards), and Marie uses that word here; however, their grapevines had generally been replaced by splendid gardens intended exclusively for the pleasure of the cosseted occupants, with statues and fountains, waterfalls and grottoes. Dulong, *Marie Mancini*, 133–34.

135. Don Giulio Savelli, prince of Albano and of Venafro, duke of Ariccia (which he sold to the Chigi family in 1661), marquis of San Martino, etc. (1626–1712). Many of the Savelli family lands were in the Alban hills near Colonna domains such as Marino, Frattocchie, and Frascati.

136. Probably Don Ludovico Sforza, duke of Onano (1618–85), who was married to the younger sister of the Duke of Bassanello, Donna Artemisia Colonna (d. 1676). Thus, the ties of family and friendship between the members of Marie's "cabal" were tightly interwoven; in fact, after Donna Artemisia's death, Don Ludovico married a sister of Philippe Mancini's wife, Adelaïde Damas de Thianges (d. 1730).

137. Don Stefano Colonna, duke of Bassanello (d. 1673), who was the first husband of the constable's younger sister Lucrezia (1652–1716). Don Stefano would probably have been born in the late 1620s or early 1630s and would thus have been closer to the age of Marie and her husband than to that of his own wife. In his will, Don Stefano stipulated that the duchy of Bassanello should pass to his wife, Donna Lucrezia, upon his death, but that in the case of her remarriage, it should remain in the Paliano branch of the Colonna family. Thus, when Lucrezia married Don Giuseppe Lotario Conti, duke of Guadagnolo, in 1677, the title of duke of Bassanello passed to Lucrezia's brother—and Marie's husband—Lorenzo Onofrio Colonna; although Lorenzo promptly bestowed it upon Don Stefano's younger brother Egidio (d. 1686), this doubtless played a part in the bitter disputes over inheritance between Lucrezia and Lorenzo, to which Dulong refers in her account of Lorenzo's death in 1689 (*Marie Mancini*, 325–26).

138. The pope during carnival 1671 was Clement X (Emilio Bonaventura Altieri, 1590–1676; papacy 1670–76). He was tolerant of the theater, and under his reign the first public theater in Rome—the Teatro Tor di Nona, which was a project of Queen Christina's and had been authorized by Clement IX Rospigliosi during his two-year reign—flourished, staging several operas by Pier Francesco Cavalli. Pippo Acciaioli presumably belonged to the old noble Florentine family of that name; he had been active in staging operas also during the reign of Clement IX. See online *Banca Dati 'Giulio Rospigliosi'* (http://www.nuovorinascimento.org/rosp-2000/home.htm). Pippo Acciaioli is mentioned in a notice from *Avvisi di Roma* dated February 4, 1668, at www.nuovorinascimento.org/rosp-2000/documenti/ar-1668-02-04-bis.htm.

139. Hortense returned to Rome in late May 1671.

of nine months, I finally had the satisfaction of seeing her, more beautiful than ever. But the pleasure of seeing her nearly cost me very dear, for
having gone to welcome her on the very day when I had taken a purgative
(because that was my mania at the time, and my brother had put it so firmly
into my head that purges helped to maintain one's health that I had ruined
my constitution by believing him), I was seized with such terrible stomach
pain that it would surely have killed me if it had gone on any longer with
such violence. My suffering, which could have touched even the most in-
sensitive hearts, made no impression whatsoever on that of the constable;
at least there was no outward sign of it throughout a whole night when he
listened very peacefully to my moaning. My sister hardly seemed any more
sympathetic, and it seemed in this instance that the Chevalier de Lorraine,
his brother, and generally everyone who knew me showed concern over my
illness, while those who were closest to me were not the least bit worried
about what would happen to me. However, my pain got no worse, and its
violence gave way to the force of the remedies that were applied, which
were every bit as effective as one could have hoped. Around that time, the
Chevalier de Lorraine presented me on behalf of Monsieur[140] with a hunting equipage worth a thousand pistoles, trimmed with loads of the richest
and most beautiful ribbons in Paris, which His Royal Highness had sent for
him to give to me purely out of recognition for a few little trifles I had
sent him, such as gloves and some other perfumed articles which are not
even worth mentioning. This present which the chevalier procured for me
is very far from the sums of money that malicious gossips have falsely rumored I lent him, since it is certain that he never needed any and that, on
the contrary, he expressed displeasure every time he learned that I had
sought money elsewhere than from him in order to pay what I owed from
gambling.[141]

The following summer, wishing to add bathing to our other pleasures,
we went—my brother, my sister, and I—to the Teberon,[142] which is a very

140. The king's brother Philippe, duc d'Orléans (1640–1701).

141. Marie seems anxious here to defend herself against the "malicious gossips," who did indeed speculate freely on the apparent intimacy between her and the Chevalier de Lorraine.

142. Marie may be referring to the section of the Tiber that flows around the Isola Tiberina,
an island in the river which is about half a mile from the Palazzo Colonna. The author of the
false memoir published under Marie's name (*Mémoires de M.L.P.M.M. Colonne*, 1676) mentions
the location of a spot where Marie went to swim with the Chevalier de Lorraine as "outside
the Porta del Popolo," which would put it a couple of miles north of the Isola Tiberina, up-
stream near the Villa Borghese. However, this place is more likely to be the "safer spot" to
which Marie says they later moved, since the false memoir also mentions a small wooden hut
which Marie had had built there. *Cendre et poussière*, 119.

dangerous stream. There was a rope attached to some pontoons to hold us, and when I tried letting go of it as the others had done, the swiftness of the current swept me away. If not for a Turkish girl who was presented to me by Monsieur Rospigliosi, general of the pope's galleys in Candia,[143] I would surely have drowned; but since she is very big and strong, and moreover since my brother also helped her quite a bit, I was happily delivered from that danger.[144]

After that we chose a safer spot in the Tiber, where in order to undress we had a hut built, with a gallery attached, which was so artfully constructed out of bamboo canes, reeds, and leaves that everyone was surprised to see it.

We spent the autumn in the country and carnival at the operas as was our custom, but with less satisfaction for me, since for some time already, as I have mentioned in various places in this history, the constable no longer showed the same solicitousness toward me or the same tenderness. He had no more esteem, no more confidence, he barely even spoke to me, and if he did, it was in such a way as to make me prefer his silence to his words; and his brother, Monsieur le prince de Sonnino,[145] who through his goodness has often calmed the private disputes of our family, and who through his prudence has often kept them from breaking out, could attest to what I had to endure.

And so, unable to hold out any longer against such oppressive troubles, I resolved to seek relief from them; and as Madame Mazarin and I had formed a closer friendship than ever through our regular swims and out-

---

143. This would be Vincenzo Rospigliosi, nephew of Pope Clement IX (Giulio Rospigliosi), to whom Hortense reported having appealed for the freedom of her lover Courbeville. See Hortense's memoir, note 109.

144. According to Dulong, Marie modifies the details of this episode, presumably in the interest of protecting her reputation once again. Dulong asserts (*Marie Mancini*, 175–76) that in fact it happened in the summer of 1670, not 1671, during the time when Hortense and Philippe were on their journey from Rome to Paris, and that it was not her brother but the Chevalier de Lorraine who had helped to pull her half nude from the waters of the Tiber. Although it does not help to confirm the timing of the event, a coy reference in one of Madame de Sévigné's letters to her daughter, dated February 12, 1672, does suggest that it was indeed the Chevalier de Lorraine who was involved in the near-drowning episode. Madame de Sévigné first reports that the marquis de Villeroy has been sent away from court, supposedly because of something he said at the home of Madame la Comtesse (Olympe Mancini); she then quotes a line from *Cinna*: "L'on parle d'eaux, de Tibre, et l'on se tait du reste" (People speak of water, of the Tiber, and they say nothing more.) Finally, she recounts an exchange between the king and his brother in which Monsieur relates that people in Paris are saying the marquis only wanted to speak up for another poor wretch; when the king asks which wretch, Monsieur responds, "The Chevalier de Lorraine." *Correspondance*, 1: 439.

145. See above, note 117.

ings, I hoped to benefit from her affection, and I implored her not to go off to France without bringing me with her. She agreed to this, but only after having represented to me, through the misfortunes that had befallen her, those to which I was exposing myself; for it is true, as can be seen in her history, that she never encouraged me in such an enterprise, and that on the contrary, she always tried to make me appreciate the grave consequences of it. Not many days later, the Chevalier de Lorraine was called back to court, where all his friends were pleasantly surprised by his return, not having expected to see him back in favor so soon. The coldness and the contempt of the constable, which grew every day, also added to my sorrows and my woes; and to cheer me up from the understandable apprehensions that this change in treatment caused me, my brother used to tell me very often that he greatly feared I might not long enjoy all the freedom I had. He added one day in the presence of Madame Mazarin that when I least expected it, I would find myself locked up in Paliano, which is a fortress belonging to the constable on the line between the Ecclesiastical State and the kingdom of Naples.[146] All these reasons, together with the natural aversion I felt for the customs of Italy and for the way of life in Rome, where dissimulation and hate among families reign more supreme than in other courts, made me hasten the execution of the plan I had formed to withdraw to France; for France was the country where I had been raised, where most of my relatives were, and finally where I felt at home in my way of thinking, since I loved novelty and vivacity, and talk of arms and soldierly subjects, rather than a peaceful place and a pacific government.

And so I set out on the twenty-ninth of May,[147] carrying no more on my person than seven hundred pistoles, my pearls,[148] and some diamond pendants, and Madame Mazarin having lost all her clothes and effects by leaving them in Rome. We got into her coach, at a time when the constable had gone to see a stud farm at Frattocchie,[149] which is a house he has in the country; and as we came out of the house we shouted to the coachman, "To Frascati!" to fool a crowd of people who were at the Mazarin Palace post station.[150] At a turn in the street, a German valet of my sister's named Pel-

146. Paliano is forty miles southeast of Rome.

147. In 1672.

148. These were a gift from Louis XIV, and they were Marie's most precious possession, which she kept with her throughout her life.

149. Frattocchie is twelve miles southeast of the center of Rome, two miles west of Marino, and five miles southwest of Frascati.

150. Marie came to collect her sister at the Palazzo Mazzarini, which was Philippe Mancini's residence in Rome, although he also owned the Palazzo Mancini; the Palazzo Mazzarini was

letier, who had had a felucca from Naples made ready at Civitavecchia, told the coachman to head straight there, and he threatened to rough him up if he did not go fast. The coachman obeyed, and we arrived on the outskirts of Civitavecchia after nightfall. Since the boatmen had made an agreement with the valet to come and pick us up five miles from town, for fear that we might be recognized at the port, we sent word to them. For we were becoming impatient waiting for the return of a footman whom we had sent to them earlier, and this delay caused us more than a little anxiety. Nevertheless, despite all our cares and all the fears we had of being found out, Madame Mazarin and I left the coach, made our way into the thick of a wood near the sea, and went to sleep; and we slept so soundly for two hours that my sister's maid Nanon and my Morène, who were keeping watch over us, were as surprised as could be to see us sleeping so peacefully.

When we awoke, we saw the valet coming from a distance; he told us that he had not found the boat, and that the footman, after having gotten drunk, had stayed at a hostelry to sleep it off. Thus, we saw fit to get back into the coach and to advance a bit further, using a path that was out of the way, for fear that we might be found if we were being followed along the most direct route. But our horses were so exhausted that they could barely stand, which led my sister to say that it would be best to send them back along with the coach to the hostelry opposite Civitavecchia, and to order the coachman to say if anyone was looking for us that he had seen us set sail, so that they would not pursue us any further; he promised to do as we asked, in return for a sum of money which we gave him. Meanwhile, we withdrew into the thick of a sort of wood which was near the main road and ordered Pelletier to go and look for the boat, or else to hire another if he could not find it; he promised to do so whatever the price. The heat of the sun, which had been pounding down on my head for five hours and which was then at high noon, a forced fast of twenty-four hours, and my worry over our lack of news about the boat all threw me into a despair which made me say to my sister that I wanted to turn back, and that I might just as well lose my life in Rome, in whatever way, as die of hunger where we were. But my sister, who is in all the world the most patient woman with the best temperament, bucked me up with her reassurances, adding in the end that if we did not have some favorable news within the half hour, we could always turn back then. And so I resolved to wait that much longer, and hardly a

---

located very near the Palazzo Colonna, on the Quirinale. By shouting, "To Frascati!" the women hoped to make people think they were heading southeast from Rome, whereas they were actually going northwest to Civitavecchia.

quarter hour had passed when we heard the sound of a horse coming at a gallop. Instantly the fear of being caught, together with the other things agitating my mind, threw me into the greatest dismay in the world; but my sister, who was holding two pistols in her hands, realized that it was little La Roche (that was the name of the postilion who had gone to look for the boat without saying anything to us), and she reassured me completely. And all my sadness was changed in a moment into joy by the news that he gave us from as far off as he could make himself heard, that the boat had been found and was waiting for us five miles from the place where we were. So he loaded our valises straightaway, which were neither terribly heavy nor very numerous. Meanwhile, we went ahead on foot, under the hot sun and in open country, where the only objects we saw were a goodly number of snakes slithering about. The indefatigable Madame Mazarin led the vanguard and kept striding along, so that when I tried to keep up with her, I had to rest from time to time, hunger, thirst, weariness, and the heat having sapped my spirit and my strength. It reached the point where I was obliged to implore a man who was plowing a field to carry me just some hundred paces toward the sea, telling him that I was a hunter who had lost my servants (for we had changed clothes, my sister and I, in the coach). At first he refused me, but when I added a few pistoles to my entreaties, he finally let himself be persuaded. So he carried me in his arms, and in that way I rejoined my sister; and almost immediately Pelletier arrived and told us that he had made a deal on another boat for the sum of one thousand écus, but that in truth he was not at all pleased with the look of the captain or of the hands, and that they had all seemed to him like very nasty folk. We replied to this that fortune had arranged things otherwise, having allowed little La Roche to find the first boat and to arrive ahead of him. Pelletier was no less pleased than we at this happy turn of events, for he had a very good opinion of the captain of the first boat. Finally, half on foot and half with the aid of the plowman, I reached the seashore, where our maids caught up to us soon afterward. But when we found there neither the first nor the second boat, seeing our hopes so miserably dashed, I gave way to anguish; my sister was no less sad than I at this cruel twist of fate; however, she hid her chagrin, for fear of increasing mine. Our only recourse in this situation was, after having flung ourselves down on a bit of straw which we found inside a hut, to send Pelletier out once more to look for the boat, while for my part I beseeched the plowman to go and fetch me a little water. A quarter of an hour later Pelletier came back, and looking worried and sounding alarmed, he told us that we were being followed and that all was lost. My weakness had left me so numb that I was nearly unmoved by this news; but my sister pressed him to tell us whether what he said was true, and when she saw from the way in which he assured her that there was nothing to it, she told him half angrily to be serious. When he replied thereupon that it was not true and that he had wanted to frighten us, she scolded him vehemently and said that he'd chosen a very bad time to make jokes. So we made our way toward the place where the boat was, where as luck would have it we also encountered the second one, which the captain and the sailors were pressing us hard to board. But since Pelletier had given me a better impression of the captain of the first one, I got right onto his boat, paying no heed to the entreaties of the others, and my sister and our maids did the same. As soon as the sailors saw this, they began to threaten us and to prevent us from leaving, so that I found myself obliged to make certain generous donations to them in order to bring them all to agree, and to get us out of this tight spot. We had hardly pulled away from the shore when I began to feel the effects of the sea, and when the captain also surprised us with a new proposition and began asking us for more money than the valet had promised him, justifying his request by the peril to which he was exposing himself in order to serve us. Pelletier was intrepid, and grieved to see that he'd been mistaken in the good opinion he had formed of the captain, and vexed that at the expense of his word the latter should demand more than he was owed, he became angry and tried to insist on the bargain that had been struck. But since the captain had force on his side, and since he backed up his arguments (valid or not) with threats of throwing us into the sea or abandoning us on some desert isle, I bade Pelletier be quiet and I shut up the captain with a hundred pistoles, as well as the additional hope I gave him that I would reward him handsomely provided he brought us safely to France, which he promised to do.

We sailed quite happily and with quite a good wind for the first six hours, but then there was a great calm during which we progressed very little. At sunrise we spied a brig, and as the captain feared that it might be a Turkish vessel, we landed at the foot of some rocks on the coast of Tuscany, where he showed us a place where we could disembark and keep under cover in case he should be attacked. Then with the help of those same rocks, he went to reconnoiter the vessel to see where it was from, and after he finally asked and learned that it was Genovese, we continued our journey amid the same calm all the way to Monaco. There my sister became quite seasick, as the sea had been made extremely rough by a tremendous wind which had blown up, and we might have been shipwrecked if our captain had not been so skillful. Since we could not disembark without having bills of health because we were coming from Civitavecchia and there was plague in that area, we disembarked at Monaco, where we obtained false bills which we used for La Ciotat. Our captain had not wanted to disembark at Marseille because of some dispute he had had there, which did us quite a good turn by causing us to avoid the feluccas and the galleys that the constable had sent after us. Since they had not managed to meet up with us at sea, thanks to the unusual route taken by our captain, who was a very clever man, they had gone to wait for us at Marseille and in the other ports, where they would surely have caught us if we had had valid bills to land there.

In short, after nine days' voyage we arrived successfully at La Ciotat, where, after having rested for about four hours, we mounted horses which we had hired, and riding all night, we arrived at a fairly early hour in Marseille. There I inquired first thing after Monsieur Arnous, *intendant des galères*,[151] in the hope that he would have a passport for me, which I had requested of the king in a letter I had written to His Majesty before leaving Rome. When I learned that he was on the verge of death, I found myself obliged to go and see him; upon entering, I told him who I was, and after having expressed how sorry I was to see him in that state, I asked him whether he did not have something for me from the king. He replied to me with considerable difficulty because of a stroke he had suffered, and gave me a sealed package containing a passport and a letter from His Majesty for me, and another from Monsieur de Pomponne,[152] who wrote to Monsieur de Grignan,[153] the king's lieutenant in Provence, urging him strongly to receive me in Aix and to assist me with his authority and with anything that I might need. Upon our return from Monsieur Arnous's house, we went to bed, and I had scarcely slept one hour when I was awakened and told that Captain Menechini was asking to speak to me on behalf of the constable. This news greatly frightened my servants, and in order to prevent anything that might happen to me, I sent word of it to Monsieur Arnous, who immediately sent me some guards, entreating me to come and stay at his house, where he

---

151. Nicolas Arnoul was *intendant des galères* at this time. The royal fleet of galleys was head-quartered in Marseille, and in charge of its maintenance was the *intendant des galères*. Although galleys were not practical war vessels on the Atlantic, their maneuverability through the use of oars made them effective in the Mediterranean battles against the Turks; the oars were manned by prisoners convicted of petty delinquency and crimes such as vagrancy, begging, counterfeiting, smuggling, and tax evasion. Nicolas Arnoul was put in place by Colbert in 1665, and he immediately began a grand project of construction of a modern arsenal complex which covered a large area around the southeast section of the Vieux Port. Arnoul remained *intendant des galères* until his death in 1673.

152. Simon Arnauld, marquis de Pomponne (1618–99), was secretary of state for foreign affairs (*secrétaire d'État aux affaires étrangères*) from 1671 to 1679.

153. François Adhémar de Monteil, comte de Grignan (1632–1714), was lieutenant general to the governor of Provence; he was married to the daughter of Madame de Sévigné, Françoise-Marguerite de Sévigné, comtesse de Grignan (1646–1705). See Hortense's memoir, note 131.

assured me I would be safer.[154] I did just that after having given an audience to the messenger, who came with nothing more to propose to me than that I return to the constable, or at the least that I wait until he could send me a train more in keeping with my quality, and all that was needed to continue my journey with greater splendor and decorum. He did not neglect to try softening me up by reminding me of my children, figuring that the love I felt for them would lead me to take the action to which he was endeavoring to induce me; but although I loved them tremendously, I feared peril even more, and having no doubt that there was some scheme hidden beneath his charming words, I told him succinctly that I had no intention of returning, and I went straightaway to the home of Monsieur Arnous, who had sent us his coach with a gentleman. And Monsieur Arnous, through his great hospitality and the fine fare he offered us and the good beds we found at his house, repaired in some way the discomfort we had suffered on the boat.

The next morning, as I had sent to Monsieur de Grignan the letter that Monsieur de Pomponne had inserted for him in the package I mentioned, I was awakened with a start and told that a gentleman had been sent by him with six guards and his coach to offer to escort me, and with the order to assist me with everything I would need. I accepted, and after having dined, Madame Mazarin and I got into a coach with the said gentleman, and we arrived in the evening in Aix. There, Monsieur de Grignan, who had come out nearly a league to meet us, accompanied us in his coach, in which he had us ride, and he expressed to us the regret he felt at not being able to lodge us in the residence of the governor, who was at that time my nephew the duc de Vendôme, son of the duc de Mercoeur and of my eldest sister, of whom I spoke at the beginning of these memoirs.[155] We thanked him for his civility and told him that he should not trouble himself over our lodgings because we had already given our word to a gentleman called Monsieur de Moriès,[156] who is in my brother's service, that we would stay with him. We went there straightaway, and he treated us for a fortnight at the home of his elder brother, the Président Castelet, and did so in the most magnificent and the most obliging manner in the world.

As my sister could not go to Paris because of a ruling by the Parlement

154. The residence of the *intendant des galères* was within the well-fortified arsenal complex, which really formed a sort of city within the city.

155. Marie's nephew was Louis-Joseph, duc de Vendôme et de Mercoeur (1654–1712), eldest son of her sister Laure. Although he assumed the title of governor of Provence from his father, the duc de Vendôme never personally performed the duties of the office, and in fact he put in only one appearance in the lands of his governorship, in 1581.

156. According to Claude Dulong, this gentleman was related to Madame de Venelle. *Marie Mancini*, 374n.

which her husband had obtained against her, I had dispatched Pelletier with a letter I wrote to the king in which I begged him to indicate to me where he wished that I go and stay in Paris. I implored His Majesty to permit Madame Mazarin to go there, too, without her having anything to fear from her husband the duc, and I also proposed that we take up residence at the Palais Mazarin,[157] where my sister desired to live with me. The return of Pelletier, whom I had sent, had been prevented by an accident which befell him along the way, in which he was robbed and nearly killed. This caused me great impatience, which was succeeded by the pique I felt at learning that Monsieur de Saint-Simon,[158] who had come through Aix and had made me similar propositions to those of Captain Menechini, and with equal success, was in Paris, where he was raging against me and where, appealing on behalf of the constable and belonging at the same time to Cardinal Altieri, the nephew of His Holiness,[159] he was backing up his negotiations with pontifical authority. Therefore, I wanted to go and fend off this attack without waiting for Pelletier's return, and despite the objections of my sister, we went to Mirabeau, where the knight who was seigneur of that place and captain of the guards to my nephew the duc de Vendôme escorted us with six of his guards and treated us splendidly.[160] While we were there, Madame Mazarin saw that I was resolved to leave and begged me to await the return of her valet for a while; I consented to this to please her, but after I had waited six days to no avail, I said resolutely that I wanted to leave and draw nearer to Paris, having always had a presentiment that I would be prevented from going there. When the knight saw that I was thus resolved, he followed us with the guards, and when we arrived at Pont-Saint-Esprit, we learned that Polastron, captain of the guards to Monsieur le Duc Mazarin, had gone through Aix and was looking for us. This news forced us to leave the main road and withdraw to a house in the country where we stayed

157. The Palais Mazarin was located near the Palais Royal on the rue de Richelieu; Cardinal Mazarin bequeathed half of the palace to the Duc and Duchesse Mazarin, his principal heirs, and the other half to Philippe Mancini, duc de Nevers, who was his only surviving male heir. In modern times, the Palais Mazarin housed the Bibliothèque Nationale until the construction of the Bibliothèque Nationale de France in the 1990s.

158. This envoy does not appear to be related to the duc de Saint-Simon or to his descendant, the memorialist Saint-Simon. Dulong, *Marie Mancini*, 195–96.

159. Pope Clement X, who reigned 1670–76, was Emilio Bonaventura Altieri (1590–1676); his nephew was Paluzzo Paluzzi Altieri degli Albertoni (1623–98), who became a cardinal in 1664 and was adopted by Clement X as a nephew on the day of the pope's election. He was the last person to hold the position of Cardinal Nephew in the history of the papacy.

160. The Chevalier de Mirabeau was Thomas Albert de Riquetti, son of Thomas de Riquetti, marquis de Mirabeau, and of Anne de Pontevès.

for the night; and that very night Madame Mazarin set out for Savoy, accompanied by the aforementioned knight, by Nanon, and by half of the guards, the other half having stayed with me.[161] This separation from my sister was very painful for me, and in return for the promise she made me to stay in Chambéry, where she was headed, until the king permitted her to live in France, I promised her not to go further than Grenoble, in order to be nearer to her and to have news of her more often.[162] So I arrived there, and after I had stayed three days in a hostelry on the other side of the water without being recognized by anyone, there finally arrived a gentleman sent by the queen,[163] to whom the king had left the government of his realm while he was at war in Holland. He handed over to me a letter from Her Majesty in which she commanded me, but in the most obliging manner in the world, to remain wherever this gentleman who gave me the letter found me, adding that she had no doubt that such would be the intention of the king. I replied to this gentleman that I did not plan to go further and that I would obey Her Majesty's orders most scrupulously.

Monsieur le duc de Lesdiguières,[164] governor of the province, to whom the same orders had been sent, came thereafter to visit me and urged me to go and stay at his house or at the Arsenal. I accepted the latter offer, not wishing to be a bother to him, and also not being eager to put myself in an uncomfortable situation. Polastron, whom I believed to have come after my sister, as we had been told in letters, came to see me at the Arsenal and conveyed to me the compliments of Monsieur Mazarin, and offered me his palace and anything at his disposal, protesting that he had no other orders from his master the duc than to convey the same compliments to the duchesse his wife. Having been assured of this upon his word and upon that of the governor, I notified my sister by a courier I dispatched to her, begging her to come and join me. But since she had taken a very long route to Chambéry, going by way of Turin and the mountains, she arrived there only after a month, so that my courier was obliged to wait for her there. She left almost as soon as she had received my letter, and I went immediately to greet her. During our meeting, she recounted to me all that she had suffered along the way, and told me that she had been repaid with interest for

---

161. Marie's account of the sisters' peregrinations in this period is a bit different from Hortense's. See Hortense's memoir, 80–81.

162. Chambéry and Grenoble are only thirty-five miles apart.

163. Marie-Thérèse of Austria (1638–83), whom Louis XIV had married in 1660.

164. François de Bonne de Créquy, duc de Lesdiguières (ca. 1596–1677), lieutenant general of the province of Dauphiné, of which Grenoble was the chief city.

all her woes and her little indignities by the honors she had received from His late Royal Highness.[165] Polastron spoke to her afterward, and when all his proposals failed to produce any effect at all, he turned back toward Paris, and we toward Grenoble. We remained there until around the beginning of August, when the king returned from the campaign and when Pelletier, after having miraculously escaped as I have said above, came to join us and gave me a letter from the king, in which he advised me to enter a convent in order to stop the malicious gossip, which was producing unsavory interpretations of my departure from Rome. He added with regard to Madame Mazarin that the conditions under which she had left, with which she was quite familiar, remained in effect.

As I was not entirely satisfied with this letter, I resolved to go to Paris unannounced to throw myself at the feet of the king, and I communicated my plan to my sister, who, out of extraordinary kindness, told me that I should disregard any considerations concerning her, that in this situation I should consult nothing but my own interest and the good of my affairs, and that as for her, she would return to Chambéry. So we set out in litters, without saying anything about our journey for fear that the governor might stop me, and we traveled together as far as Lyon, where we parted ways, she to make her way toward Chambéry, and I to go to Paris. I was accompanied there by a *courrier du cabinet* whom I had met in Rome, called Marguein, a man of character, expert and loyal, who took charge of everything related to my journey and did the most honest job in the world of it, going so far as to advance all the money that was needed. I sped along in a *chaise roulante,* and Morène and he followed me on horseback. When I was one day beyond Lyon, I took a boat in order to travel more comfortably, but the water was so low and that vehicle was so ill suited to my impatience that I got out at the first village, where, finding no post horses, I was obliged to use those that some peasants lent us. As luck would have it, not one was fit to pull the *chaise roulante,* so a man had to lead by hand the one to which it was hitched, which caused me to despair, seeing that by some twist of fate I could never go fast, either by post or by relay, and that some obstacle always kept me from making haste. We finally arrived at Nevers, where I learned without being recognized that my brother and his wife were at Saint-Eloy, located three leagues from the city, and where I encountered a problem I had not foreseen when I arrived at the post station, although

165. Charles-Emmanuel II, duke of Savoy (1634–75), the sovereign protector and benefactor to whom Hortense addressed her memoir.

I came through it fairly successfully. For when I asked for horses, they refused to give me any, saying that they could not do so without notifying a gentleman who had forbidden them to give horses to anyone without his order and who, I believe, had placed the same prohibitions on the other post stations that were on my route. Since I had been aware from Lyon on that the king had sent out a gentleman, I strongly suspected that he was coming not to greet me but only to prevent me from going to Paris. Thus, in order to render his precautions useless, I told Marguein that whatever the cost, we needed to gain the cooperation of the people at the post station; and this he did so skillfully that we were given all the mounts necessary for our journey, while Monsieur de la Gibertière, who was the gentleman in question, waited for me on the bridge by which he believed I would have to pass, since he had learned that I had embarked in a boat at Roanne,[166] and it did not occur to him that my impatience might have made me change routes.

With the aid of a good horse which made my *chaise roulante* fly along, which had tired me much more than it had tired the post horses, I was thinking about making up the time I had lost on the water by traveling all night. But just when I thought I would have no more mishaps to endure, when I thought I would get off with just those I have reported, and with having tipped over twice although I did not hurt myself at all, to top off my bad luck, by that cruel fate that I mentioned above, which seems inseparable from all my travels, upon our arrival in Montargis at around noon, Morène had an attack of colic, and Marguein was seized by an affliction which was much more dangerous for me than for him. He filled his mind with circumspection and politic considerations, and reflected very seriously on the negative repercussions that could result from my undertaking, for me as well as for him, and for his whole family, if we arrived in this way, against the will and the orders of the king; and adding to that the fact that Morène was in no condition to come with me, he concluded that it would be more appropriate that I go no further. The fatigue of the journey and the sleepiness with which I was overcome led me to savor these arguments, which would not have been able to persuade me under other circumstances; and thus, giving in as much to my need for rest as to his insinuations, I came to an agreement with him that while he went to Paris to present a letter to the

166. Roanne is 55 miles northwest of Lyon, and the Loire flows through it. Nevers is 95 miles northwest of Roanne, also along the Loire, so that Marie could conceivably have traveled all the way there and beyond by water. Paris is a further 150 miles north of Nevers, with Montargis about halfway between Nevers and Paris; in turn, Fontainebleau is about halfway between Montargis and Paris, or about 40 miles south of Paris.

king on my behalf, and another to Monsieur de Louvois,[167] I would go to Fontainebleau. I made my way there with Morène, whom I took into my chair, Marguein having left us as a substitute for himself a boy of his acquaintance, loyal but as dim-witted as they come, who, since he did not know me and judged me by my train, took me for what I appeared to be with such a meager equipage. At every post station, he had new disputes with the postilions, whom he was paying from the money that Marguein had left him and who, because they did not want to pull two people in the same chair, were cursing copiously about the overload. Nevertheless, despite all their bad temper, we arrived at Fontainebleau at seven o'clock in the evening, where Monsieur de la Gibertière was able to catch up with me because of the rest I had taken at Montargis. Having already been informed that we had been given post horses, he had wanted to punish the postilions, but in the end he had pardoned them, considering perhaps that clemency is the virtue of noble spirits, or else not wishing to take the time. For he had made such good time that after having left Nevers at noon, he arrived two hours after we did at Fontainebleau, where he forbade anyone to give us horses, and where I did not learn of his arrival until five o'clock in the morning, when he sent word to me that he was there on behalf of the king and that he needed to speak to me. So I had him shown in, and after he had given me a letter of credentials from his master the king, he tried to persuade me to return to the constable, as the best course of action that I could possibly choose, given that things were not really disposed to my advantage in France since the king had been given to believe I was flattering myself that I had a strong hold over his mind. He added to this that the king was very irritated to have granted me his protection upon frivolous pretexts and for reasons founded on nothing but my whims; and he concluded that if I was not resolved to go back home, I should return to Grenoble and enter the abbey of Montfleury. Those were the exact terms of his legation, to which I replied that I had not left home only to return so soon; that I had not made this decision based on frivolous pretexts but for good and solid reasons which I could not and would not relate except to the king, and that I hoped from the mind and the sense of justice of His Majesty that, provided I could speak to him just once, which was all I asked, he would easily be disabused of all the bad impressions that people had given him of me; that I was very far from flattering myself that I held the kind of power he had just mentioned; that I had neither enough merit nor enough ability to claim even the

---

167. François-Michel Le Tellier, marquis de Louvois (1641–91), secretary of state for military affairs (*secrétaire d'État à la guerre*). See Hortense's memoir, note 56.

slightest role in the handling of his affairs; that I asked nothing more than to withdraw to Paris, and I restricted my ambitions to the space of a cloister, where I implored His Majesty to let me live among my relatives, as Madame la grande duchesse de Toscane[168] and the princesse de Chalais[169] lived today and as a thousand other ladies had lived who were widowed or separated from their husbands; that as for returning to Grenoble, I was too tired to undertake another journey; and that moreover I would wait for a reply from

168. The grand duchess of Tuscany was Marguerite-Louise d'Orléans (1645–1721), daughter of Louis XIII's brother Gaston d'Orléans and stepsister of Anne-Marie-Louise d'Orléans, duchesse de Montpensier (1627–93). Like Marie, Marguerite-Louise was married in 1661 (they were wed within days of each other, in April), into a powerful Italian family, and like Marie she was not enthusiastic about the marriage. Marguerite-Louise's husband was Côme de Médicis (1642–1723), who became grand duke of Tuscany in 1670. The marriage was unhappy, and after having borne three children, the grand duchess obtained her husband's permission in 1675 to return to France, on the condition that she be strictly confined to a convent and that she be allowed to go out of it only when the king summoned her to court. The similarity between the Mancini sisters' case and that of the grand duchess was not lost on observers at the time. Madame de Sévigné, for instance, wrote in July 1675, as the grand duchess was making her way toward Paris, "She's expected here like a sort of Colonna and Mazarin, because of the folly of her having left her husband after fifteen years with him." Letter to Madame de Grignan dated July 3, 1675, *Correspondance,* 1: 748. And Mademoiselle de Montpensier attests that the queen harbored suspicions about the grand duchess similar to those she had about Marie: "The queen did me the honor of telling me that my sister had only come to France and had only had such a strong desire to come because of a horoscope that had been done for her, in which it was said that she would hold sway over the king. For that reason, the queen could not abide her, but she had nothing to fear, for she only wanted enough sway over him to induce him to return the States to Monsieur de Lorraine so that she could marry him." Montpensier, *Mémoires,* 2: 446–47. Indeed, the grand duchess had the additional point in common with Marie that she had had an involvement with the prince de Lorraine before her marriage.

169. Anne-Marie de La Trémouille (or Marie-Anne de La Trémoille), princesse de Chalais (1642–1722), was married in 1657 to Adrien-Blaise de Talleyrand, prince de Chalais, and was widowed in 1670 in Italy. She stayed in Italy, and in 1675 she married Flavio degli Orsini, duke of Bracciano (1620–98). After his death, she assumed the title of princesse des Ursins, although it had no legal existence, and through her complicated political maneuvering she managed to establish herself as *camerera mayor* to Marie-Louise Gabrielle of Savoy (granddaughter of Hortense's benefactor, Charles-Emmanuel II of Savoy), the thirteen-year-old bride of the young Spanish king, Philip V (who was himself the grandson of Louis XIV). From 1701 to 1714, the princesse des Ursins was the most powerful figure in Spain, holding sway as she did over the young queen and through her over the king. However, Marie's reference here to the princesse de Chalais is meant to point out the freedom which she claimed for herself as a young widow in Italy. And like the freedom that the Mancini sisters had appropriated, it was looked upon with disapproval by such contemporaries as Madame de Sévigné, who wrote in 1672: "Madame de Chalais is mad; that is how she is seen in this country. The fine idea of going from town to town, in Italy, like a hapless wretch of a princess, instead of coming back peacefully to Paris to her mother who adores her, and who counts among all the misfortunes of her family the extravagance of her daughter! She is right; I have never seen a more ridiculous one." Letter to Madame de Grignan dated April 20, 1672, *Correspondance,* 1: 484.

His Majesty and then take my measures accordingly. Having made this rejoinder, I took my guitar and he his leave. A short time later, I received a letter from Marguein, by which I learned that Monsieur le duc de Créqui[170] was coming to see me on behalf of the king, and that he was charged with responding to my propositions. And so he arrived, and Marguein too, at almost the same time. I had him shown in, and when he saw me in a bed and in a hostelry room, remembering the grandeur in which he had seen me in Rome, he confessed that he was surprised and touched by the change, and he lamented for me over the sad state of my fortune. But I mocked his lamentations straightaway and beseeched him to come right to the point, upon which he began to speak quite plainly. He told me that the king did not want me to enter Paris, or to see him, as he had given his word to Monsieur le Nonce[171] and the constable that he would allow me neither the one nor the other, for reasons of which I was certainly not unaware; and he told me that I could go back to Grenoble in the meantime until I returned home, which was the safest and most decent course of action I could take. I was deeply hurt by this declaration, and I replied that the king could certainly prevent me from seeing him and from entering Paris, but that he could not decently force me to return to Grenoble in the state in which I found myself, having been as ill used by the heat as by the haste with which I had traveled. I added that it was quite harsh and quite severe of the king thus to forbid me the honor of his presence, but that since I had to obey, I implored His Majesty to permit me at the least to enter the Lys, which is an abbey situated some ten leagues from Paris.[172] Thereupon, Monsieur de Créqui had me write a note in which I begged him to obtain this favor from His Majesty, and after he returned to Paris, a page came the following day to bring me from him the permission that I had requested, along with an order to the abbess to receive me, and one to Monsieur de la Gibertière to escort me. At almost the same time, there came a gentleman sent by Monsieur Colbert with two purses containing five hundred pistoles each, which His Majesty had ordered him to send me, and which sum he continued to have me receive every six months during the time when I was under his protection.[173]

170. Charles, duc de Créquy (1624–87), was first gentleman of the king's chamber (*premier gentilhomme de la chambre du Roi*) and governor of Paris at this time, but Marie knew him well because of his stint during the 1660s as French ambassador to Rome.

171. Francesco Nerli the Younger (1636–1708) was nuncio in France beginning in April 1672; he was created cardinal in 1673.

172. See above, note 133.

173. It was reported that when she received this money from Colbert's envoy, Marie remarked, "I had certainly heard that people gave money to ladies in order to see them, but

So I went straightaway to the Lys, where the abbess received me with all possible kindness and civility, and where my sisters came to see me and gave me magnificent presents. I felt inconceivable joy at seeing them, and the kindness they showed by remaining three or four days in a row with me every time they came to see me was no small relief for my woes; and a few days later, Madame la comtesse de Soissons, her husband, and Monsieur le duc de Bouillon[174] also came to visit me, after having first obtained the king's permission, as nobody would dare to do so without his consent. I spent my time quite pleasantly in that monastery, since the nuns, who were the finest people in the world, treated me as well as the abbess did, with a gentleness, a kindness, and an affection beyond all expression, and since they always behaved so generously toward me that I will never forget my debt to them. Nevertheless, as fortune cannot suffer me to enjoy for long the advantages I possess, it decided to use me against myself and to trouble my repose with the feelings of resentment and grief that it inspired in me against the king, causing me to write Monsieur Colbert a letter complaining of His Majesty's lack of kindness toward me, to which I added that since he refused to allow me to go to Paris, he might at least grant me the freedom to go anywhere else I pleased. This letter, which Monsieur Colbert showed to His Majesty, made him supremely angry with me, and my enemies, taking this opportunity to stoke the fire, impressed upon him that I was too close to Paris, that from one hour to the next I could escape and go there; and with their malicious insinuations they convinced him to give Monsieur Colbert the order to tell me on his behalf that I should choose a convent sixty leagues from Paris, and that after the letter I had written, I did not deserve his protection.

This response showed me only too well the mistake I had made, and I repented, though belatedly, of my fit of pique. I wrote to Monsieur Colbert that in truth I should not have written the letter I had sent him, but that neither should he have shown it to the king, and that since he had brought his indignation down on me by showing it to him, he should now take it upon himself to placate him by pointing out to him the regret I felt over my imprudence, and in short that he should ask him to pardon my mistake. So he did what he could to put it right, and the following day I learned from a

---

never in order not to see them" (J'avais bien ouï dire qu'on donnait de l'argent aux dames pour les voir, mais jamais pour ne les voir point). Dulong, *Marie Mancini*, 212. In a letter to Madame de Scudéry, Bussy-Rabutin wrote appreciatively of the remark, but libertine though he was, he disapproved of Marie's behavior (Dulong, *Marie Mancini*, 212–13).

174. In other words, Marie's sister Olympe came with her husband and the husband of their youngest sister, Marie-Anne.

letter he wrote me that he had obtained the king's pardon for me, but that His Majesty was still persisting in his decision to keep me sixty leagues away from Paris; thereupon, I replied to him with great submission that I did not know the map well enough to choose a convent at that distance, and that if His Majesty was inflexible on this point, he might be kind enough to name one for me, and that I would obey him blindly, although to tell the truth I found it quite harsh and quite difficult to leave a convent to which I was already accustomed and where I was so comfortable. The only response to that letter that I received was Monsieur de la Gibertière, who came after four or five days with a coach and an order to the abbess to let me out. So I obeyed and left with four maids I had at the time, the constable having sent me three who had remained in Rome, whom I had requested of him, and of whom there are still two in my service; and all together we set out for Avenay,[175] which is an abbey three leagues from Reims, where the king had ordered that I go, having spared me thirty leagues. The abbess welcomed me with all the expressions of esteem and friendship that one could desire; and one month later the archbishop of Reims,[176] brother of Monsieur le marquis de Louvois, came to visit me, and he pressed me hard to reveal to him my reasons for leaving Rome, which I wanted to relate to the king. When I declined to do so because of the difference there was between us,[177] he asked me in a fairly disagreeable way whether I wanted to remind His Majesty of things past, to which I retorted that that was the last thing on my mind, as it should be.

The abbess continually gave me evidence of her generosity and kindness, and all the nuns, who had great wit and merit, strove ceaselessly to

---

175. The Benedictine abbey of Avenay, which was founded in 660, was completely destroyed during the Revolution. The village of Avenay-Val-d'Or where it was located is eighteen miles south of Reims.

176. Charles-Maurice Le Tellier (1642–1710) was archbishop of Reims from 1671 until his death; like Louvois (1641–91), he was the son of Michel Le Tellier (1603–85), who was secretary of state for military affairs (*secrétaire d'État à la guerre*) and later chancellor of France (*chancelier de France*).

177. Never mind that the archbishop of Reims was the prelate to whom the kings of France had come to be consecrated ever since Clovis, that his ecclesiastical office gave him the rank of duke and peer, and that this particular archbishop of Reims was both the brother of Louvois and the son of Michel Le Tellier, Marie regards him as vastly inferior to her in rank and refuses to entrust him with her message for Louis XIV. Dulong considers this to be perhaps the gravest of Marie's myriad misjudgments, speculating that if she had given this emissary from the king credible evidence of her reasons for fleeing Italy, she would have won Louis's strong and durable protection; as it was, she succeeded in dooming her cause (Dulong, *Marie Mancini*, 222–23).

make the time pass pleasantly for me during the interval of three months when I enjoyed their amiable company, at the end of which time my brother received permission from the king to come and fetch me and bring me to Nevers. The hope of obtaining the freedom to go to Paris someday caused me to undertake this little trip with great satisfaction, but my hopes were soon dashed; for I had given my word to my brother that I would enter a convent in the event that he left Nevers, and he told me after a week that business obliged him to leave immediately for Venice and that he hoped I would not go back on what I had promised him. This unexpected journey pained me greatly, as much because it took away the hope that I had conceived of returning to Paris as because it was going to make me leave a place where I was fairly comfortable and deprive me of the company of his wife the duchesse, who is assuredly one of the kindest and most solicitous people on earth, and who did all she could to soothe my sorrows. Nevertheless, despite all these considerations, since I am a woman of my word, I was determined to keep it to him even at the expense of my own satisfaction, and I went to visit all the convents in Nevers, to see if there were any that pleased me. But when I did not find any to my liking, because I was used to big and beautiful abbeys, and since my brother was pressing me every day besides, more for political reasons, to tell the truth, than because of the business he had in Venice, I told him that I saw no better expedient to give him what he desired of me than to go to Lyon, and that there I would find convents to choose. He was not averse to this resolution, hoping that it would give him the opportunity to bring me even further away, as he did. Thus, we set out for Lyon, where Monsieur le marquis de Villeroy[178] sent us his coaches,

---

178. François de Neufville, marquis and then (as of 1675) duc de Villeroy (1644–1730), was the son of Nicolas de Neufville, duc and maréchal de Villeroy (1597–1685). The father had been *gouverneur* of Louis XIV, and the son would become *gouverneur* of Louis XV; he was also named *maréchal de France* in 1693. The marquis de Villeroy was raised at court with Louis XIV, and the king maintained his affection for Villeroy throughout his life, even despite the latter's lack of success and sometimes calamitous losses as a military commander between 1695 and 1706. Villeroy was known at court as *le Charmant*, and he was regularly involved in amorous intrigue there; he was closely linked with Olympe Mancini, comtesse de Soissons, and replaced the marquis de Vardes as her lover. Indeed, according to Madame de Sévigné's version of events, Villeroy's exile in February 1672 was due to some indiscrete remark he had made at Madame la Comtesse's house; and that remark appears to have been about the scandal of Marie's near drowning in the Tiber, in the company of the Chevalier de Lorraine. See above, note 144. Sévigné to Madame de Grignan, February 10 and 12, 1672 (*Correspondance*, 1: 435, 439). The Marquis de Villeroy was exiled to Lyon, where he had succeeded his father (though his father was still alive) as governor; he had also succeeded his father in other governorships in the Lyonnais, Forez, and Beaujolais regions.

and after we had rested, I went to reconnoiter the convents, including that of Sainte Marie de la Visitation,[179] situated on a height from which one can see the whole city. I would have stayed there if my fate, which always runs counter to my well-being, had not inspired Monsieur le marquis de Villeroy and my brother to dissuade me; they managed so successfully to exaggerate to me everything that I had had to endure in France and the ill treatment I had received there that I made the decision to leave the country and to withdraw to Italy, without however telling them the place. And since at that time the marquis de Villeroy was called back from exile, we set out all together, he for Paris and we for Italy. But scarcely was I outside of France when I recognized the mistake I had made in leaving and not staying in Lyon; and in order to remedy it in some way, I resolved to remain in Turin once I arrived there, in the hope that His Royal Highness would approve. I revealed this plan to no one, except to my sister when I passed through Chambéry, where she was; I implored her earnestly to write to His Royal Highness on my behalf in order to facilitate the execution of my plan, and she very obligingly did so. When I was beyond the Alps, I informed my brother of my resolution, and he was rather surprised by it but did not oppose it, recognizing that it was then neither the time nor the place to do so. Therefore, I dispatched Monsieur Boniel, who was a chaplain I had engaged in Grenoble and who had later come to join me in Avenay and had followed me to Turin; his knowledge and his loyalty I cannot praise highly enough, as he certainly possesses both the one and the other in the highest degree. I entrusted to him a letter for His Royal Highness in which I begged him to permit me to withdraw to some convent within his states, assuring him that the king would not object. To this he replied very obligingly the next day that he was most willing to grant me his protection, provided that the king did not disapprove, as I assured him he would not; and he sent me his compliments by way of a gentleman, who came to fetch me with a coach and to bring me to Turin. My brother took leave of me then to continue

---

179. The convent of the Visitation in Lyon was the first convent of this order to be established (in 1615), after the original one in Annecy, in the duchy of Savoy. Marie and Hortense had both stayed in other convents of the Visitation before in their lives: both were placed in one in the faubourg Saint-Jacques in Paris when they first came to court as young girls, and Hortense stayed for a time in Sainte Marie de la Bastille, also in Paris, where she spent her time with the marquise de Courcelles. See above, 87–88; Hortense's memoir, 50-51. The Order of the Visitation was founded in 1610 by Jeanne de Chantal (1572–1641), paternal grandmother of Madame de Sévigné, under the direction of François de Sales (1567–1622). It was a contemplative order, with a very mild rule regarding external, physical mortifications, but a strict devotion to "internal" mortifications, including an absolute prohibition against the ownership of any property, no matter how small, by individual sisters.

his journey and preferred not to pass through that city, in order to avoid the encounter with His Royal Highness, who came to greet me one league from the city; he had me ride in his coach, where there were also some seigneurs from his court. Followed by a great many gentlemen on horseback, the prince conducted me himself to the convent of the Visitation,[180] where he had had an apartment furnished for me and had disposed the abbess to receive me, by way of the archbishop, who was there to see me in. The nuns of that monastery, who have the sweetest and most accommodating nature in the world, gave me evidence of their affection over and over throughout the three months that I spent with them. At the end of that time, as I had received word toward the end of April[181] that Madame Mazarin was to leave for Paris soon, my desire to see her, and in part my plan to make up, if possible, for the mistake I had made not long before, induced me to undertake a journey to Chambéry. Thus, I beseeched His Royal Highness to prevent any courier from leaving for two days, for fear that I might be followed; the prince granted me this very graciously, although he could not refrain from expressing his disapproval of my decision, and he even appeared to be hurt by it. With the word of His Royal Highness, I set out with Morène and Monsieur Boniel, whom I have already mentioned; I took with me the thousand pistoles that the king had had delivered to me, which was the sum that he gave me every six months, as I have said above. Attended by this small retinue, I arrived in Chambéry more fatigued than ever, and my only consolation after all this was to find myself frustrated in the hope of seeing my sister, as her affection had given way to circumspection and politic caution, and she had hid from me for fear of being drawn into supporting my intentions. I stayed the night at the château where she was living,[182] and I inquired of all her servants where she was and when she would return, but I was unable to learn anything. This made me resolve, for fear of giving up a sure thing for an uncertain reward, to return to Turin and to enjoy the protection of His Royal Highness, with whom I had reason to be pleased,

180. The convent of the Visitation in Turin; following the order's founding in Annecy in 1610, the convents of the Visitation continued throughout the seventeenth century to be particularly concentrated in the duchy of Savoy and in southeastern France.

181. In 1673. Actually, Marie left Turin for Chambéry on April 9; after spending one night in the château de Chambéry without seeing her sister, she set out to return to Turin on April 12 (Dulong, *Marie Mancini*, 233–36).

182. From 1563 when the capital of Savoy was moved from Chambéry to Turin, the Château des Ducs de Savoie had remained a ducal residence and had also housed various administrative organs of the government of the duchy. Charles-Emmanuel II maintained his residence in Turin, but he had offered his hospitality to Hortense in the château de Chambéry.

as he had shown me for some time, and particularly at that moment, favors and indulgences which left nothing to be desired. So I wrote to him and asked him to send a coach for me to the foot of the Alps, which he did with his usual punctuality. The Marquis Drone[183] and one of the constable's gentlemen called Don Mauritio Bologna,[184] who was attending me then by his order, came to meet me near Turin; they were delighted to see me come back, and since they had feared nothing so much as the execution of what I had contemplated, they had already dispatched couriers to several places in order to bar my way. It was around that time that the king, at the constable's urging and solicitation, forbade all the governors of the borders and provinces of his realm to allow me entrance.

Upon my arrival in Turin, I went to the home of Monsieur le prince de Carignan,[185] where my nephews were, the comte de Dreux and the Chevalier de Savoie,[186] the first of whom, who held great promise, died a short time ago. I took possession of an apartment without saying anything, for fear that he might refuse to receive me if I notified him beforehand. I stayed there for more than a month, while waiting for permission from Rome to return to the convent and to have the freedom to go out once a week, which I obtained through the agency of Monsieur le Cardinal Porto Carrero.[187] During this interval, I went to court and visited the house called La

---

183. Prince Carlo Filiberto I d'Este, marquis de Dronero (1649–1703), rose progressively in the service of the dukes of Savoy and eventually became the duke's ambassador to Portugal. Dronero is located sixty miles southwest of Turin.

184. Don Maurizio Bologna had been Marie's Italian secretary in Rome, and he was sent to her in Turin by the constable in late February 1673, more to spy on her than to serve her. Dulong, *Marie Mancini*, 233–37.

185. Emmanuel-Philibert de Savoie-Carignan, prince de Carignan (1628–1709), was the first cousin of Duke Charles-Emmanuel II; he was also the brother of Olympe Mancini's husband, Eugène-Maurice de Savoie-Carignan, comte de Soissons. Thus, Marie's nephews were also the nephews of the prince de Carignan, who had no children of his own in 1673, as he did not marry until 1684.

186. Marie's sister Olympe, the comtesse de Soissons, gave birth to eight children between 1657 and 1668; the two sons mentioned here were the third and fourth of her children. The comte de Dreux was the younger of the two: Emmanuel-Philibert (1662–76), who had indeed died shortly before the composition of Marie's memoir in 1677. The Chevalier de Savoie was Louis-Jules (1660–83), although Roger Duchêne, in his edition of the letters of Madame de Sévigné (citing Dangeau's *Journal* for November 21–22, 1684), contends that the Chevalier de Savoie was rather Olympe's second child, Philippe (1659–1693), whom Madame de Sévigné refers to as the Chevalier de Soissons (*Correspondance*, 3: 161 nn. 4–5). The reason why both Dangeau and Madame de Sévigné were talking about Philippe in November 1684 was that he had created a sensation by going to London, promptly falling in love there with his aunt Hortense, and killing in a duel a rival for her affections, a Swedish gentleman known as Baron Banér (or Bannier). Rosvall, *Mazarine Legacy*, 192–93.

187. Luis Manuel Fernández de Portocarrero (1635–1709), who was created cardinal in 1669, and who lived until 1677 in Rome as cardinal protector of the Spanish nation. In 1677 he was

Vénerie,[188] where there were all kinds of entertainments, and I can say that I have scarcely ever spent my time more pleasantly than I did then, as His late Royal Highness and Madame Royale[189] regularly made toward me all the gestures of friendship and esteem that I could have desired.

This happiness was too great, and fortune, which seems to take an interest in tormenting me, took good care not to allow it to last; and so to interrupt its course, fortune inspired sentiments of a political nature in His late Royal Highness and obliged him to propose that I return home.[190] He tried to convince me that I would be much better off there than in a cloister and suggested that if the only obstacle to my return was the discord between the constable and me, he would offer himself as guarantor of our reunion. These propositions, together with some other little things which he said to me at La Vénerie, shocked me so thoroughly that on the impulse of my quick temper, I determined to leave that very instant and return to the convent, and I would have done so if not for Madame Royale, who prevented me and kept me there for another week, at the end of which time

---

elected archbishop of Toledo. Like the princesse des Ursins, he later became a key figure in the struggles over the Spanish succession, supporting the accession of Louis XIV's grandson Philippe, duc d'Anjou. See above, note 169.

188. The name of the house means "The Hunt." La Vénerie, or La Veneria reale by its Italian name, was one of the country houses belonging to the dukes of Savoy in the vicinity of Turin.

189. Marie-Jeanne Baptiste de Savoie-Nemours (1644–1724) was the second wife of Charles-Emmanuel II and the mother of his one legitimate child, Victor-Amédée II (1666–1732), who became duke of Savoy after his father's death in 1675; Madame Royale acted as regent for her son until 1685. Charles-Emmanuel had five illegitimate children with three other women; he legitimized the three eldest of those children, all of whom were by Marie-Jeanne de Trecesson, marquise de Cavour, and were born before his marriage to Marie-Jeanne Baptiste. They were born before and during his first marriage, to his first cousin, Françoise-Madeleine de Bourbon d'Orléans (1648–64), known as Mademoiselle de Valois, daughter of Louis XIII's brother Gaston d'Orléans. That marriage lasted less than a year, as Françoise-Madeleine died very young on January 14, 1664, two days after the birth of Charles-Emmanuel's third child with the marquise de Cavour. Charles-Emmanuel had two more children with two other women during his marriage to Marie-Jeanne Baptiste; given her husband's philandering, it is not surprising that Madame Royale promptly asked Hortense to leave Chambéry after his death, although by Marie's account here, she seems to have treated the latter quite civilly.

190. Although Charles-Emmanuel had withstood them for some time while offering Marie his hospitality, the political pressures on him were considerable. The constable was urging him to send Marie back to Rome, and Louis XIV himself had written to that effect as soon as he had learned that Marie was planning to stay in Savoy. The king's letter read as follows: "My Brother [sovereign princes addressed each other as "brother"; Louis and Charles-Emmanuel were in fact first cousins], It is most honorable of you to write to me about the arrival of my cousin the Constabless Colonna in your states. I am very glad that she has taken a path which will lead her to a place where she can negotiate her reconciliation in person. You will do me a very great favor by exhorting her to go there as soon as she finds it possible, as I am convinced that this is the true way toward the happiness I desire for her. I look forward to this sign of your friendship." Dulong, *Marie Mancini*, 228.

they both accompanied me back to the convent. On our way there we had yet another quarrel over something, and since I will not tolerate very much and the prince was not terribly patient himself, our attitudes grew more embittered than ever; and when he let go of my hand at the entrance to the convent, he told me after a long silence that despite my escapades and my whims, he would continue to protect me. The manner in which he made me this offer irritated me instead of mollifying me, so that I replied to him fairly disobligingly that his protection was as indifferent to me as his person. This reply stung him so sharply that he left without saying any more to me, and as my enemies saw in this a good opportunity to ruin me in his mind, they used it thereafter with considerable success. It was at around this time that I endeavored, through various letters which I wrote to the ministers of France, to impel the king to revoke the order he had given not to let me enter the kingdom; but all my efforts were useless, and he persisted in his resolution. Meanwhile, His late Royal Highness spent the whole summer at La Vénerie without sending me the slightest message, and when he came to see me with Madame Royale to convey their condolences for the death of Monsieur le comte de Soissons,[191] he discharged the duty most admirably, and his visit was as serious and as solemn as the cause which had brought him there. And so when I saw that I could have no hope from France, and that I was held in less esteem than in the past by the sovereign in Savoy, I took the opportunity presented by a trip which Monsieur le marquis de Borgomeinero[192] made to Turin to implore him to appeal to the constable as his best friend and to obtain his permission for me to enter France; for I was convinced that the king would not refuse the constable this favor, if the latter did me that of requesting it for me from His Majesty. Thus, he returned to Milan with the intention of serving me in this matter, and of coming to fetch me as soon as he had permission from Spain, for which he told me that he preferred to write to the court; he did not wish to request it of the gov-

191. The comte de Soissons, Olympe Mancini's husband, died on June 6, 1673, at the age of forty. In January 1680 when Olympe was implicated in the Affair of the Poisons and fled the country, one of the accusations being leveled against her was that she had poisoned her husband. See letters from Bussy-Rabutin to La Rivière dated January 27, 1680, and from La Rivière to Bussy-Rabutin dated February 5, 1680. Roger de Rabutin, *Correspondance*, 5: 43–45, 51–53.

192. Prince Don Carlo Emanuele d'Este, marquis de Borgomanero (1622–95), was, like Lorenzo Onofrio Colonna, an Italian nobleman in the service of Spain. He was a grandee of Spain and a knight of the Order of the Golden Fleece, and he later became the king of Spain's ambassador to England and to the emperor, the viceroy of Galicia, and a *conseiller d'État*. Borgomanero also had close family connections to the dukes of Savoy, as his father had been in their service and his nephew was the "Marquis Drone"—or marquis de Dronero—whom Marie mentions. See above, 148.

ernor of Milan, who was at that time Monsieur le duc d'Ossune,[193] for fear that he would refuse it, since he was not in favor with the duc and since through his own fault he had lost his place in his esteem and his good graces. Meanwhile, the constable wrote to me of the hope that the king would permit me to return to France and continually asserted that he had written to His Majesty about it; and since we readily believe what we desire, I was easily convinced, especially considering that it was consistent with his political interests to contribute to getting me out of Turin, where despite the minor annoyances I had had, my interests were preferred over his. Finally, the marquis de Borgomeinero came back in early autumn with permission from Spain, which the Queen Regent[194] had granted him; seeing that the constable was still writing me that he had no response from France, and supposing moreover that he would find it more acceptable that I withdraw to Flanders than to any other country, I resolved to go there and to leave in a week, and I disclosed my plan to the marquis, who approved of it. In the interval, the late duc de Savoie came to see me very assiduously, but it gave me less satisfaction than before because I was already so put off by his uneven manners that I did not even want to tell him of the decision I had made, although he pressed me considerably to declare it to him. Therefore, he was so hurt that Madame Royale, having noticed it, did not fail to ask me when I went to take my leave of her what I had done to him to make him come back from the convent in such ill humor; to which I replied that he had only himself and his moodiness to blame for anything that I might have done, and that he would always have been pleased with me if he had not given me reason to complain of him. Nonetheless, in the morning before I left, since the marquis de Borgomeinero had pressed me to say good-bye to him, I went to acquit myself of this duty, more for the sake of decorum than out of inclination. During this farewell, he reproached me at length and showed

---

193. Don Gaspar Téllez Girón Gómez de Sandoval Enríquez de Rivera, duke of Osuna, marquis of Peñafiel, count of Ureña (d. 1694), was governor of Milan from 1670 to 1674. He was reputed to have seduced several ladies of the Milanese nobility.

194. Queen Marie-Anne of Austria (1634–96) married Philip IV of Spain (1605–65) in 1649; she was his second wife and also his niece—the daughter of his sister, Maria Anna (1606–46), with her cousin and husband, the Holy Roman Emperor Ferdinand III (1608–57). Inbreeding was the rule in the Habsburg family, and it was probably largely responsible for the physical and mental debility of Charles II of Spain (1661–1700), who was Philip IV's only surviving legitimate son at his death in 1665. Queen Marie-Anne (or Mariana) acted as regent for her son, and because of his incompetence she effectively remained in control until her death in 1696, except for a period of less than two years (1677–79) when Philip IV's illegitimate son, Don Juan of Austria, led a revolt against her and forced her into exile. See below, 164–66, 169, and note 226.

himself to be very hurt by my resolution to leave, entreating me vehemently to tell him where I was going and assuring me that in no country would I find a prince more devoted to me, nor one who would protect me more highly. I listened to his reproach and his offers very attentively, and when I took my leave of him, I politely declined the latter, since the plan I had formed to leave his states left me no grounds for accepting them; so he gave me his hand and escorted me to the coach in which we left, and we set off for Rone,[195] in the state of Milan, in order to cross into Switzerland from there. But one day after leaving Turin, the marquis de Borgomeinero and the abbé Oliva,[196] who had come from Rome in place of Monsieur Boniel in order to accompany me on my journey (a learned man, to be sure, but quite far from the zeal and the loyalty of the first), began to dissuade me from going by way of the state of Milan, telling me that they were sure there was some plot against me, that I should avoid while I still could whatever traps had been laid for me there, and that Monsieur le duc d'Ossune would doubtless have me arrested. It took me a long time to be persuaded in the least by what they told me, but in the end I gave in to their eloquence and to the strength of their arguments and took the road for Saint Bernard,[197] along with the said marquis and the abbé, Morène, and a Swiss valet called Martin, and I sent my train and my personal effects by way of Rone. It was not long before I saw confirmation of what they had told me. Monsieur le duc d'Ossune had been informed of my departure from Turin by a courier which Don Maurice[198] had dispatched to him, and he had received letters from the constable in which the latter beseeched him earnestly to have me detained in the castle of Milan; thinking that I was in Rone because, as I have already said, I had sent my servants there, he gave the order to detain them. One of my maids called Nanette received in my stead all the honors of this arrest, until a knight of the Order of Malta named Cavanago,[199] whom the duc had

195. It is not clear which town Marie means to designate by this name, but it is most probably Arona, located forty miles northwest of Milan at the southern end of the Lago Maggiore. Presumably, the plan would have been to travel by boat from Arona into Switzerland.

196. Gian Paolo Oliva (1600–1681) became general of the Society of Jesus in 1664. He was a noted preacher and an art lover who had close ties to the Colonna family, even as he worked consistently to limit the influence of the nobility on the Jesuit order.

197. The Great Saint Bernard pass is on the border between Italy and Switzerland, roughly ninety miles northwest of Turin.

198. Don Maurizio Bologna; see above, note 184.

199. The false memoir published under Marie's name (*Mémoires de M.L.P.M.M. Colonne*, 1676) mentions Cavanago as one of Marie's companions in Venice and acknowledges the rumor that he was her lover. This passage helps to illustrate why Marie would have felt the outrage she expresses at the opening of *La Vérité dans son jour*: the author of the false memoir—speaking

sent to identify me, discovered the mix-up and withdrew them from the sweetest captivity in the world; for throughout the week that it had lasted they had been magnificently wined and dined, and even after their release they had enjoyed all sorts of pleasures, so generously did this duc treat them. We were not exactly having so pleasant a time on the mountain of Saint Bernard, where we were then and where we were walking through snow and along dreadful paths lined with precipices. Nevertheless, we arrived safely in Basel, where we learned of my servants' adventures; one week after having regained their freedom thanks to the clarification that I have related, they came to join us in Mainz. From there we went to Frankfurt and then to Cologne, going far off the most direct path in order to please the marquis de Borgomeinero and the abbé Oliva, who did not wish to run into the siege of Bonn and who wanted to avoid encountering the Spanish and French troops who had set out with provisions at the same time as we had.[200] During the three days we spent in Frankfurt, I had the pleasure of seeing Madame la duchesse de Lorraine[201] and of receiving all the expressions of friendship from her that I could have desired. After having enjoyed the pleasant company of this princess during that whole time, I wished to satisfy my impatience to continue the journey, and I resolved to set out again. On the road I was made to suffer more than I can say and more than can be imagined from the contrary nature, the unbearable slowness, and the unnecessary precautions of the marquis; and because misfortunes never come

---

as Marie—is ostensibly defending against such calumny, but the text lays out at length the many activities that Marie and Cavanago shared, and it goes on to note that similar rumors were circulating about her and Cardinal Chigi as well as about her and the Chevalier de Lorraine (*Cendre et poussière*, 89–91).

200   As Marie was wending her way across Europe, Louis XIV and his allies (England, Sweden, Bavaria) were waging the Franco-Dutch War against the Quadruple Alliance of the Dutch Republic, Spain, the Holy Roman Empire, and Brandenburg. The war began in the spring of 1672 and did not end until the Treaty of Nijmegen was signed on August 10, 1678. In 1667–68, Louis had fought the War of Devolution to press his claim to the Spanish Netherlands (present-day Belgium), and he began the Franco-Dutch War to continue in that pursuit but also to defend French commercial interests against Dutch competition and to champion the Catholic faith over Dutch Protestantism. The siege of Bonn was not a particularly significant event in the war, but the tactic of laying siege to cities in order to take control of them was characteristic of the wars fought by Louis XIV's armies.

201.   This would be Marie Louise d'Aspremont (1652–92), who was married to Charles IV, duke of Lorraine (1604–75), in 1665 at the age of thirteen. At this meeting in the fall of 1673, then, the duchess of Lorraine would have been twenty-one and Marie, thirty-four. On August 30, 1673, Duke Charles had allied himself with the Dutch, Spanish, Austrian, and German side of the war; thus, as she pursued her journey here and in the later stages she recounts, Marie was consorting primarily with the enemies of Louis XIV. See above, note 52; Hortense's memoir, note 33.

singly, the abbé Oliva, who had taken his side less by inclination than out of fear, contributed not a little to causing me grief. My trials lasted until Cologne, where the marquis deemed it neither safe nor opportune to cause me any more; he adopted other methods with me, since doubtless he was not unaware that the ambassadors of various crowns had offered to serve me, and since he feared perhaps that the insinuations of some of them might cause me to change my plans. That is precisely what would inevitably have happened if fortune, which, as I have said so many times, takes an interest in making me unhappy, had not rendered me skeptical of what Monsieur Courtin and Monsieur Barillon[202] predicted would happen if I went to Flanders, and if it had not prevented me from following the advice they gave me not to go there. Meanwhile, the marquis and the abbé, apprehensive that the interviews and conversations I was having with these ambassadors might become obstacles to their plans and might even prevent their fruition, marshaled all their credit and their eloquence to persuade me to leave. The marquis could not rest until he saw us under way, after having received word from Don Emanuel de Lira, special envoy from Spain, that a regiment which had come to escort a convoy of money was to return, and that a more favorable opportunity could not have presented itself for us to be escorted to the camp of Monsieur le marquis d'Assentar, *maître de camp général*, who was killed at the battle of Seneffe.[203] Borgomeinero had even written to the latter, who was one of his good friends, to ask that he receive us and permit us to follow him with the said regiment all the way to Flanders, for fear that we might otherwise be surprised by the French, who were spread out all over the countryside and were ravaging the entire land.

Before we arrived at the camp of the marquis, fortune, which wished to use Borgomeinero as an apt instrument for my persecution, produced the opportunity for it through the episode that I shall relate. Since our coach

202. French plenipotentiaries at the peace negotiations in Cologne (1673–74), which were broken off two months later, in February 1674. Both men subsequently became French ambassadors to the court of Charles II in England, where they were much preoccupied by the influence of the Duchesse Mazarin over the English king, since she quickly usurped the place of the mistress whom Louis XIV had tasked with defending French interests—Louise de Kéroualle, duchess of Portsmouth. Honoré Courtin (1626–1703) was ambassador to England in 1676 and 1677, followed by Paul de Barillon d'Amoncourt (d. 1691), who remained as ambassador from 1677 to 1689.

203. Seneffe is in Belgium, twenty-five miles south of Brussels. The battle of Seneffe, between the French army led by *le Grand Condé* (Louis II de Bourbon, prince de Condé, 1621–86) and the allied Dutch, Spanish, and Austrian forces under William III of Orange (1650–1702), took place on August 11, 1674. Although it ended in a drawn battle after sixteen hours of intense fighting and great losses on both sides, it was seen as a French victory because of the inferior numbers of French troops and cannon going into battle.

had broken down in such a way that we had neither the time nor what we needed to repair it, we were offered horses. However, not only was the road very dangerous, the cold great, and the night well advanced and dark, but neither I nor my maids had boots or spurs, and since without that equipment our mounts would have been more a hindrance than a help to us, I did not care to accept them. I opted for the solution offered to me by the marquis de Morbec,[204] *maître de camp* of the regiment in question and member of one of the most illustrious families of Flanders, and I rode pillion on a very good and very steady horse which he had at the time, as did two of my maids, after I had sent the others and the rest of my servants along with my personal effects and some valid passports by way of Holland. That horse, good and steady as it was, had neither of those qualities for me, since it was the cause of what I suffered subsequently, and since it threw me into misfortunes which I had not foreseen. For after that ride, Borgomeinero could think of nothing but doing me ill, and he managed it so adroitly that it was impossible for me to parry any of his blows.

Throughout this whole journey, all the principal officers, whether Spanish, Dutch, or Flemish, showed all imaginable care and consideration, endeavoring to entertain me, now with gaming, now with conversation. While I was having quite a pleasant time and was even enjoying Borgomeinero's nasty temper and his profound reveries—while, as I say, I was scarcely concerned about the plots he was hatching with the marquis d'Assentar, and I knew nothing of the traps he had laid for me with the comte de Monterey,[205] then governor of Flanders, whom he had prejudiced against me—we arrived in Malines,[206] where the governor of the city came to tell me that the comte de Monterey had sent written orders to him to detain me until everything was in place to receive me in Brussels in a convent, for that was the specious pretext for the arrest. I cannot express how much these compliments surprised me, or how great was the apprehension that this unforeseen

204. This is apparently Marie's spelling of the Flemish Moerbeke, which is located twelve miles northeast of Ghent.

205. Don Juan Domingo de Haro y Guzmán, younger son of Don Luis de Haro, with whom Cardinal Mazarin had negotiated the Peace of the Pyrenees in 1659–60. The count of Monterey was a grandee of Spain, through his mother; he acquired the title of count of Monterey from his wife, Doña Ines Alvarez de Toledo Fonseca Zuniga Azevedo y Claërhoot, countess of Ayala, Monterey, and Fuentes, marquise of Tarazona, and baroness of Maldeghen. As Marie says, he was governor of Flanders at this time, and he later became president of the council of Flanders. Perey cites the following description of his character: "He was a man of superior genius in everything, but haughty, mean, and dangerous." *Une princesse romaine,* 322 n. 1.

206. Mechelen (Malines, in French) is located twenty miles north of Brussels, in the Flemish part of present-day Belgium.

reception caused me. Borgomeinero, fearing that I might believe him to be the author of it, pretended to be astonished and added oaths and protests to his feigned surprise. I believed these to be so sincere that I beseeched him to go immediately to Brussels to beg the comte to permit me to enter the city, so that I might retire to the convent of Barlement[207] and recover in some way the freedom that the governor of Malines had taken from me by placing guards around my house on the pretext of doing honor to me. So the marquis promised to use all his good offices with the comte on my behalf, and to tell the truth, the confidence that I placed in him on this occasion, despite the suspicions that my detention had caused me, should have wiped his soul clean of all feelings of vengeance and impelled him to serve me in good faith, or at least to remain neutral. But it goes to show that, contrary to the sentiment of a poet of yore, there are men who enjoy vengeance as much as and even more than women do; for he and his colleague Oliva inspired in the comte de Monterey everything that hate is capable of suggesting, going so far as to advise him to put me in the castle of Antwerp to keep me from slipping into France or England. So at the time when I firmly believed that these two individuals were working for my freedom—and in order to convince myself of it, I imagined that everything that had happened to me in Malines was just a misunderstanding—Borgomeinero came the next day with one of the comte de Monterey's gentlemen, who told me that His Excellency, who was leaving the following day with the army to go and meet the French troops, desired that I go to Antwerp until his return. The marquis backed up this compliment, or rather, this order, pretending to be vexed by it and saying that I had to obey but that it would be only for a few days, until I received letters from the constable and a brief from His Holiness so that I could enter the convent. He also said that he was bitterly disappointed not to have managed to win the comte over to allowing me to enter Brussels at that time, and that I ought to blame that setback on the nasty impressions that people had given him of me, adding that it would take time to change those impressions, but that he would undertake to do so. Still suspecting nothing and considering his conduct as honest as it appeared, and as it should have been, I expressed my gratitude to him for the offers he had made me; and seeing that for the moment there was no other course of action to take than the one I was being forced to accept, I embarked with the admiral, who came to collect me in a very beautiful boat. At daybreak the next day, we arrived at the port of Antwerp, where I began to suspect something sinister and feared that I had been betrayed when I saw that they were slow to let me disembark. However, after three hours, when I was

207. Or rather, the convent of Berlamont, the most "fashionable" convent in Brussels.

informed that the marquis d'Ossera, commander of the fortress, awaited me with his coach, I was a bit reassured, judging from all appearances that it was to do me honor. Thus, having disembarked, I got into the coach with Borgomeinero and the commander, who brought me straight to the castle, where, still continuing in my error, I believed I was free and thought of nothing but relaxing on the first day. On the second, I asked the commander to order me a coach because I wanted to go out, upon which he glanced at Borgomeinero and then said to me, looking fairly disconcerted, that the weather was too bad and it would be better if I rested. I did not protest, out of an innocent gratitude for his concern for my health, but the following day, after the marquis de Borgomeinero had left to go and join Monsieur le comte de Monterey in the army, and Oliva had gone to Brussels on the pretext of returning to Rome, two soldiers and an officer were stationed at my door. I then realized the deceit and treachery, and that the marquis had had this treatment put off until after his departure so that I would not think he had ordered it. That was not all: as if I had been a common criminal, all my letters were intercepted, and I did not receive a single one that had not first been opened. Even that was not enough, and the marquis, not thinking himself sufficiently avenged for the contempt I had shown him, which he had brought upon himself through his lack of consideration for me, found out that I had received a letter from the constable and a brief from the pope, in which His Holiness permitted the archbishop of Malines to let me enter the convent of my choice, and he advised the comte de Monterey to wait for the replies regarding my arrival. He said he was sure that everything they had done would meet with the approval not only of the constable but even of the Queen Regent, who would not disapprove of his conduct in my regard; and thus he broke off the deal at the very time when I thought it was concluded. The comte was not mistaken in the opinion that Borgomeinero led him to conceive, for the reports against me that the latter had sent to Spain and to Italy met with all the success that his vindictive mind could have desired. The queen gave the order to the said comte to apprehend me, and the constable praised his actions highly and wrote to me privately, in order to justify them, that he had been obliged to detain me in this manner because of the notice he had received that I intended to flee to France or to England. It was no use trying to defend myself against these false accusations when Monsieur le comte de Monterey came to see me at the castle, or telling him, as I had also written to the constable, that if I had had the plan of which I was suspected, it would have been very easy for me to carry it out in Cologne, where as they must both be aware, I wanted neither for friends nor for protection.

That argument alone could have disabused any other minds than theirs, but Borgomeinero's information proved more powerful than my innocence and my excuses. Nevertheless, when the comte came to visit me upon his return from the army, I complained to him of the continuation of this rigorous treatment, and I pressed him to allow me to go to Brussels, as I had been given to hope at the time of my arrest and as he himself had promised me; so he resolved to grant my request, and Borgomeinero, having received this assignment, took an apartment adjoining a convent called Les Anglaises, where he had more metal bars installed than there were on the monastery itself, and then he left for Burgundy following this heroic expedition. I was notified straightaway of the lodgings that had been prepared for me, and when two of my maids whom I had sent to Brussels to speak in my favor to the comte de Monterey reported to me all the details of that worthy prison and said that the one where I was was much better, I refused to believe them, being unable to conceive that I could really be deprived both of the freedom to go out and move around the city and of the freedom even to enter the convent itself. When everything was ready and that lovely dwelling was all in order, the comte sent his captain of the guards to collect me, and I embarked with him for Brussels, where I was very eager to be. I was informed in greater detail about my future home, and I began to think seriously about ways to avoid staying there. Thus, I resolved to resort to the sanctuary which was near this residence; and when a very handsome coach belonging to the comte came to meet me in order to conduct me there without allowing me to go to the palace and see Madame la Comtesse, or even to speak to the comte, I went into the church of the convent on the pretext of saying my prayers there, and I immediately declared to the captain of the guards who was escorting me that I would not leave the spot where I was except to enter the monastery, in accordance with the promise that the comte had given me at the castle. The captain went straightaway to tell this to the comte, who came at once to find me and who, when his entreaties and even his threats did nothing to draw me out of the church, became provoked by my resistance and called for the internuncio and the archbishop, in order to obtain permission from them to remove me by force. After some conferring, he came to speak to me once again; when he obtained nothing from that second attempt except words as bitter as those he used with me, he finally went away and left several guards around me as well as four sentinels at the door of the church, having first forbade the abbess, in the name of the Queen Regent, to receive me in the convent.

Thus, I was resolved to sleep in the church when Monsieur Bruneau, *Aman* of the city of Brussels, advised me to come out of my own accord, assuring me that he knew from very good sources that His Excellency had ordered the soldiers to remove me as soon as I fell asleep. I put faith in what he told me because I knew him to be a man of probity, and allowing myself to be persuaded by his arguments, I finally went to the famous dwelling, which I found to be more heavily reinforced and guarded than the tower of Danae;[208] there, despite my unhappiness which was not inconsiderable, overwhelmed with fatigue and drowsiness, I went to bed and slept better than I have ever done in my life. Apparently, all these precautions did not suffice, the bars and sentinels and guards were not enough, and for fear that I might dig myself a tunnel into the convent, Monsieur le comte de Monterey sent me a guard to be witness to all my actions, who was a Spanish gentleman named Monsieur de Saint Laurent. In this pitiful state, having managed to obtain nothing from the governor of Flanders either by my pleas or by my tears, I finally made up my mind to ask to withdraw to Madrid, to a convent, knowing full well that this request would be granted; and indeed, the comte accepted the proposition and dispatched a courier to the constable, to inform him of it and to obtain permission for me, which I also requested of him most earnestly, as much out of the passion I had to see that court as out of a desire to improve my conditions.

While we were waiting for the reply, the comte found himself obliged to go to Antwerp for some business which had come up, and he pressed me to return to the castle because he needed his guards, assuring me that I would be treated there with less rigor and that he would allow me to go out from time to time accompanied by the lieutenant of the castle. I had him sign the conditions of this agreement for me during a visit he made to me before leaving for Antwerp, since experience had made me wiser and I did not wish to go through everything I had gone through the first time; the next day I took the same road, accompanied by Monsieur Bruneau and Monsieur de Saint Laurent. Thereafter I lived in greater freedom in that castle, and particularly after the arrival of Monsieur l'abbé Don Ferdinand Colonna,[209] whom the constable had sent to me to attend to my person and accompany me to Madrid; he contributed greatly through his efforts to having me treated more gently than I had been until then, as he pointed out to the comte that it was certainly possible to hold me in a more decent

---

208. In Greek mythology, Danae was a princess of Argos, daughter of Eurydice and Acrisius. When an oracle declared that her father would be killed by his own grandson, Acrisius imprisoned Danae in a bronze tower. However, Zeus loved her and was metamorphosed into a shower of gold in order to enter the tower; Perseus was born of their union.

209. Don Fernando Colonna was the illegitimate half-brother of Lorenzo Onofrio Colonna. Their father had recognized Fernando and helped to establish him in an ecclesiastical career; Marie was well acquainted with him from her time in Rome.

manner, and to keep me detained without resorting to such disagreeable and rigorous precautions.

As soon as my journey was organized, I wrote a letter to the Almirante,[210] in which I begged him to do me the favor of receiving me at his home upon my arrival, and of persuading the queen to see fit that I retire to a convent in Madrid. And when everything was finally arranged for my departure, I set out for Ostend, where during the week that I spent waiting for a boat there I was treated sumptuously by Don Ferdinand de Valladares, commander of the fortress; in the end, I left on an English vessel which, thanks to a good wind, landed in nine days at San Sebastian.[211]

No sooner had I arrived than, finding no reply from the Almirante, or consequently from the queen (since it was he who was to obtain it for me), I wrote him a second letter with the same content as the first and waited a week to see whether I would hear from him. During that time, Don Balthasar Pantoja, commander of the fortress, at whose home I was staying, treated me and all my servants in the most obliging manner in the world. The week having passed, my impatience at having received no reply pushed me to continue my journey, in the hope that I would receive one along the way. One day's journey short of Burgos, as I had still seen nothing of what I was waiting for, I dispatched an express messenger to the Almirante, to find out whether I should count on the favor that I had asked of him in my letters from Antwerp and San Sebastian; and continuing on my way, I arrived at Alcovendas,[212] which is a town three leagues from Madrid, where the courier came to find me with two letters, one from the queen in which Her Majesty did me all the honor I could have desired, and the other from the Almirante in which he granted me most graciously the house that I had requested of him, adding that he would come himself to meet me in order to reiterate the offer of it. The evening of that same day, I left for Madrid, and along the way I encountered Madame la duchesse d'Alburquerque

---

210. The Almirante (Admiral) of Castile was the second highest dignitary in the kingdom, after the Queen Regent herself. He was Don Juan Gaspar Enriquez de Cabrera, duke of Medina de Rioseco, count of Melgar and of Módica, hereditary Almirante of Castile (1625–91); the dukes of Medina de Rioseco were descended from an illegitimate line of the royal house of Castile. The Almirante was known for his sumptuous hospitality: he was acclaimed, for instance, for the splendor with which he had received the French envoys who came in 1659 to ask officially for the hand of the Infanta Marie-Thérèse. In his youth he had engaged in bullfighting in the way that great seigneurs did—not pursuing the fight to the death—and he had even written a short treatise on the art. He was also a generous patron of the visual arts and of literature and, finally, a great lover of women; indeed, several of his mistresses lived in his Madrid palace along with his wife. Dulong, *Marie Mancini*, 254–60.

211. In early June 1674.

212. Alcobendas is twelve miles north of the center of Madrid.

and the daughter-in-law of the Almirante, wife of Monsieur le marquis d'Alcagniças, who had come to welcome me quite near Alcovendas, in a coach followed by another in which were riding the Almirante, the marquis d'Alcagniças,[213] his second son, and the late duc d'Alburquerque;[214] and all together they escorted me to a country house belonging to the said Almirante, situated at the edge of Madrid, which was superbly furnished and decorated with a very great number of the richest and most beautiful paintings there are in all of Europe.[215] I stayed in that delicious dwelling for around two months, after which I feared I was becoming a burden to the Almirante, who was treating me quite splendidly, and I noted moreover that due to a certain slowness which is rather part of his nature, he was not presenting my request to the queen to have me enter a convent as Her Majesty had given me to hope. And so I went myself to speak to her and to beg her to have an order sent to the nuns of Saint Dominic to receive me or to give me a house which belongs to them, situated between their convent and the monastery of Our Lady of the Angels, of the order of Saint Francis.[216] The queen received me then very obligingly, and granting my request, she sent them an order the next day to receive me or to give me the house I have just mentioned; they replied to this that they would obey but that they humbly beseeched Her Majesty to have a decree sent stating that the favor I was being accorded would not set a precedent. Her Majesty granted them one declaring the maintenance of their privileges and also setting out very advantageous conditions for me.[217] Thus, I entered the convent on the last day of August,[218] and I was accompanied there by Monsieur le Nonce, now Car-

---

213. The son's title was passed to him by his mother, the wife of the Almirante, Doña Teresa d'Almanza y Borja, marquise of Alcañizas and of Oropeza, countess of Almanza.

214. The dukes of Alburquerque were also grandees of Spain. Marie refers here to Francisco Fernández de la Cueva, eighth duke of Alburquerque (1618–76), who had been governor of New Spain from 1653 to 1660. His grandson (who was also his nephew, since his brother married the eighth duke's daughter), Francisco Fernández de la Cueva Enríquez, tenth duke of Alburquerque, was governor of New Spain from 1702 to 1711; the city of Albuquerque, New Mexico, was named for him in 1706.

215. The house, called Casa de Huerta for its exquisite gardens, was located east of the city, near the Prado and next to the park Buen Retiro.

216. The convent of Santo Domingo el Real in Madrid was founded in 1218 by Santo Domingo de Guzmán, and it still is known today as a "posh" establishment. The Franciscan convent of Nuestra Señora de los Angeles, on the other hand, no longer exists.

217. As this passage suggests, the heads of Spanish convents jealously guarded their privileges, and one privilege which had been accorded the various female religious communities in Madrid was the right not to house secular ladies.

218. August 31, 1674. Marie found her apartment hung with fine tapestries from the collection of Don Pedro d'Aragon, who knew her from his time as viceroy of Naples. However, a remark in a letter from Marie to her husband Lorenzo reveals the tension that underlay her

dinal Marescoti,[219] by the Almirante, and by the marquis d'Alcagniças. So that I would not disturb or be disturbed in my new household, I was given the house that adjoins the convent; half of it was made into my apartment, to which a hatch and metal bars were added, and the other half was left for the abbé Don Ferdinand Colonna and for the rest of my servants. At first, I felt rather ill at ease in this new home, not knowing the language and being unfamiliar with the customs of the land; if it had not been for Donna Victoria Porcia Orosco, sister of the marquis de Mortara,[220] who was then abbess, who understands Italian fairly well, and who is a woman of infinite wit, I would have had quite a bad time of it during those first days. Later I made new acquaintances in the convent and felt fairly happy there, until I asked permission to go out once a week, as I had been given to hope when I entered there and as I had obtained in Turin, and I discovered that it had been refused me from Rome. I learned subsequently that the constable was far from giving me satisfaction for my earnest entreaties that he send me my second son[221] so that I could travel with him to Flanders, where the two companies of cavalry that Her Majesty had granted him immediately upon my request obliged him to go. Vowing, doubtless, to make me return to Rome by thwarting me in everything, he had written to Her Majesty and to the Almirante, who had endeavored in their letters to make him condescend to what I asked, that he did not wish me to go out of the convent, that he begged Her Majesty not to permit me to do so, that I was safe and secure in Madrid, and that he did not want to risk seeing me at liberty anywhere else. I have already said somewhere in this history that it is in my nature to be infuriated when I am thwarted, so one can well imagine the resentment and the pique that this news caused me; and to get a clearer picture of it, one should add the care with which I was constantly observed by loads of people who kept watch on my actions by order of Don Ferdinand Colonna, who was perhaps following the constable's orders overly strictly. On top of that, certain malicious individuals, in order to do me a bad turn and thereby

---

relations with Don Pedro: "It took . . . a whole song and dance to make Don Pedro lend me a tapestry—which he ought to have offered me himself after the favors he has received from our family. It is as if the favors were due them, and they do not even remember them." Letter dated July 9, 1675, in appendix to Cholakian and Goldsmith, eds., *La Vérité dans son jour*, 99; the letter was translated from the Italian by Giovanna Suhl.

219. Galeazzo Marescotti (1627–1726) was nuncio in Spain from 1670 to 1675; he was created cardinal in 1675.

220. Again, Don Francisco de Orozco, marquis of Mortara, who had been governor of Milan for a brief stint in 1668. See above, note 109.

221. Marcantonio Colonna (1664–1715).

gain his good graces, wrote to him that I wanted to run away and that I would do it inevitably if I were not closely watched. These rumors, together with the other reasons which I have declared above, made me decide to go out of the convent, to show that the efforts to hold me would keep me locked up there only so long as I was willing. So one day when Don Ferdinand had gone out with all my servants, I had my maids open in an instant— and it was my maids, mind you—those strong, those thick, and those high walls which the author of my history contends were the only obstacle to my flight.[222] Next I sent word to Monsieur le duc d'Ossune, the Almirante, and the prince d'Astillane,[223] my relatives, by writing a note to each of them, imploring them to assist me in this situation, since my plan was not, as my enemies had falsely spread it around, to flee to France or to England, but only to live without enclosure in the house where I was dwelling, as it was not right that I should be held by force in a place I had entered of my own free will. The duc d'Ossune, though he was a man of great worth and very obliging toward ladies, waited for the storm to pass; merely sending me his compliments the next day, when everything was put right, he did not come to see me until a few days later, preferring in this instance to appear circumspect rather than overzealous and solicitous. The prince d'Astillane went a full week without visiting me, proffering the excuse that he had not learned of it until very late and that for that reason he had not come earlier. Monsieur le Nonce Mellini[224] and the Almirante, for whom Don Ferdinand had

222. One of the subtexts to Marie's memoir resurfaces here, namely, the spurious *Mémoires de M.L.P.M.M. Colonne*, which Marie cites at the beginning of her text as the impetus for her writing. The false memoir ends with her arrival at Santo Domingo el Real and with her speculation about what she might do next. The author, assuming Marie's voice, says: "I don't know if I should tell you my secret. It is that I am always thinking about how I can get away from this convent. Its walls are thick and its location, problematic. Nevertheless, I plan to follow the example of the comte de Lauzun, who kept digging at Pignerol for two whole years in order to get away. It is true that he had the misfortune of being discovered, but perhaps that will not happen to me. In any event, I have a room which is as well suited as can be to digging, and that is what makes me want to try my luck." *Cendre et poussière*, 139.

223. Don Nicolas de Guzmán y Caraffa, marquis of Toral, duke of Medina de Las Torres, prince of Stigliano, duke of Sabionetta and of Mondragone (d. 1689). Marie transcribes and gallicizes "di Stigliano" as "d'Astillane." She refers to these men as her relatives because they were indeed all related to the family of her husband. One sister of Lorenzo Onofrio Colonna's great-grandfather (Donna Vittoria Colonna—not the famous poetess, who was also a member of this family but who lived a century earlier) was the grandmother of both the Almirante and the wife of the duke of Osuna; another of his great-grandfather's sisters (Donna Giovanna Colonna) was the great-great-grandmother of the prince of Stigliano.

224. Savo Millini (or Mellini) (1644–1701) replaced Marescotti as nuncio in Spain beginning in 1675; he was created cardinal in 1681. Although he arrived in Madrid strongly predisposed against Marie, he was quickly won over to the justice of her requests. He was a young man

sent, begging them to come quickly, came straightaway, not to further my plan but rather to carry out theirs, which was to make me go back into the convent. I did all I could to avoid it, and the nuns contributed not a little to my efforts with the objections they raised to taking me in. Nevertheless, seeing that I had no protection, and that I had everything to fear from the very people in whom I had vainly placed my hope, I made up my mind to go back in, the nuns' resistance having been overcome in the end by the fear of excommunication with which the Nuncio was threatening them. The Almirante, very happy to see me locked up again after this coup d'état, continued his efforts before Their Majesties in order to have my enclosure continued; but the constable was incomparably more pleased with this happy outcome, my loss of freedom serving as a reward for him, and it is certain that, with a sentiment quite opposite to those I saw in him in the past, he will always be pleased with the court so long as I do not obtain satisfaction from it.

I had already been back in the convent for a few months, where I was suffering very impatiently the violence with which they endeavored to hold me, and my woes were all the greater because I saw no prospect of relief for them under the regency of the queen. For Her Majesty had replied to me one day when I was pressing her very earnestly to remove me from the oppression I was enduring, that she would willingly do so, provided that the constable was agreeable; and the Almirante, who had control over the mind of Don Ferdinand Valenzuela[225] at that time, was too tightly linked with the constable to countenance anything that might be contrary to the decisions the latter had made, for the execution of which he had given the Almirante absolute power.

I was in this pitiful state when heaven, moved by that of the monarchy and interested in its preservation, inspired in the leading seigneurs of that

---

with pleasant looks and manners, and he established a much more cordial relationship with Marie than had the nuncio Marescotti.

225. Fernando de Valenzuela, marquis of Villa Sierra (1630–92), was the favorite of Queen Marie-Anne and held sway over her government. He was born in Naples, the son of a fairly obscure Andalusian gentleman, but he was placed as a page in a ducal household and eventually came to Madrid in 1659. Two years later, he contracted a marriage with Maria de Uceda, a lady-in-waiting to the queen, and with her help he obtained the post of introducer of ambassadors in the royal household. He became the trusted advisor of the queen, who favored him with the marquisate of Villa Sierra and eventually named him chief minister, gave him quarters in the palace, and made him a grandee. Much like Cardinal Mazarin with Anne of Austria, Valenzuela was regarded by many as the queen's lover; also like Mazarin, he was reviled as an upstart by the powerful nobles of the country, and his influence was bitterly resented. He was eventually stripped of his grandeeship and possessions and forced to leave Spain; he went first to the Philippines and then to Mexico, where he died.

court the plan to make the king see fit that they call His Highness Don Juan of Austria,[226] his brother, as the sole cure for the ills with which the kingdom was then threatened through the disorder of the government. It was during this time that I saw a ray of hope, recalling that Father Vintimilla,[227] as illustrious by his ability and his rare talents as by the nobility of his birth, had told me any number of times (before he was distanced from the court, from which Valenzuela had found a way to oblige him to withdraw on some specious pretext involving the public good, but in truth because he had been so inseparably attached to the interests of His Highness that he had sung his praises in all his sermons) that my freedom would have to be the work of this prince, and that his return would restore it to me without fail. I thought seriously about making use of such favorable circumstances, having no doubt that they would produce the effect he had led me to expect. The esteem that I have always had for the singular merit of this prince has always made me desire advantage for him,[228] but I desired it much more ardently when I could hold some hope of benefiting from it, and when I considered my freedom to be an inevitable consequence of his return. All I can say is that I

226. Don Juan (1629–79) was the illegitimate son of Philip IV with the actress Maria Calderon; his father recognized him and gave him a princely education. Don Juan had a number of military successes and stayed in his father's favor until Philip IV's death in 1665, but thereafter he went into opposition against the government of the queen. He led an uprising in 1669 which expelled Marie-Anne's favorite, the German Jesuit Nithard, but he did not come to power himself at that time. He remained viceroy of Aragon until 1677, when the widespread resentment of the queen's new favorite, Valenzuela, helped Don Juan to push them out and take over the government himself. As Marie did, many people hoped for great things from Don Juan, but his rule was cut short by his death in 1679.

227. Father Vintimilla (or Vintimiglia) was Marie's confessor. He came from a Sicilian noble family and was the superior of the Theatine monastery of San Gaetano in Madrid. The Theatines were an order founded in Italy in the sixteenth century to counter Protestant influences, and Cardinal Mazarin had brought them to France and acted as their protector there. Mazarin had given them a house in Paris, where Father Vintimiglia had spent a considerable length of time, and he spoke fluent French as a result. He would likely have been an enthusiastic and devoted servant of Marie's if for no other reason than out of deference for her uncle. Dulong, *Marie Mancini*, 272.

228. Well, perhaps not *always*. Lucien Perey recounts how Marie had done her utmost to turn Louis XIV against Don Juan when, in March 1659, the latter had come to Paris as part of the Spanish effort to negotiate the peace and the marriage of the king with the Infanta. In fact, Marie's wrath had come down most heavily on Don Juan's favorite, a female jester (*folle*) called Capitor whose incisive wit was greatly admired by all at the French court, including the king. Capitor was full of praise for the Infanta, which caused Marie to treat her very coldly and haughtily; when the sharp-tongued fool ridiculed Marie in return, Louis quickly turned against her and demanded that she be sent away. (*Le Roman du Grand Roi*, 133–34). Evidently, Marie is counting on the passage of time and the generosity of Don Juan to permit him to be favorably disposed toward her now, almost twenty years later.

desired it, being in no position to do anything else, and being unable to be of use to him or to contribute in any way to heightening his glory, except through my wishes or my insinuations. I did not spare the latter in speaking with the duc d'Ossune, who was the one who visited me the most assiduously of all my relatives. The Almirante, like certain others, had discontinued his visits, for fear that I might push him into engagements which would be contrary to the good relations he wished to maintain with the constable; and as the good of the state is the sole guide for the actions of this duc, I found him so well disposed toward this great undertaking that he burned with desire to put his hand to it himself. So with things already quite far along, and Father Vintimilla having written me that His Highness had left Saragossa, I thought that it was time to put into action what I had resolved to do. I estimated the time of the prince's arrival based on the shortest days I imagined he could possibly put in, and then I went out of the convent in broad daylight, and not as I had the first time, but through the gate, in plain sight of all the portresses; I climbed into a coach with a lady friend of mine, who was waiting for me for that purpose, and I went straight to the home of the marquise de Mortare,[229] whom I did not find in but who, upon her return, treated me very obligingly, although she was very surprised to see me, and my visit was the last thing in the world that she had expected.

I had given notice of my second exit from the convent, as I had of the first, to the same people whom I mentioned above, and the marquise had made it known that I was at her house to Monsieur le président de Castille;[230] Don Ferdinand Colonna had previously suggested to him that he send orders in all directions to arrest me and force me back into a convent, not knowing where I was and being convinced that my intention was to leave the kingdom. The Almirante, at the solicitation of Don Ferdinand or else moved by the same spirit, which had long been leading him to take action against me, no sooner learned where I was than he could think of nothing but how to deprive me once again of my freedom. During the short time that I enjoyed it, I was visited by no one but Monsieur le duc d'Ossune, whom the marquise had notified and who said nothing in particular to me during his visit, except that I could not have done better to repair the mistake I had made by coming out of the convent than to withdraw as I had done to a house which had all the sanctity of a convent without the austerity or the

229. The marquise of Mortara was the wife of the former governor of Milan, Don Francisco de Orozco, and the sister-in-law of the abbess of Santo Domingo el Real, Donna Victoria Porcia Orozco. See above, 119, 162. Perey refers to her as "the most respected and the most respectable woman in Madrid" (*Une princesse romaine*, 382).

230. The president of the council of Castile.

constraint. The prince d'Astillane neither came nor replied, but he behaved very gallantly all the same, sending Don Ferdinand my note and writing to him that he would serve the constable in any way he could. The Almirante, who behaved in just as generous a manner, did not come to see me because he was extremely occupied with business which concerned me; it was (if the inquiring reader wishes to know) a *consulte*[231] which was being conducted against me, until the conclusion of which he put off visiting me. However, I knew nothing of all these actions of which I have since learned, because there had been no one there who might have given me any knowledge of them at the time, except Monsieur de Lindenau, special envoy of the king of Denmark, a man of probity and honor who sent a number of messages with one of my maids about what was brewing against me. But since I was not able to speak to him, I attributed these warnings to his zeal and did nothing to guard against their effects; and although the continual apprehensions that I felt were like inner warnings which should have confirmed the others for me, the ambassadress of Denmark, an intelligent and resolute woman, and Monsieur le duc d'Ossune reassured me and told me so positively that I had nothing to fear that I believed I was safe. Nevertheless, two days later the Nuncio, the Almirante, and Don Garcie de Medrano,[232] from the royal council and the chamber of Castile, came to speak to me on behalf of the king when I least expected it. The purpose of this visit was to make me return to the convent, which they said I should not have left without the permission of His Majesty, since I had entered it by his order. The Almirante, who was the first to speak, told me that he had come solely as the representative of the king's will; when it was the Nuncio's turn, he added that he had come to facilitate the execution of that will and to overcome any obstacles that the nuns might put up against it; and the last, speaking as minister of justice, told me rather haughtily that he had orders to take me away, and that should I refuse to consent, he would not leave my person and would keep me under very tight guard. I would not have been very worried that he might keep his word, and that threat alone would never have made me give an inch. But the marquise for her part was entreating me most earnestly to go, expressing to me how unhappy she would be if any violence were done to me in her house because of my refusal to obey the king's orders, saying that I would do

231. A *consulte* was an administrative body convened to deliberate on a specific issue. Marie uses the word here to refer to the deliberations and below (170), to mean the ruling that resulted.

232. Perey identifies the third member of this delegation as the president of the council of Castile, although it is not clear from Marie's phrasing that that was Garcia de Medrano's function (*Une princesse romaine*, 383–84).

better to follow them and that once I was in the convent, I could come out again later with the consent and the authorization of His Majesty, so that in the end she compelled me through her timid reasoning to condescend to return there. And so she accompanied me in a coach belonging to the king. The Nuncio wanted to take the nuns by surprise, so he went ahead and had the gate opened, ordering that it should remain open as if he had had the intention of leading in some seigneur. I arrived at this time and found the duc d'Aveiro,[233] who had learned along the way as he was coming to see me at the marquise de Mortare's house that I was returning to the convent, and so he had followed the Nuncio there to wait for me. He gave me his hand as soon as he saw me and escorted me all the way into the convent, where several nuns who had recognized me as soon as I had taken off my mantle began to fill the air with their cries, pouring out to the Nuncio all their displeasure at seeing their privileges violated. The Nuncio finally found himself obliged to send his coach to fetch the Provincial, who lives at Notre Dame d'Atocha, outside the gates of Madrid, and who came straightaway.[234] He made them see reason and compelled them to conform to His Majesty's decree, which the Nuncio read out to them once the two of them had quieted the din that the differences between factions had raised among them; for it is practically impossible that in a community of one hundred thirty people, all with different inclinations, the opinions should not be similarly divided. That day I sided with the faction who opposed me, and despite my despair over the violence that was being done to me, I took pleasure in their division, and to foment it I pointed out to them how strange and unheard-of it was that there should be so little regard shown for their privileges, and that as if it were not enough that these had been violated when they were obliged to receive me the first time, they had been compelled to do it again after my first exit, and they were being forced to do it once more after my second.

At last this internecine war died down, and of all these riled minds, only mine remained troubled and agitated, because my periodic reflection on the violence with which people insisted on keeping me in the convent, under

---

233. The title of duke of Aveiro was associated with the royal house of Portugal. Don Pedro de Lancastre (or Lencastre), duke of Aveiro, archbishop of Evora, Grand Inquisitor of Portugal, died in 1673, after which the title passed to his elder brother's daughter, Doña Maria Guadalupe de Lancastre (1630–1715). Thus, the duke of Aveiro to whom Marie refers here was Doña Maria's husband, Don Manuel Ponce de León, duke of Arcos (d. 1693).

234. The Provincial is the presiding member of a religious order in a given province or district. Evidently, the Dominican Provincial, who had authority over the nuns of Santo Domingo el Real, was based at the royal basilica of Nuestra Señora de Atocha. The basilica is near the Atocha train station, just south of the Prado and the royal botanical gardens.

nettlesome conditions which were very different from those I had been given to expect, gave me cause for bitter anxiety. And yet I did not lose heart for having seen my two attempts at freeing myself turn out so badly, and conscious that freedom is the richest treasure in the world and that a noble and generous spirit must stop at nothing to acquire it or to recover it after having lost it, I applied my efforts once again to obtaining it. I had · already been working on this for about a week when fortune finally brought forth that day for which the people of this great realm had so yearned. That day, I say, when His Highness made his glorious entry after the expulsion and imprisonment of Valenzuela.[235] I will not speak here of the details of that famous negotiation, or of the circumstances that preceded the entry of the prince, and I leave it to other pens than mine to describe them. I will say only that even if I participated less than others in this undertaking, nobody took a greater interest than I in its success, or expressed more joy over it. And I have no doubt that if not for Don Ferdinand Colonna, my joy would have been complete and His Highness would have given me satisfaction for the petition I had presented to the Queen Regent during the time of her government and again soon after I had returned to the convent, and which had been submitted by His Majesty to Monsieur le président de Castille and had been drawn out until the arrival of His Highness. However, Don Ferdinand Colonna, in order to prevent the blow that this prince was going to strike in my favor at the behest of the ducs d'Ossune and de Médina Sidonia,[236] had impressed upon him that the constable desired nothing more zealously than to see me in a cloister and that it would be an inestimable favor to him to keep me there. Since that declaration had made His Highness suspend his decision and had obliged this prince to put my freedom back at the disposition of Monsieur le président de Castille, who did not attend to the matter any more actively than he had done before, I found it necessary to present another petition to His Majesty along with another for His Highness, which was submitted to him by the duc de Médina Sidonia. But when this prince was resolved to grant me everything for which I could have hoped from his justice, a letter came from the constable, who had learned of my last exit from the convent and asked His Majesty earnestly to please have me put in a castle.[237] Thereupon, His Highness, in order to ex-

---

235. In January 1677.

236. Don Juan Clarós de Guzmán, duke of Medina Sidonia, marquis of Cazaza and of Valverde, count of Niebla (1642–1713).

237. The constable's request that his wife be put into "a castle" (*un château*) was in effect a request that she be imprisoned in a fortress.

tricate himself from this delicate pass with his usual prudence, declined to resolve anything, and submitted my petition and the constable's letter to the Council of State; I sent an appeal to the councilors and drew promises from Messieurs les ducs d'Ossune and d'Albe,[238] and from Monsieur le marquis d'Astorga,[239] that they would do all they could for me. They kept their word to me, and most councilors expressed opinions in my favor and concluded that I would be granted complete freedom and placed in a house where I would be served in accordance with my rank and my quality. As soon as I was informed of this favorable *consulte,* I wrote to Don Hieronime d'Eguia,[240] secretary of universal dispatches, begging him not to defer putting it into the king's hands, so that His Majesty might issue orders in the matter as it pleased him. He did not reply to me in writing but had me told very obligingly that he would do what I desired of him without delay; he acquitted himself of his promise, and two days later I learned, to use the terms of that court, that the *consulte* was "upstairs." Soon afterward, I received from Monsieur Don Barthelemy de Legasa, secretary of state, a sort of decree, the content of which was that His Majesty, after having seen my petition and the letter from the constable, had seen fit to suspend his decision until he had written to him, but that in the meantime, if it pleased me to choose some small place in the vicinity of Madrid where the air would be good and healthy, His Majesty would consent to my withdrawing there until the final decision. However, the abbé Don Ferdinand Colonna, who was informed of everything that was happening and to whom the constable had given a very strict directive to make all possible efforts to have me put into a castle in the event that there were no way to keep me enclosed, did everything he could think of to prevent my freedom. He even presented a written chronicle in which he laid out at great length the disadvantages to granting it to me and expressed how important it was to the constable's peace of mind that I stay in a cloister or that I be put in a castle. Fearing therefore that this opposition

238. Don Antonio Álvarez de Toledo, seventh duke of Alba (or Alba de Tormes) and of Huesca, marquis of Coria, count of Salvatierra, seigneur of Valdecorneja, etc. (1615–90). Don Antonio's ancestor Fernando Álvarez de Toledo, third duke of Alba de Tormes (1507–82), was a notoriously brutal governor of the Low Countries in the mid-sixteenth century, who was known as the Iron Duke because of his ruthless repression of Protestants and other rebels against Spanish rule.

239. Don Antonio Davila y Osorio, marquis of Astorga, of Velada, and of San Roman, count of Trastamara, and seigneur of Villalobos.

240. Don Geronimo d'Eguya had the post of secretary of state *del despacho,* a lucrative office which was directly attached to the persons of the king and of the chief minister. Perey cites the estimation of Don Geronimo by the marquis de Villars, the French ambassador to Spain: "He was an intellect of limited capacities, muddle-headed, neither punctual in business nor trustworthy in what he promises." *Une princesse romaine,* 384 n. 1.

by Don Ferdinand might have an outcome which would not be favorable for me, and that it might cause a change in the decision that had already been made (and there was a fair chance of this, for I had learned from a good source that the councilors had been quite swayed by what he had put forward), I felt obliged to avoid by my exit the blow with which I saw myself threatened. I gave notice of my plan to Monsieur le Nonce, to Monsieur le duc d'Ossune, and to Donna Victoria Porcia Orosco, whom I have already mentioned and who did not disapprove of it, since she believed the decree that had been sent to me was entirely in due form and valid; after having given this notice, I got up extremely early, for fear that a nun friend of mine who slept in the same apartment might discover my intention, which she did not fail to do anyway despite all my precautions, and I left at six o'clock. I went first to the parlor, to converse with some nuns whom I had summoned there while I waited for the coach I had hired to arrive; for the marquise de Mortare, from whom I had requested a coach in writing the day before, and whom I had begged to send me one of her women, had declined to do so with a reply she had sent the evening before to Donna Victoria Porcia, her sister-in-law, on the advice that some of her lady friends had given her not to get mixed up in my affairs, so as not to find herself in the same trouble she had encountered before because of me. When the coach finally came after two hours, I went with two of my maids as far as Atocha, where I found the procurator[241] of the convent from which I had just come, who had arrived there ahead of me in order to say mass for me as I had asked him to do. Four days before my exit from the convent, I had notified Don Barthelemy de Legasa that I had chosen as my retreat the town of Ballecas[242] (which belongs to the king and is located one league from Madrid), so that he could inform His Majesty of it, and I had requested another coach from Monsieur le marquis de Camarassa,[243] with the excuse that I wanted to send two of my maids there to have a residence prepared in the house of Donna Cicilia de Vera, who had given it to me with the exception of an apartment which is occupied by Monsieur le prince de Montesarchio[244] and where he is more or less a prisoner on his honor. This coach made no more haste than

---

241. The *père procureur* is the friar responsible for the temporal interests of a religious establishment.

242. Vallecas is located seven miles southeast of the center of Madrid.

243. The marquis of Camarasa at this time was Don Baltasar Gomez Manrique de Mendoza Los Cobos y Luna (or Don Baltasar de Los Cobos Sarmiento de Mendoza, or Don Baltasar de Los Cobos Luna Sarmiento de Mendoza Zúñiga y Manrique), fifth marquis of Camarasa (d. 1715). He was also viceroy of Aragon in 1692–93 and again in 1696–99.

244. Don Andrea d'Avalos d'Aquino d'Aragona, prince of Montesarchio, and grandee of Spain of the first class in 1707 (1618–1709).

the first, and after I had heard four masses while I waited, it finally arrived with a gentleman whom I had taken into my service, and who had been recommended to me formerly by the constable. We went all together to the house I have just mentioned, where we found at that time only the servants of Monsieur le prince de Montesarchio; they left his apartment to us because it was the better one, and they had a very good dinner prepared for us. After the meal, Monsieur le Nonce came at four or five o'clock, accompanied by the abbé Don Ferdinand Colonna; after having given me absolution for the excommunication that I had incurred for having left the convent without permission, he convinced me with such keen arguments of the good reasons that Don Ferdinand had had for presenting to the council of state the petition that I mentioned above, and he made such tactful excuses for the declarations that the latter had made there against my freedom and in favor of the constable, that I could not afterward refuse his plea that I take Don Ferdinand into my good graces. I slept that night at Ballecas, where the dampness of the apartment I was in gave me a cold which kept me from sleeping all night long; and when it was followed the next day by a fever, it made me resolve to go to Madrid and stay in the house of Don Ferdinand Colonna, which I knew to be very good and very comfortable. Thus I dispatched a page straightaway to the duc d'Ossune, asking him to send me posthaste a six-mule coach (for they do not speak of horses here); a moment later Don Ferdinand came into my apartment, and I told him of my plan and begged him not to oppose it. He made me that promise, and not only did he keep his word, but he even wrote to Monsieur le Nonce about the matter; impressing upon him the miserable state in which he had found me and pointing out that it would be more appropriate that I be in Madrid and that I await His Majesty's orders at his house, he asked him to send me a coach as soon as possible. I was extremely happy about this request, since I feared that the duc d'Ossune might use his capacity as minister as a reason to refrain from sending me one. The Nuncio immediately relayed the letter that Don Ferdinand had written him to Don Barthelemy de Legasa, who, after having conferred about it with a number of councilors, replied that they had not seen fit that the Nuncio should grant me what he was being asked to grant. However, he did not stop at this refusal but showed the letter to Don Hieronime d'Eguia, who showed it to His Highness; Don Hieronime received the order from this prince to tell Monsieur le Nonce that he saw no reason not to grant me what Don Ferdinand had requested of him. Thereupon he dispatched a coach and some other carriages for my train, after I had waited in vain for the one from the duc d'Ossune; after having detained my page for a full eight hours because of the various meetings with which he was occupied, the duc had sent him back to me with assurances that he would come to see me. I appreciated very much the honor that he was offering to do me, but to be frank, I would have appreciated his coach more, in my impatience to return to Madrid, and with the apprehension I had felt all day that some order forbidding me to go there might arrive at any moment. My apprehension was especially strong when I saw one of His Highness's footmen come in with a letter, in which the prince pointed out to me that I had not properly interpreted His Majesty's orders and that other procedures should rightly have preceded my exit from the convent, both in regard to the choice of place and as concerned the way for me to reside there in all the splendor that His Majesty considered to be due my person. However, I recovered a bit from my fright when I saw that it was not an order but a little reprimand; and after I had been on pins and needles for a long time, Monsieur le Nonce's coach came, and I climbed in straightaway in an incredible rush, still apprehensive that I might be detained where I was. About halfway through my journey, I encountered Messieurs les ducs d'Ossune, de Veraguas,[245] and d'Uzeda,[246] and Father Vintimilla, who were coming to see me followed by four coaches and a great many servants on horseback. When I teased the first about his punctuality, he told me that I had no reason to complain, that it was much more proper for civility's sake to come himself than to send a coach, and that he had gone above and beyond what I had asked of him, since instead of one coach he was bringing me four, of which I could dispose as I wished so long as Don Ferdinand agreed to accompany me. His coach and mine traveled side by side as far as the gates of Madrid, where we went our separate ways, and then I came across Monsieur le Nonce, who was on foot and who approached my coach most obligingly and gave me some advice which I have since followed and which has come out well for me. Following this fortuitous meeting, I went straight to Don Ferdinand's house, where I am at present, awaiting His Majesty's decision on my fate. I do not know yet what will become of me, although I have reason to hope from the goodness and the justice of this

---

245. Don Pedro II Manuel Nuno Colon de Portugal y Sandoval, duke of Veragua and of La Vega, count of Gelves, marquis of Jamaica and of Villamizar (1651–1710). The duchy of Veragua was given by Charles V to Don Diego Colon (1474–1526), son of Christopher Columbus.

246. The man to whom Marie refers as the duke of Uceda was in fact the son-in-law of the duke of Osuna, married to his daughter, Doña Isabel María Téllez Girón (or Isabel María de Sandoval y Girón), duchess of Uceda (1653–1711). Doña Isabel inherited the title from her mother, Doña Felice de Sandoval, who died in 1671; Doña Isabel was married to Don Juan Francisco Téllez Girón, count of la Puebla de Montalbán (b. 1649).

prince, and from the great prudence of His Highness, that I will come to the end of all my woes and will find the peace that I desire with a passion as great as is my need for it.[247]

247. Of course, Marie's woes continued for years after the composition of this memoir in 1677. Her husband came to Spain in 1678 to take up the post of viceroy of Aragon and also to negotiate the marriage of their eldest son, Filippo, to a daughter of the duke of Medinaceli (Don Juan Francisco de la Cerda y Enríquez de Ribera, duke of Medinaceli and of Alcalá de los Gazules, 1637–91). Lorenzo stayed in Spain, sometimes in Madrid and sometimes at his post in Saragossa, until after Filippo's wedding, which took place in April 1681 in Madrid. During that period, Marie was compelled to live for a time in her husband's house in Madrid, and from there, strangely enough, she was forcibly removed and imprisoned in the *alcazar* of Segovia by order of the duke of Medinaceli himself. She was released from this imprisonment only when she agreed to take religious vows and enter a convent as a nun; she remained there as a novice from February 1681 until 1686, when the pope ordered that she leave because she had not taken orders. She actually went to live briefly at the home of the duke of Medinaceli, to whom she was then related through the marriage of their children, but eventually was allowed to take up residence again in another Madrid convent. Meanwhile, her sister Olympe sojourned in Madrid from 1686 until 1689, after having fled France in January 1680 in the wake of the Affair of the Poisons. Lorenzo died in 1689, and Marie returned to Rome in 1691, but she stayed there only a few months before returning to Madrid. From then until her death in Pisa in May 1715, she made several trips back and forth between Spain and Italy. She passed through southern France on more than one occasion, but she never tried again to see Louis XIV, who died himself just four months after she did.

APPENDIX A

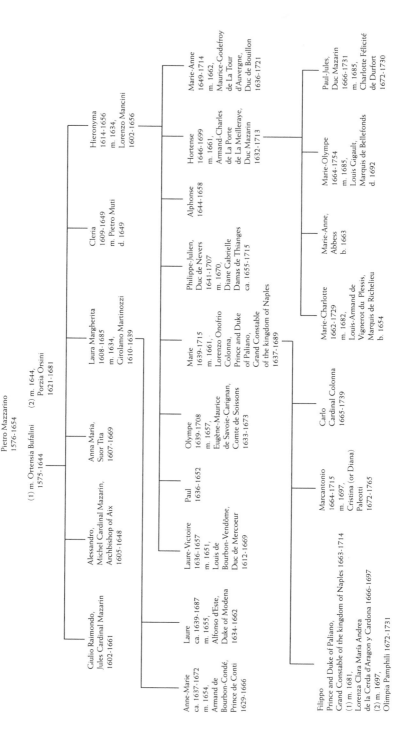

Pietro Mazzarino
1576-1654

(1) m. Ortensia Bufalini
1575-1644

(2) m. 1644,
Porzia Orsini
1621-1681

Giulio Raimondo,
Jules Cardinal Mazarin
1602-1661

Alessandro,
Michel Cardinal Mazarin,
Archbishop of Aix
1605-1648

Anna Maria,
Suor Tita
1607-1669

Laura Margherita
1608-1685
m. 1634,
Girolamo Martinozzi
1610-1639

Cleria
1609-1649
m. Pietro Muti
d. 1649

Hieronyma
1614-1656
m. 1634,
Lorenzo Mancini
1602-1656

Anne-Marie
ca. 1637-1672
m. 1654,
Armand de
Bourbon-Condé,
Prince de Conti
1629-1666

Laure
ca. 1639-1687
m. 1655,
Alfonso d'Este,
Duke of Modena
1634-1662

Laure-Victoire
1636-1657
m. 1651,
Louis de
Bourbon-Vendôme,
Duc de Mercoeur
1612-1669

Paul
1636-1652

Olympe
1639-1708
m. 1657,
Eugène-Maurice
de Savoie-Carignan,
Comte de Soissons
1633-1673

Marie
1639-1715
m. 1661,
Lorenzo Onofrio
Colonna,
Prince and Duke
of Paliano,
Grand Constable
of the kingdom of Naples
1637-1689

Philippe-Julien,
Duc de Nevers
1641-1707
m. 1670,
Diane Gabrielle
Damas de Thianges
ca. 1655-1715

Alphonse
1644-1658

Hortense
1646-1699
m. 1661,
Armand-Charles
de La Porte
de La Meilleraye,
Duc Mazarin
1632-1713

Marie-Anne
1649-1714
m. 1662,
Maurice-Godefroy
de La Tour
d'Auvergne,
Duc de Bouillon
1636-1721

Filippo
Prince and Duke of Paliano,
Grand Constable of the kingdom of Naples 1663-1714
(1) m. 1681,
Lorenza Clara María Andrea
de la Cerda d'Aragon y Cardona 1666-1697
(2) m. 1697,
Olimpia Pamphili 1672-1731

Marcantonio
1664-1715
m. 1697,
Cristina (or Diana)
Paleotti
1672-1765

Carlo
Cardinal Colonna
1665-1739

Marie-Charlotte
1662-1729
m. 1682,
Louis-Armand de
Vignerot du Plessis,
Marquis de Richelieu
b. 1654

Marie-Anne,
Abbess
b. 1663

Marie-Olympe
1664-1754
m. 1685,
Louis Gigault,
Marquis de Bellefonds
d. 1692

Paul-Jules,
Duc Mazarin
1666-1731
m. 1685,
Charlotte Félicité
de Durfort
1672-1730

APPENDIX A: Genealogical chart of the Mazzarino and Mancini families, including the children of Marie and of Hortense Mancini (but not those of their siblings and cousins).

APPENDIX B

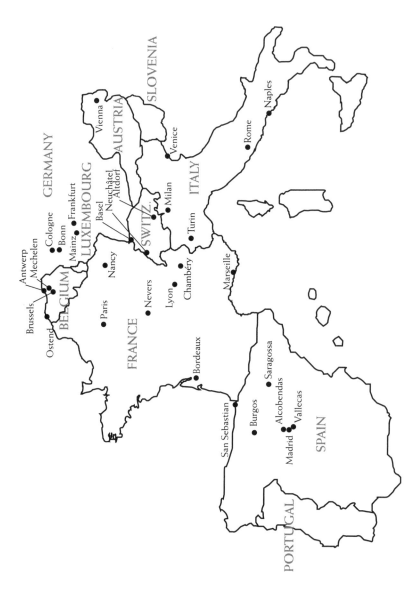

APPENDIX B: Map of present-day Western Europe with places mentioned in the memoirs of Hortense and of Marie Mancini.

APPENDIX C

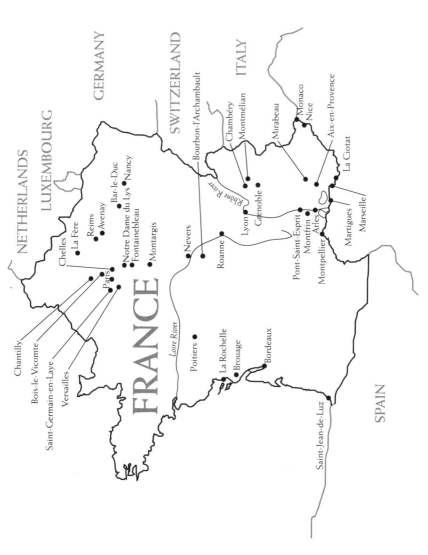

APPENDIX C: Map of present-day France with places mentioned in the memoirs of Hortense and of Marie Mancini.

APPENDIX D

APPENDIX D: Map of present-day Italy with places mentioned in the memoirs of Hortense and of Marie Mancini.

SERIES EDITORS' BIBLIOGRAPHY

PRIMARY SOURCES

Alberti, Leon Battista (1404–72). *The Family in Renaissance Florence.* Trans. Renée Neu Watkins. Columbia, SC: University of South Carolina Press, 1969.

Arenal, Electa, and Stacey Schlau, eds. *Untold Sisters: Hispanic Nuns in Their Own Works.* Trans. Amanda Powell. Albuquerque, NM: University of New Mexico Press, 1989.

Astell, Mary (1666–1731). *The First English Feminist: Reflections on Marriage and Other Writings.* Ed. and Introd. Bridget Hill. New York: St. Martin's Press, 1986.

Atherton, Margaret, ed. *Women Philosophers of the Early Modern Period.* Indianapolis, IN: Hackett Publishing Co., 1994.

Aughterson, Kate, ed. *Renaissance Woman: Constructions of Femininity in England: A Source Book.* London and New York: Routledge, 1995.

Barbaro, Francesco (1390–1454). *On Wifely Duties.* Trans. Benjamin Kohl in Kohl and R. G. Witt, eds., *The Earthly Republic.* Philadelphia: University of Pennsylvania Press, 1978, 179–228. Translation of the preface and book 2.

Behn, Aphra. *The Works of Aphra Behn.* 7 vols. Ed. Janet Todd. Columbus, OH: Ohio State University Press, 1992–96.

Blamires, Alcuin, ed. *Woman Defamed and Woman Defended: An Anthology of Medieval Texts.* Oxford: Clarendon Press, 1992.

Boccaccio, Giovanni (1313–75). *Famous Women.* Ed. and trans. Virginia Brown. The I Tatti Renaissance Library. Cambridge, MA: Harvard University Press, 2001.

———. *Corbaccio or the Labyrinth of Love.* Trans. Anthony K. Cassell. Second revised edition. Binghamton, NY: Medieval and Renaissance Texts and Studies, 1993.

Booy, David, ed. *Autobiographical Writings by Early Quaker Women.* Aldershot and Brookfield: Ashgate Publishing Co., 2004.

Brown, Sylvia. *Women's Writing in Stuart England: The Mother's Legacies of Dorothy Leigh, Elizabeth Joscelin and Elizabeth Richardson.* Thrupp, Stroud, Gloceter: Sutton, 1999.

Bruni, Leonardo (1370–1444). "On the Study of Literature (1405) to Lady Battista Malatesta of Moltefeltro." In *The Humanism of Leonardo Bruni: Selected Texts.* Trans. and Introd. Gordon Griffiths, James Hankins, and David Thompson. Binghamton, NY: Medieval and Renaissance Studies and Texts, 1987, 240–51.

Castiglione, Baldassare (1478–1529). *The Book of the Courtier.* Trans. George Bull.

New York: Penguin, 1967; *The Book of the Courtier*. Ed. Daniel Javitch. New York: W. W. Norton & Co., 2002.

Christine de Pizan (1365–1431). *The Book of the City of Ladies*. Trans. Earl Jeffrey Richards. Foreword Marina Warner. New York: Persea Books, 1982.

———. *The Treasure of the City of Ladies*. Trans. Sarah Lawson. New York: Viking Penguin, 1985. Also trans. and introd. Charity Cannon Willard. Ed. and introd. Madeleine P. Cosman. New York: Persea Books, 1989.

Clarke, Danielle, ed. *Isabella Whitney, Mary Sidney and Aemilia Lanyer: Renaissance Women Poets*. New York: Penguin Books, 2000.

Couchman, Jane, and Ann Crabb, eds. *Women's Letters Across Europe, 1400–1700*. Aldershot and Brookfield: Ashgate Publishing Co., 2005.

Crawford, Patricia and Laura Gowing, eds. *Women's Worlds in Seventeenth-Century England: A Source Book*. London and New York: Routledge, 2000.

"Custome Is an Idiot": Jacobean Pamphlet Literature on Women. Ed. Susan Gushee O'Malley. Afterword Ann Rosalind Jones. Chicago and Urbana: University of Illinois Press, 2004.

Daybell, James, ed. *Early Modern Women's Letter Writing, 1450–1700*. Houndmills, England and New York: Palgrave, 2001.

De Erauso, Catalina. *Lieutenant Nun: Memoir of a Basque Transvestite in the New World*. Trans. Michele Ttepto and Gabriel Stepto; foreword by Marjorie Garber. Boston: Beacon Press, 1995.

Elizabeth I: Collected Works. Ed. Leah S. Marcus, Janel Mueller, and Mary Beth Rose. Chicago: University of Chicago Press, 2000.

Elyot, Thomas (1490–1546). *Defence of Good Women: The Feminist Controversy of the Renaissance*. Facsimile Reproductions. Ed. Diane Bornstein. New York: Delmar, 1980.

Erasmus, Desiderius (1467–1536). *Erasmus on Women*. Ed. Erika Rummel. Toronto: University of Toronto Press, 1996.

Female and Male Voices in Early Modern England: An Anthology of Renaissance Writing. Ed. Betty S. Travitsky and Anne Lake Prescott. New York: Columbia University Press, 2000.

Ferguson, Moira, ed. *First Feminists: British Women Writers 1578–1799*. Bloomington, IN: Indiana University Press, 1985.

Galilei, Maria Celeste. *Sister Maria Celeste's Letters to her father, Galileo*. Ed. and trans. Rinaldina Russell. Lincoln, NE, and New York: Writers Club Press of Universe. com, 2000; *To Father: The Letters of Sister Maria Celeste to Galileo, 1623–1633*. Trans. Dava Sobel. London: Fourth Estate, 2001.

Gethner, Perry, ed. *The Lunatic Lover and Other Plays by French Women of the 17th and 18th Centuries*. Portsmouth, NH: Heinemann, 1994.

Glückel of Hameln (1646–1724). *The Memoirs of Glückel of Hameln*. Trans. Marvin Lowenthal. New Introd. Robert Rosen. New York: Schocken Books, 1977.

Harline, Craig, ed. *The Burdens of Sister Margaret: Inside a Seventeenth-Century Convent*. Abridged ed. New Haven: Yale University Press, 2000.

Henderson, Katherine Usher, and Barbara F. McManus, eds. *Half Humankind: Contexts and Texts of the Controversy about Women in England, 1540–1640*. Urbana: University of Illinois Press, 1985.

Hoby, Margaret. *The Private Life of an Elizabethan Lady: The Diary of Lady Margaret Hoby 1599–1605*. Phoenix Mill: Sutton Publishing, 1998.

Humanist Educational Treatises. Ed. and trans. Craig W. Kallendorf. The I Tatti Renaissance Library. Cambridge, MA: Harvard University Press, 2002.

Hunter, Lynette, ed. *The Letters of Dorothy Moore, 1612–64.* Aldershot and Brookfield: Ashgate Publishing Co., 2004.

Joscelin, Elizabeth. *The Mothers Legacy to her Unborn Childe.* Ed. Jean leDrew Metcalfe. Toronto: University of Toronto Press, 2000.

Kaminsky, Amy Katz, ed. *Water Lilies, Flores del agua: An Anthology of Spanish Women Writers from the Fifteenth Through the Nineteenth Century.* Minneapolis: University of Minnesota Press, 1996.

Kempe, Margery (1373–1439). *The Book of Margery Kempe.* Trans. and ed. Lynn Staley. A Norton Critical Edition. New York: W. W. Norton, 2001.

King, Margaret L., and Albert Rabil, Jr., eds. *Her Immaculate Hand: Selected Works by and about the Women Humanists of Quattrocento Italy.* Binghamton, NY: Medieval and Renaissance Texts and Studies, 1983; second revised paperback edition, 1991.

Klein, Joan Larsen, ed. *Daughters, Wives, and Widows: Writings by Men about Women and Marriage in England, 1500–1640.* Urbana, IL: University of Illinois Press, 1992.

Knox, John (1505–72). *The Political Writings of John Knox: The First Blast of the Trumpet against the Monstrous Regiment of Women and Other Selected Works.* Ed. Marvin A. Breslow. Washington: Folger Shakespeare Library, 1985.

Kors, Alan C., and Edward Peters, eds. *Witchcraft in Europe, 400-1700: A Documentary History.* Philadelphia: University of Pennsylvania Press, 2000.

Krämer, Heinrich, and Jacob Sprenger. *Malleus Maleficarum* (ca. 1487). Trans. Montague Summers. London: Pushkin Press, 1928; reprinted New York: Dover, 1971.

Larsen, Anne R., and Colette H. Winn, eds. *Writings by Pre-Revolutionary French Women: From Marie de France to Elizabeth Vigée-Le Brun.* New York and London: Garland Publishing Co., 2000.

de Lorris, William, and Jean de Meun. *The Romance of the Rose.* Trans. Charles Dahlbert. Princeton: Princeton University Press, 1971; reprinted University Press of New England, 1983.

Marcus, Leah S., Janel Mueller, and Mary Beth Rose, eds. *Elizabeth I: Collected Works.* Chicago: University of Chicago Press, 2000.

Marguerite d'Angoulême, Queen of Navarre (1492–1549). *The Heptameron.* Trans. P. A. Chilton. New York: Viking Penguin, 1984.

Mary of Agreda. *The Divine Life of the Most Holy Virgin.* Abridgment of *The Mystical City of God.* Abr. by Fr. Bonaventure Amedeo de Caesarea, M.C. Trans. from French by Abbé Joseph A. Boullan. Rockford, IL: Tan Books, 1997.

Mullan, David George. *Women's Life Writing in Early Modern Scotland: Writing the Evangelical Self, c. 1670–c. 1730.* Aldershot and Brookfield: Ashgate Publishing Co., 2003.

Myers, Kathleen A., and Amanda Powell, eds. *A Wild Country Out in the Garden: The Spiritual Journals of a Colonial Mexican Nun.* Bloomington: Indiana University Press, 1999.

Russell, Rinaldina, ed. *Sister Maria Celeste's Letters to Her Father, Galileo.* San Jose and New York: Writers Club Press, 2000.

Teresa of Avila, Saint (1515–82). *The Life of Saint Teresa of Avila by Herself.* Trans. J. M. Cohen. New York: Viking Penguin, 1957.

———. *The Collected Letters of St. Teresa of Avila. Volume One: 1546–1577,* trans. Kieran Kavanaugh. Washington, DC: Institute of Carmelite Studies, 2001.

Travitsky, Betty, ed. *The Paradise of Women: Writings by Entlishwomen of the Renaissance.* Westport, CT: Greenwood Press, 1981.

Weyer, Johann (1515–88). *Witches, Devils, and Doctors in the Renaissance: Johann Weyer, De praestigiis daemonum.* Ed. George Mora with Benjamin G. Kohl, Erik Midelfort, and Helen Bacon. Trans. John Shea. Binghamton, NY: Medieval and Renaissance Texts and Studies, 1991.

Wilson, Katharina M., ed. *Medieval Women Writers.* Athens: University of Georgia Press, 1984.

———, ed. *Women Writers of the Renaissance and Reformation.* Athens: University of Georgia Press, 1987.

———, and Frank J. Warnke, eds. *Women Writers of the Seventeenth Century.* Athens: University of Georgia Press, 1989.

Wollstonecraft, Mary. *A Vindication of the Rights of Men and a Vindication of the Rights of Women.* Ed. Sylvana Tomaselli. Cambridge: Cambridge University Press, 1995. Also *The Vindications of the Rights of Men, The Rights of Women.* Ed. D. L. Macdonald and Kathleen Scherf. Peterborough, Ontario, Canada: Broadview Press, 1997.

Woman Defamed and Woman Defended: An Anthology of Medieval Texts. Ed. Alcuin Blamires. Oxford: Clarendon Press, 1992.

Women Critics 1660–1820: An Anthology. Edited by the Folger Collective on Early Women Critics. Bloomington, IN: Indiana University Press, 1995.

Women Writers in English 1350–1850: 15 published through 1999 (projected 30-volume series suspended). Oxford University Press.

Women's Letters Across Europe, 1400–1700. Ed. Jane Couchman and Ann Crabb. Aldershot and Brookfield: Ashgate Publishing Co., 2005.

Wroth, Lady Mary. *The Countess of Montgomery's Urania.* 2 parts. Ed. Josephine A. Roberts. Tempe, AZ: MRTS, 1995, 1999.

———. *Lady Mary Wroth's "Love's Victory": The Penshurst Manuscript.* Ed. Michael G. Brennan. London: The Roxburghe Club, 1988.

———. *The Poems of Lady Mary Wroth.* Ed. Josephine A. Roberts. Baton Rouge: Louisiana State University Press, 1983.

de Zayas Maria. *The Disenchantments of Love.* Trans. H. Patsy Boyer. Albany: State University of New York Press, 1997.

———. *The Enchantments of Love: Amorous and Exemplary Novels.* Trans. H. Patsy Boyer. Berkeley: University of California Press, 1990.

SECONDARY SOURCES

Abate, Corinne S., ed. *Privacy, Domesticity, and Women in Early Modern England.* Aldershot and Brookfield: Ashgate Publishing Co., 2003.

Ahlgren, Gillian. *Teresa of Avila and the Politics of Sanctity.* Ithaca: Cornell University Press, 1996.

Akkerman, Tjitske, and Siep Sturman, eds. *Feminist Thought in European History, 1400–2000.* London and New York: Routledge, 1997.

Allen, Sister Prudence, R.S.M. *The Concept of Woman: The Aristotelian Revolution, 750 B.C. – A.D. 1250.* Grand Rapids, MI: William B. Eerdmans Publishing Company, 1997.

————. *The Concept of Woman: Volume II: The early Humanist Reformation, 1250–1500.* Grand Rapids, MI: William B. Eerdmans Publishing Company, 2002.

Altmann, Barbara K., and Deborah L. McGrady, eds. *Christine de Pizan: A Casebook.* New York: Routledge, 2003.

Ambiguous Realities: Women in the Middle Ages and Renaissance. Ed. Carole Levin and Jeanie Watson. Detroit: Wayne State University Press, 1987.

Amussen, Susan D, and Adele Seeff, eds. *Attending to Early Modern Women.* Newark: University of Delaware Press, 1998.

Andreadis, Harriette. *Sappho in Early Modern England: Female Same-Sex Literary Erotics 1550–1714.* Chicago: University of Chicago Press, 2001.

Architecture and the Politics of Gender in Early Modern Europe. Ed. Helen Hills. Aldershot and Brookfield: Ashgate Publishing Co., 2003.

Armon, Shifra. *Picking Wedlock: Women and the Courtship Novel in Spain.* New York: Rowman and Littlefield Publishers, Inc., 2002.

Attending to Early Modern Women. Ed. Susan D. Amussen and Adele Seeff. Newark: University of Delaware Press, 1998.

Backer, Anne Liot. *Precious Women.* New York: Basic Books, 1974.

Ballaster, Ros. *Seductive Forms.* New York: Oxford University Press, 1992.

Barash, Carol. *English Women's Poetry, 1649–1714: Politics, Community, and Linguistic Authority.* New York and Oxford: Oxford University Press, 1996.

Barker, Alele Marie, and Jehanne M. Gheith, eds. *A History of Women's Writing in Russia.* Cambridge: Cambridge University Press, 2002.

Battigelli, Anna. *Margaret Cavendish and the Exiles of the Mind.* Lexington: University of Kentucky Press, 1998.

Beasley, Faith. *Revising Memory: Women's Fiction and Memoirs in Seventeenth-Century France.* New Brunswick: Rutgers University Press, 1990.

————. *Salons, History, and the Creation of Seventeenth-Century France.* Aldershot and Brookfield: Ashgate Publishing Co., 2006.

Becker, Lucinda M. *Death and the Early Modern Englishwoman.* Aldershot and Brookfield: Ashgate Publishing Co., 2003.

Beilin, Elaine V. *Redeeming Eve: Women Writers of the English Renaissance.* Princeton: Princeton University Press, 1987.

Bennett, Lyn. *Women Writing of Divinest Things: Rhetoric and the Poetry of Pembroke, Wroth, and Lanyer.* Pittsburgh: Duquesne University Press, 2004.

Benson, Pamela Joseph. *The Invention of Renaissance Woman: The Challenge of Female Independence in the Literature and Thought of Italy and England.* University Park: Pennsylvania State University Press, 1992.

————— and Victoria Kirkham, eds. *Strong Voices, Weak History? Medieval and Renaissance Women in their Literary Canons: England, France, Italy.* Ann Arbor: University of Michigan Press, 2003.

Berry, Helen. *Gender, Society and Print Culture in Late-Stuart England.* Aldershot and Brookfield: Ashgate Publishing Co., 2003.

Beyond Isabella: Secular Women Patrons of Art in Renaissance Italy. Ed. Sheryl E. Reiss and David G. Wilkins. Kirksville, MO: Turman State University Press, 2001.

Beyond Their Sex: Learned Women of the European Past. Ed. Patricia A. Labalme. New York: New York University Press, 1980.

Bicks, Caroline. *Midwiving Subjects in Shakespeare's England.* Aldershot and Brookfield: Ashgate Publishing Co., 2003.

Bilinkoff, Jodi. *The Avila of Saint Teresa: Religious Reform in a Sixteenth-Century City.* Ithaca: Cornell University Press, 1989.

————. *Related Lives: Confessors and Their Female Penitents, 1450–1750.* Ithaca, NY: Cornell University Press, 2005.

Bissell, R. Ward. *Artemisia Gentileschi and the Authority of Art.* University Park: Pennsylvania State University Press, 2000.

Blain, Virginia, Isobel Grundy, and Patricia Clements, eds. *The Feminist Companion to Literature in English: Women Writers from the Middle Ages to the Present.* New Haven: Yale University Press, 1990.

Blamires, Alcuin. *The Case for Women in Medieval Culture.* Oxford: Clarendon Press, 1997.

Bloch, R. Howard. *Medieval Misogyny and the Invention of Western Romantic Love.* Chicago: University of Chicago Press, 1991.

Bogucka, Maria. *Women in Early Modern Polish Society, Against the European Background.* Aldershot and Brookfield: Ashgate Publishing Co., 2004.

Bornstein, Daniel, and Roberto Rusconi, eds. *Women and Religion in Medieval and Renaissance Italy.* Trans. Margery J. Schneider. Chicago: University of Chicago Press, 1996.

Brant, Clare, and Diane Purkiss, eds. *Women, Texts and Histories, 1575–1760.* London and New York: Routledge, 1992.

Briggs, Robin. *Witches and Neighbours: The Social and Cultural Context of European Witchcraft.* New York: HarperCollins, 1995; Viking Penguin, 1996.

Brink, Jean R., ed. *Female Scholars: A Traditioin of Learned Women before 1800.* Montréal: Eden Press Women's Publications, 1980.

————, Allison Coudert, and Maryanne Cline Horowitz. *The Politics of Gender in Early Modern Europe.* Sixteenth Century Essays and Studies, 12. Kirksville, MO: Sixteenth Century Journal Publishers, 1989.

Broude, Norma, and Mary D. Garrard, eds. *The Expanding Discourse: Feminism and Art History.* New York: HarperCollins, 1992.

Brown, Judith C. *Immodest Acts: The Life of a Lesbian Nun in Renaissance Italy.* New York: Oxford University Press, 1986.

———— and Robert C. Davis, eds. *Gender and Society in Renaisance Italy.* London: Addison Wesley Longman, 1998.

Burke, Victoria E. Burke, ed. *Early Modern Women's Manuscript Writing.* Aldershot and Brookfield: Ashgate Publishing Co., 2004.

Burns, Jane E., ed. *Medieval Fabrications: Dress, Textiles, Cloth Work, and Other Cultural Imaginings.* New York: Palgrave Macmillan, 2004.

Bynum, Carolyn Walker. *Fragmentation and Redemption: Essays on Gender and the Human Body in Medieval Religion.* New York: Zone Books, 1992.

————. *Holy Feast and Holy Fast: The Religious Significance of Food to Medieval Women.* Berkeley: University of California Press, 1987.

Campbell, Julie DeLynn. "Renaissance Women Writers: The Beloved Speaks her Part." Ph.D diss., Texas A&M University, 1997.

Catling, Jo, ed. *A History of Women's Writing in Germany, Austria and Switzerland.* Cambridge: Cambridge University Press, 2000.

Cavallo, Sandra, and Lyndan Warner. *Widowhood in Medieval and Early Modern Europe.* New York: Longman, 1999.

Cavanagh, Sheila T. *Cherished Torment: The Emotional Geography of Lady Mary Wroth's Urania*. Pittsburgh: Duquesne University Press, 2001.

Cerasano, S. P., and Marion Wynne-Davies, eds. *Readings in Renaissance Women's Drama: Criticism, History, and Performance 1594–1998*. London and New York: Routledge, 1998.

Cervigni, Dino S., ed. *Women Mystic Writers. Annali d'Italianistica* 13 (1995) (entire issue).

———and Rebecca West, eds. *Women's Voices in Italian Literature*. Special issue. *Annali d'Italianistica* 7 (1989).

Charlton, Kenneth. *Women, Religion and Education in Early Modern England*. London and New York: Routledge, 1999.

Chojnacka, Monica. *Working Women in Early Modern Venice*. Baltimore: Johns Hopkins University Press, 2001.

Chojnacki, Stanley. *Women and Men in Renaissance Venice: Twelve Essays on Patrician Society*. Baltimore: Johns Hopkins University Press, 2000.

Cholakian, Patricia Francis. *Rape and Writing in the* Heptameron *of Marguerite de Navarre*. Carbondale and Edwardsville: Southern Illinois University Press, 1991.

———. *Women and the Politics of Self-Representation in Seventeenth-Century France*. Newark: University of Delaware Press, 2000.

Christine de Pizan: A Casebook. Ed. Barbara K. Altmann and Deborah L. McGrady. New York: Routledge, 2003.

Clogan, Paul Maruice, ed. *Medievali et Humanistica: Literacy and the Lay Reader*. Lanham, MD: Rowman & Littlefield, 2000.

Clubb, Louise George (1989). *Italian Drama in Shakespeare's Time*. New Haven: Yale University Press

Clucas, Stephen, ed. *A Princely Brave Woman: Essays on Margaret Cavendish, Duchess of Newcastle*. Aldershot and Brookfield: Ashgate Publishing Co., 2003.

Conley, John J., S.J. *The Suspicion of Virtue: Women Philosophers in Neoclassical France*. Ithaca, NY: Cornell University Press, 2002.

Crabb, Ann. *The Strozzi of Florence: Widowhood and Family Solidarity in the Renaissance*. Ann Arbor: University of Michigan Press, 2000.

The Crannied Wall: Women, Religion, and the Arts in Early Modern Europe. Ed. Craig A. Monson. Ann Arbor: University of Michigan Press, 1992.

Creative Women in Medieval and Early Modern Italy. Ed. E. Ann Matter and John Coakley. Philadelphia: University of Pennsylvania Press, 1994.

Crowston, Clare Haru. *Fabricating Women: The Seamstresses of Old Regime France, 1675–1791*. Durham, NC: Duke University Press, 2001.

Cruz, Anne J. and Mary Elizabeth Perry, eds. *Culture and Control in Counter-Reformation Spain*. Minneapolis: University of Minnesota Press, 1992.

Datta, Satya. *Women and Men in Early Modern Venice*. Aldershot and Brookfield: Ashgate Publishing Co., 2003.

Davis, Natalie Zemon. *Society and Culture in Early Modern France*. Stanford: Stanford University Press, 1975.

———. *Women on the Margins: Three Seventeenth-Century Lives*. Cambridge, MA: Harvard University Press, 1995.

DeJean, Joan. *Ancients against Moderns: Culture Wars and the Making of a Fin de Siècle*. Chicago: University of Chicago Press, 1997.

————. *Fictions of Sappho, 1546–1937.* Chicago: University of Chicago Press, 1989.

————. *The Reinvention of Obscenity: Sex, Lies, and Tabloids in Early Modern France.* Chicago: University of Chicago Press, 2002.

————. *Tender Geographies: Women and the Origins of the Novel in France.* New York: Columbia University Press, 1991.

————. *The Reinvention of Obscenity: Sex, Lies, and Tabloids in Early Modern France.* Chicago: University of Chicago Press, 2002.

D'Elia, Anthony F. *The Renaissance of Marriage in Fifteenth-Century Italy.* Cambridge, MA: Harvard University Press, 2004.

Dictionary of Russian Women Writers. Ed. Marina Ledkovsky, Charlotte Rosenthal, and Mary Zirin. Westport, CT: Greenwood Press, 1994.

Dixon, Laurinda S. *Perilous Chastity: Women and Illness in Pre-Enlightenment Art and Medicine.* Ithaca: Cornell University Press, 1995.

Dolan, Frances, E. *Whores of Babylon: Catholicism, Gender and Seventeenth-Century Print Culture.* Ithaca: Cornell University Press, 1999.

Donovan, Josephine. *Women and the Rise of the Novel, 1405–1726.* New York: St. Martin's Press, 1999.

Early [English] Women Writers: 1600–1720. Ed. Anita Pacheco. New York and London: Longman, 1998.

Eigler, Friederike and Susanne Kord, eds. *The Feminist Encyclopedia of German Literature.* Westport, CT: Greenwood Press, 1997.

Engendering the Early Modern Stage: Women Playwrights in the Spanish Empire. Ed. Valeria (Oakey) Hegstrom and Amy R. Williamsen. New Orleans: University Press of the South, 1999.

Erdmann, Axel. *My Gracious Silence: Women in the Mirror of Sixteenth-Century Printing in Western Europe.* Luzern: Gilhofer and Rauschberg, 1999.

Erickson, Amy Louise. *Women and Property in Early Modern England.* London and New York: Routledge, 1993.

Extraordinary Women of the Medieval and Renaissance World: A Biographical Dictionary. Ed. Carole Levin, et al. Westport, CT: Greenwood Press, 2000.

Ezell, Margaret J. M. *The Patriarch's Wife: Literary Evidence and the History of the Family.* Chapel Hill: University of North Carolina Press, 1987.

————. *Social Authorship and the Advent of Print.* Baltimore: Johns Hopkins University Press, 1999.

————. *Writing Women's Literary History.* Baltimore: Johns Hopkins University Press, 1993.

Farrell, Michèle Longino. *Performing Motherhood: The Sévigné Correspondence.* Hanover, NH and London: University Press of New England, 1991.

Feminism and Renaissance Studies. Ed. Lorna Hutson. New York: Oxford University Press, 1999.

The Feminist Companion to Literature in English: Women Writers from the Middle Ages to the Present. Ed. Virginia Blain, Isobel Grundy, and Patricia Clements. New Haven: Yale University Press, 1990.

Feminist Encyclopedia of Italian Literature. Edited by Rinaldina Russell. Westport, CT: Greenwood Press, 1997.

Feminist Thought in European History, 1400–2000. Ed. Tjitske Akkerman and Siep Sturman. London and New York: Routledge, 1997.

Ferguson, Margaret W. *Dido's Daughters: Literacy, Gender, and Empire in Early Modern England and France.* Chicago: University of Chicago Press, 2003.

———, Maureen Quilligan, and Nancy J. Vickers, eds. *Rewriting the Renaissance: The Discourses of Sexual Difference in Early Modern Europe.* Chicago: University of Chicago Press, 1987.

Ferraro, Joanne M. *Marriage Wars in Late Renaissance Venice.* Oxford: Oxford University Press, 2001.

Fletcher, Anthony. *Gender, Sex and Subordination in England 1500–1800.* New Haven: Yale University Press, 1995.

Franklin, Margaret. *Boccaccio's Heroines.* Aldershot and Brookfield: Ashgate Publishing Co., 2006.

French Women Writers: A Bio-Bibliographical Source Book. Ed. Eva Martin Sartori and Dorothy Wynne Zimmerman. Westport, CT: Greenwood Press, 1991.

Frye, Susan and Karen Robertson, eds. *Maids and Mistresses, Cousins and Queens: Women's Alliances in Early Modern England.* Oxford: Oxford University Press, 1999.

Gallagher, Catherine. *Nobody's Story: The Vanishing Acts of Women Writers in the Marketplace, 1670–1820.* Berkeley: University of California Press, 1994.

Garrard, Mary D. *Artemisia Gentileschi: The Image of the Female Hero in Italian Baroque Art.* Princeton: Princeton University Press, 1989.

Gelbart, Nina Rattner. *The King's Midwife: A History and Mystery of Madame du Coudray.* Berkeley: University of California Press, 1998.

Giles, Mary E., ed. *Women in the Inquisition: Spain and the New World.* Baltimore: Johns Hopkins University Press, 1999.

Gill, Catie. *Somen in the Seventeenth-Century Quaker Community.* Aldershot and Brookfield: Ashgate Publishing Co., 2005.

Glenn, Cheryl. *Rhetoric Retold: Regendering the Tradition from Antiquity Through the Renaissance.* Carbondale and Edwardsville, IL: Southern Illinois University Press, 1997.

Goffen, Rona. *Titian's Women.* New Haven: Yale University Press, 1997.

Going Public: Women and Publishing in Early Modern France. Ed. Elizabeth C. Goldsmith and Dena Goodman. Ithaca: Cornell University Press, 1995.

Goldberg, Jonathan. *Desiring Women Writing: English Renaissance Examples.* Stanford: Stanford University Press, 1997.

Goldsmith, Elizabeth C. *Exclusive Conversations: The Art of Interaction in Seventeenth-Century France.* Philadelphia: University of Pennsylvania Press, 1988.

———, ed. *Writing the Female Voice.* Boston: Northeastern University Press, 1989.

——— and Dena Goodman, eds. *Going Public: Women and Publishing in Early Modern France.* Ithaca: Cornell University Press, 1995.

Grafton, Anthony, and Lisa Jardine. *From Humanism to the Humanities: Education and the Liberal Arts in Fifteenth-and Sixteenth-Century Europe.* London: Duckworth, 1986.

The Graph of Sex and the German Text: Gendered Culture in Early Modern Germany 1500–1700. Ed. Lynne Tatlock and Christiane Bohnert. Amsterdam and Atlanta: Rodolphi, 1994.

Grassby, Richard. *Kinship and Capitalism: Marriage, Family, and Business in the English-Speaking World, 1580–1740.* Cambridge: Cambridge University Press, 2001.

Greer, Margaret Rich. *Maria de Zayas Tells Baroque Tales of Love and the Cruelty of Men.* University Park: Pennsylvania State University Press, 2000.

Grossman, Avraham. *Pious and Rebellious: Jewish Women in Medieval Europe.* Trans. Jonathan Chipman. Brandeis/University Press of New England, 2004.

Gutierrez, Nancy A. *"Shall She Famish Then?" Female Food Refusal in Early Modern England.* Aldershot and Brookfield: Ashgate Publishing Co., 2003.

Habermann, Ina. *Staging Slander and Gender in Early Modern England.* Aldershot and Brookfield: Ashgate Publishing Co., 2003.

Hacke, Daniela. *Women Sex and Marriage in Early Modern Venice.* Aldershot and Brookfield: Ashgate Publishing Co., 2004.

Hackel, Heidi Brayman. *Reading Material in Early Modern England: Print, Gender, Literacy.* Cambridge: Cambridge University Press, 2005.

Hackett, Helen. *Women and Romance Fiction in the English Renaissance.* Cambridge: Cambridge University Press, 2000.

Hall, Kim F. *Things of Darkness: Economies of Race and Gender in Early Modern England.* Ithaca, NY: Cornell University Press, 1995.

Hamburger, Jeffrey. *The Visual and the Visionary: Art and Female Spirituality in Late Medieval Germany.* New York: Zone Books, 1998.

Hampton, Timothy. *Literature and the Nation in the Sixteenth Century: Inventing Renaissance France.* Ithaca, NY: Cornell University Press, 2001.

Hannay, Margaret, ed. *Silent But for the Word.* Kent, OH: Kent State University Press, 1985.

Hardwick, Julie. *The Practice of Patriarchy: Gender and the Politics of Household Authority in Early Modern France.* University Park: Pennsylvania State University Press, 1998.

Harris, Barbara J. *English Aristocratic Women, 1450–1550: Marriage and Family, Property and Careers.* New York: Oxford University Press, 2002.

Harth, Erica. *Ideology and Culture in Seventeenth-Century France.* Ithaca: Cornell University Press, 1983.

————. *Cartesian Women. Versions and Subversions of Rational Discourse in the Old Regime.* Ithaca: Cornell University Press, 1992.

Harvey, Elizabeth D. *Ventriloquized Voices: Feminist Theory and English Renaissance Texts.* London and New York: Routledge, 1992.

Haselkorn, Anne M., and Betty Travitsky, eds. *The Renaissance Englishwoman in Print: Counterbalancing the Canon.* Amherst: University of Massachusetts Press, 1990.

Hawkesworth, Celia, ed. *A History of Central European Women's Writing.* New York: Palgrave Press, 2001.

Hegstrom (Oakey), Valerie, and Amy R. Williamsen, eds. *Engendering the Early Modern Stage: Women Playwrights in the Spanish Empire.* New Orleans: University Press of the South, 1999.

Hendricks, Margo, and Patricia Parker, eds. *Women, "Race," and Writing in the Early Modern Period.* London and New York: Routledge, 1994.

Herlihy, David. "Did Women Have a Renaissance? A Reconsideration." *Medievalia et Humanistica* 13 n.s. (1985): 1–22.

Hill, Bridget. *The Republican Virago: The Life and Times of Catharine Macaulay, Historian.* New York: Oxford University Press, 1992.

Hills, Helen, ed. *Architecture and the Politics of Gender in Early Modern Europe.* Aldershot and Brookfield: Ashgate Publishing Co., 2003.

A History of Central European Women's Writing. Ed. Celia Hawkesworth. New York: Palgrave Press, 2001.

A History of Women in the West.

> Volume 1: *From Ancient Goddesses to Christian Saints.* Ed. Pauline Schmitt Pantel. Cambridge, MA: Harvard University Press, 1992.

> Volume 2: *Silences of the Middle Ages.* Ed. Christiane Klapisch-Zuber. Cambridge, MA: Harvard University Press, 1992.

> Volume 3: *Renaissance and Enlightenment Paradoxes.* Ed. Natalie Zemon Davis and Arlette Farge. Cambridge, MA: Harvard University Press, 1993.

A History of Women Philosophers. Ed. Mary Ellen Waithe. 3 vols. Dordrecht: Martinus Nijhoff, 1987.

A History of Women's Writing in France. Ed. Sonya Stephens. Cambridge: Cambridge University Press, 2000.

A History of Women's Writing in Germany, Austria and Switzerland. Ed. Jo Catling. Cambridge: Cambridge University Press, 2000.

A History of Women's Writing in Italy. Ed. Letizia Panizza and Sharon Wood. Cambridge: University Press, 2000.

A History of Women's Writing in Russia. Edited by Alele Marie Barker and Jehanne M. Gheith. Cambridge: Cambridge University Press, 2002.

Hobby, Elaine. *Virtue of Necessity: English Women's Writing, 1646–1688.* London: Virago Press, 1988.

Horowitz, Maryanne Cline. "Aristotle and Women." *Journal of the History of Biology* 9 (1976): 183–213.

Howell, Martha. *The Marriage Exchange: Property, Social Place, and Gender in Cities of the Low Countries, 1300–1550.* Chicago: University of Chicago Press, 1998.

Hufton, Olwen H. *The Prospect before Her: A History of Women in Western Europe, 1: 1500–1800.* New York: HarperCollins, 1996.

Hull, Suzanne W. *Chaste, Silent, and Obedient: English Books for Women, 1475–1640.* San Marino, CA: Huntington Library, 1982.

Hunt, Lynn, ed. *The Invention of Pornography: Obscenity and the Origins of Modernity, 1500–1800.* New York: Zone Books, 1996.

Hutner, Heidi, ed. *Rereading Aphra Behn: History, Theory, and Criticism.* Charlottesville: University Press of Virginia, 1993.

Hutson, Lorna, ed. *Feminism and Renaissance Studies.* New York: Oxford University Press, 1999.

The Invention of Pornography: Obscenity and the Origins of Modernity, 1500–1800. Ed. Lynn Hunt. New York: Zone Books, 1996.

Italian Women Writers: A Bio-Bibliographical Sourcebook. Edited by Rinaldina Russell. Westport, CT: Greenwood Press, 1994.

Jaffe, Irma B., with Gernando Colombardo. *Shining Eyes, Cruel Fortune: The Lives and Loves of Italian Renaissance Women Poets.* New York: Fordham University Press, 2002.

James, Susan E. *Kateryn Parr: The Making of a Queen.* Aldershot and Brookfield: Ashgate Publishing Co., 1999.

Jankowski, Theodora A. *Women in Power in the Early Modern Drama.* Urbana, IL: University of Illinois Press, 1992.

Jansen, Katherine Ludwig. *The Making of the Magdalen: Preaching and Popular Devotion in the Later Middle Ages.* Princeton: Princeton University Press, 2000.

Jed, Stephanie H. *Chaste Thinking: The Rape of Lucretia and the Birth of Humanism.* Bloomington: Indiana University Press, 1989.

Jones, Ann Rosalind and Peter Stallybrass. *Renaissance Clothing and the Materials of Memory.* Cambridge: Cambridge University Press, 2000.

Jordan, Constance. *Renaissance Feminism: Literary Texts and Political Models.* Ithaca: Cornell University Press, 1990.

Kagan, Richard L. *Lucrecia's Dreams: Politics and Prophecy in Sixteenth-Century Spain.* Berkeley: University of California Press, 1990.

Kehler, Dorothea and Laurel Amtower, eds. *The Single Woman in Medieval and Early Modern England: Her Life and Representation.* Tempe, AZ: MRTS, 2002.

Kelly, Joan. "Did Women Have a Renaissance?" In her *Women, History, and Theory.* Chicago: University of Chicago Press, 1984. Also in Renate Bridenthal, Claudia Koonz, and Susan M. Stuard, eds., *Becoming Visible: Women in European History.* Third edition. Boston: Houghton Mifflin, 1998.

———. "Early Feminist Theory and the *Querelle des Femmes.*" In *Women, History, and Theory.*

Kelso, Ruth. *Doctrine for the Lady of the Renaissance.* Foreword by Katharine M. Rogers. Urbana: University of Illinois Press, 1956, 1978.

Kendrick, Robert L. *Celestical Sirens: Nuns and their Music in Early Modern Milan.* New York: Oxford University Press, 1996.

Kermode, Jenny, and Garthine Walker, eds. *Women, Crime and the Courts in Early Modern England.* Chapel Hill: University of North Carolina Press, 1994.

King, Catherine E. *Renaissance Women Patrons: Wives and Widows in Italy, c. 1300–1550.* New York and Manchester: Manchester University Press (distributed in the U.S. by St. Martin's Press), 1998.

King, Margaret L. *Women of the Renaissance.* Foreword by Catharine R. Stimpson. Chicago: University of Chicago Press, 1991.

Krontiris, Tina. *Oppositional Voices: Women as Writers and Translators of Literature in the English Renaissance.* London and New York: Routledge, 1992.

Kuehn, Thomas. *Law, Family, and Women: Toward a Legal Anthropology of Renaissance Italy.* Chicago: University of Chicago Press, 1991.

Kunze, Bonnelyn Young. *Margaret Fell and the Rise of Quakerism.* Stanford: Stanford University Press, 1994.

Labalme, Patricia A., ed. *Beyond Their Sex: Learned Women of the European Past.* New York: New York University Press, 1980.

Lalande, Roxanne Decker, ed. *A Labor of Love: Critical Reflections on the Writings of Marie-Catherine Desjardina (Mme de Villedieu).* Madison, NJ: Fairleigh Dickinson University Press, 2000.

Lamb, Mary Ellen. *Gender and Authorship in the Sidney Circle.* Madison: University of Wisconsin Press, 1990.

Laqueur, Thomas. *Making Sex: Body and Gender from the Greeks to Freud.* Cambridge, MA: Harvard University Press, 1990.

Larsen, Anne R., and Colette H. Winn, eds. *Renaissance Women Writers: French Texts/American Contexts.* Detroit, MI: Wayne State University Press, 1994.

Laven, Mary. *Virgins of Venice: Enclosed Lives and Broken Vows in the Renaissance Convent.* London: Viking, 2002.

Ledkovsky, Marina, Charlotte Rosenthal, and Mary Zirin, eds. *Dictionary of Russian Women Writers.* Westport, CT: Greenwood Press, 1994.

Lehfeldt, Elizabeth A. *Religious Women in Golden Age Spain: The Permeable Cloister.* Aldershot and Brookfield: Ashgate Publishing Co., 2005.

Lerner, Gerda. *The Creation of Patriarchy* and *Creation of Feminist Consciousness, 1000–1870*. Two vols. New York: Oxford University Press, 1986, 1994.

Levack. Brian P. *The Witch Hunt in Early Modern Europe*. London: Longman, 1987.

Levin, Carole, and Jeanie Watson, eds. *Ambiguous Realities: Women in the Middle Ages and Renaissance*. Detroit: Wayne State University Press, 1987.

Levin, Carole, Jo Eldridge Carney, and Debra Barrett-Graves. *Elizabeth I: Always Her Own Free Woman*. Aldershot and Brookfield: Ashgate Publishing Co., 2003.

Levin, Carole, et al. *Extraordinary Women of the Medieval and Renaissance World: A Biographical Dictionary*. Westport, CT: Greenwood Press, 2000.

Levy, Allison, ed. *Widowhood and Visual Culture in Early Modern Europe*. Aldershot and Brookfield: Ashgate Publishing Co., 2003.

Lewalsky, Barbara Kiefer. *Writing Women in Jacobean England*. Cambridge, MA: Harvard University Press, 1993.

Lewis, Gertrud Jaron. *By Women for Women about Women: The Sister-Books of Fourteenth-Century Germany*. Toronto: University of Toronto Press, 1996.

Lewis, Jayne Elizabeth. *Mary Queen of Scots: Romance and Nation*. London: Routledge, 1998.

Lindenauer, Leslie J. *Piety and Power: Gender and Religious Culture in the American Colonies, 1630–1700*. London and New York: Routledge, 2002.

Lindsey, Karen. *Divorced Beheaded Survived: A Feminist Reinterpretation of the Wives of Henry VIII*. Reading, MA: Addison-Wesley Publishing Co., 1995.

Lochrie, Karma. *Margery Kempe and Translations of the Flesh*. Philadelphia: University of Pennsylvania Press, 1992.

Longino Farrell, Michèle. *Performing Motherhood: The Sévigné Correspondence*. Hanover, NH: University Press of New England, 1991.

Lougee, Carolyn C. *Le Paradis des Femmes: Women, Salons, and Social Stratification in Seventeenth-Century France*. Princeton: Princeton University Press, 1976.

Love, Harold. *The Culture and Commerce of Texts: Scribal Publication in Seventeenth-Century England*. Amherst: University of Massachusetts Press, 1993.

Lowe, K. J. P. *Nuns' Chronicles and Convent Culture in Renaissance and Counter-Reformation Italy*. Cambridge: Cambridge University Press, 2003.

Lux-Sterritt, Laurence. *Redefining Female Religious Life: French Ursulines and English Ladies in Seventeenth-Century Catholicism*. Aldershot and Brookfield: Ashgate Publishing Co., 2005.

MacCarthy, Bridget G. *The Female Pen: Women Writers and Novelists 1621–1818*. Preface by Janet Todd. New York: New York University Press, 1994. (Originally published by Cork University Press, 1946–47).

Mack, Phyllis. *Visionary Women: Ecstatic Prophecy in Seventeenth-Century England*. Berkeley: University of California Pres, 1992.

Maclean, Ian. *Woman Triumphant: Feminism in French Literature, 1610–1652*. Oxford: Clarendon Press, 1977.

———. *The Renaissance Notion of Woman: A Study of the Fortunes of Scholasticism and Medical Science in European Intellectual Life*. Cambridge: Cambridge University Press, 1980.

MacNeil, Anne. *Music and Women of the Commedia dell'Arte in the Late Sixteenth Century*. New York: Oxford University Press, 2003.

Maggi, Armando. *Uttering the Word: The Mystical Performances of Maria Maddalena de' Pazzi, a Renaissance Visionary*. Albany: State University of New York Press, 1998.

Maids and Mistresses, Cousins and Queens: Women's Alliances in Early Modern England. Ed. Susan Frye and Karen Robertson. Oxford: Oxford University Press, 1999.

Marshall, Sherrin, ed. *Women in Reformation and Counter-Reformation Europe: Public and Private Worlds.* Bloomington: Indiana University Press, 1989.

Masten, Jeffrey. *Textual Intercourse: Collaboration, Authorship, and Sexualities in Renaissance Drama.* Cambridge: Cambridge University Press, 1997.

Matter, E. Ann, and John Coakley, eds. *Creative Women in Medieval and Early Modern Italy.* Philadelphia: University of Pennsylvania Press, 1994.

McGrath, Lynette. *Subjectivity and Women's Poetry in Early Modern England.* Aldershot and Brookfield: Ashgate Publishing Co., 2002.

McIver, Katherine A. *Women, Art, and Architecture in Northern Italy, 1520–1580.* Aldershot and Brookfield: Ashgate Publishing Co., 2006.

McLeod, Glenda. *Virtue and Venom: Catalogs of Women from Antiquity to the Renaissance.* Ann Arbor: University of Michigan Press, 1991.

McTavish, Lianne. *Childbirth and the Display of Authority in Early Modern France.* Aldershot and Brookfield: Ashgate Publishing Co., 2005.

Medieval Women's Visionary Literature. Ed. Elizabeth A. Petroff. New York: Oxford University Press, 1986.

Medwick, Cathleen. *Teresa of Avila: The Progress of a Soul.* New York: Doubleday, 1999.

Meek, Christine, ed. *Women in Renaissance and Early Modern Europe.* Dublin and Portland: Four Courts Press, 2000.

Mendelson, Sara, and Patricia Crawford. *Women in Early Modern England, 1550–1720.* Oxford: Clarendon Press, 1998.

Merchant, Carolyn. *The Death of Nature: Women, Ecology and the Scientific Revolution.* New York: HarperCollins, 1980.

Merrim, Stephanie. *Early Modern Women's Writing and Sor Juana Inés de la Cruz.* Nashville, TN: Vanderbilt University Press, 1999.

Messbarger, Rebecca. *The Century of Women: The Representations of Women in Eighteenth-Century Italian Public Discourse.* Toronto: University of Toronto Press, 2002.

Miller, Nancy K. *The Heroine's Text: Readings in the French and English Novel, 1722–1782.* New York: Columbia University Press, 1980.

Miller, Naomi J. *Changing the Subject: Mary Wroth and Figurations of Gender in Early Modern England.* Lexington: University Press of Kentucky, 1996.

——— and Gary Waller, eds. *Reading Mary Wroth: Representing Alternatives in Early Modern England.* Knoxville: University of Tennessee Press, 1991.

Monson, Craig A. *Disembodied Voices: Music and Culture in an Early Modern Italian Convent.* Berkeley: University of California Press, 1995.

———., ed. *The Crannied Wall: Women, Religion, and the Arts in Early Modern Europe.* Ann Arbor: University of Michigan Press, 1992.

Moore, Cornelia Niekus. *The Maiden's Mirror: Reading Material for German Girls in the Sixteenth and Seventeenth Centuries.* Wiesbaden: Otto Harrassowitz, 1987.

Moore, Mary B. *Desiring Voices: Women Sonneteers and Petrarchism.* Carbondale: Southern Illinois University Press, 2000.

Mujica, Bárbara. *Women Writers of Early Modern Spain.* New Haven: Yale University Press, 2004.

Musacchio, Jacqueline Marie. *The Art and Ritual of Childbirth in Renaissance Italy.* New Haven: Yale University Press, 1999.

Newman, Barbara. *God and the Goddesses: Vision, Poetry, and Belief in the Middle Ages.* Philadelphia: University of Pennsylvania Press, 2003.

Newman, Karen. *Fashioning Femininity and English Renaissance Drama.* Chicago: University of Chicago Press, 1991.

O'Donnell, Mary Ann. *Aphra Behn: An Annotated Bibliography of Primary and Secondary Sources.* Aldershot and Brookfield: Ashgate Publishing Co., 2nd ed., 2004.

Okin, Susan Moller. *Women in Western Political Thought.* Princeton: Princeton University Press, 1979.

Ozment, Steven. *The Bürgermeister's Daughter: Scandal in a Sixteenth-Century German Town.* New York: St. Martin's Press, 1995.

———. *Flesh and Spirit: Private Life in Early Modern Germany.* New York: Penguin Putnam, 1999.

———. *When Fathers Ruled: Family Life in Reformation Europe.* Cambridge, MA: Harvard University Press, 1983.

Pacheco, Anita, ed. *Early [English] Women Writers: 1600–1720.* New York and London: Longman, 1998.

Pagels, Elaine. *Adam, Eve, and the Serpent.* New York: Harper Collins, 1988.

Panizza, Letizia, and Sharon Wood, eds. *A History of Women's Writing in Italy.* Cambridge: University Press, 2000.

Panizza, Letizia, ed. *Women in Italian Renaissance Culture and Society.* Oxford: European Humanities Research Centre, 2000.

Parker, Patricia. *Literary Fat Ladies: Rhetoric, Gender and Property.* London and New York: Methuen, 1987.

Pernoud, Regine, and Marie-Veronique Clin. *Joan of Arc: Her Story.* Rev. and trans. Jeremy DuQuesnay Adams. New York: St. Martin's Press, 1998.

Perry, Mary Elizabeth. *Crime and Society in Early Modern Seville.* Hanover, NH: University Press of New England, 1980.

———. *Gender and Disorder in Early Modern Seville.* Princeton: Princeton University Press, 1990.

———. *The Handless Maiden: Moriscos and the Politics of Religion in Early Modern Spain.* Princeton: Princeton University Press, 2005.

Petroff, Elizabeth A., ed. *Medieval Women's Visionary Literature.* New York: Oxford University Press, 1986.

Perry, Ruth. *The Celebrated Mary Astell: An Early English Feminist.* Chicago: University of Chicago Press, 1986.

The Practice and Representation of Reading in England. Ed. James Raven, Helen Small, and Naomi Tadmor. Cambridge: University Press, 1996.

Quilligan, Maureen. *Incest and Agency in Elizabeth's England.* Philadelphia: University of Pennsylvania Press, 2005.

Rabil, Albert. *Laura Cereta: Quattrocento Humanist.* Binghamton, NY: MRTS, 1981.

Ranft, Patricia. *Women in Western Intellectual Culture, 600–1500.* New York: Palgrave, 2002.

Rapley, Elizabeth. *A Social History of the Cloister: Daily Life in the Teaching Monasteries of the Old Regime.* Montreal: McGill-Queen's University Press, 2001.

———. *The Devotés: Women and Church in Seventeenth-Century France.* Kingston, Ontario: Mc-Gill-Queen's University Press, 1989.

Raven, James, Helen Small, and Naomi Tadmor, eds. *The Practice and Representation of Reading in England.* Cambridge: University Press, 1996.

Reading Mary Wroth: Representing Alternatives in Early Modern England. Ed. Naomi Miller and Gary Waller. Knoxville: University of Tennessee Press, 1991.

Reardon, Colleen. *Holy Concord within Sacred Walls: Nuns and Music in Siena, 1575–1700.* Oxford: Oxford University Press, 2001.

Recovering Spain's Feminist Tradition. Ed. Lisa Vollendorf. New York: MLA, 2001.

Reid, Jonathan Andrew. "King's Sister—Queen of Dissent: Marguerite of Navarre (1492–1549) and Her Evangelical Network." Ph.D diss., University of Arizona, 2001.

Reiss, Sheryl E,. and David G. Wilkins, ed. *Beyond Isabella: Secular Women Patrons of Art in Renaissance Italy.* Kirksville, MO: Turman State University Press, 2001.

The Renaissance Englishwoman in Print: Counterbalancing the Canon. Ed. Anne M. Haselkorn and Betty Travitsky. Amherst: University of Massachusetts Press, 1990.

Renaissance Women Writers: French Texts/American Contexts. Ed. Anne R. Larsen and Co-lette H. Winn. Detroit, MI: Wayne State University Press, 1994.

Rereading Aphra Behn: History, Theory, and Criticism. Ed. Heidi Hutner. Charlottesville: University Press of Virginia, 1993.

Rheubottom, David. *Age, Marriage, and Politics in Fifteenth-Century Ragusa.* Oxford: Oxford University Press, 2000.

Richardson, Brian. *Printing, Writers and Readers in Renaissance Italy.* Cambridge: University Press, 1999.

Riddle, John M. *Contraception and Abortion from the Ancient World to the Renaissance.* Cambridge, MA: Harvard University Press, 1992.

———. *Eve's Herbs: A History of Contraception and Abortion in the West.* Cambridge, MA: Harvard University Press, 1997.

Roper, Lyndal. *The Holy Household: Women and Morals in Reformation Augsburg.* New York: Oxford University Press, 1989.

Rose, Mary Beth. *The Expense of Spirit: Love and Sexuality in English Renaissance Drama.* Ithaca, NY: Cornell University Press, 1988.

———. *Gender and Heroism in Early Modern English Literature.* Chicago: University of Chicago Press, 2002.

———, ed. *Women in the Middle Ages and the Renaissance: Literary and Historical Perspectives.* Syracuse: Syracuse University Press, 1986.

Rosenthal, Margaret F. *The Honest Courtesan: Veronica Franco, Citizen and Writer in Sixteenth-Century Venice.* Foreword by Catharine R. Stimpson. Chicago: University of Chicago Press, 1992.

Rublack, Ulinka, ed. *Gender in Early Modern German History.* Cambridge: Cambridge University Press, 2002.

Russell, Rinaldina, ed. *Feminist Encyclopedia of Italian Literature.* Westport, CT: Greenwood Press, 1997.

———. *Italian Women Writers: A Bio-Bibliographical Sourcebook.* Westport, CT: Greenwood Press, 1994.

Sackville-West, Vita. *Daughter of France: The Life of La Grande Mademoiselle.* Garden City, NY: Doubleday, 1959.

Sage, Lorna, ed. *Cambridge Guide to Women's Writing in English.* Cambridge: University Press, 1999.

Sánchez, Magdalena S. *The Empress, the Queen, and the Nun: Women and Power at the Court of Philip III of Spain.* Baltimore: Johns Hopkins University Press, 1998.

Sartori, Eva Martin, and Dorothy Wynne Zimmerman, eds. *French Women Writers: A Bio-Bibliographical Source Book*. Westport, CT: Greenwood Press, 1991.

Scaraffia, Lucetta, and Gabriella Zarri. *Women and Faith: Catholic Religious Life in Italy from Late Antiquity to the Present*. Cambridge, MA: Harvard University Press, 1999.

Scheepsma, Wybren. *Medieval Religious Women in the Low Countries: The 'Modern Devotion', the Canonesses of Windesheim, and Their Writings*. Rochester, NY: Boydell Press, 2004.

Schiebinger, Londa. *The Mind has no sex?: Women in the Origins of Modern Science*. Cambridge, MA: Harvard University Press, 1991.

———. *Nature's Body: Gender in the Making of Modern Science*. Boston: Beacon Press, 1993.

Schutte, Anne Jacobson, Thomas Kuehn, and Silvana Seidel Menchi, eds. *Time, Space, and Women's Lives in Early Modern Europe*. Kirksville, MO: Truman State University Press, 2001.

Schofield, Mary Anne, and Cecilia Macheski, eds. *Fetter'd or Free? British Women Novelists, 1670–1815*. Athens: Ohio University Press, 1986.

Schutte, Anne Jacobson. *Aspiring Saints: pretense of Holiness, Inquisition, and Gender in the Republic of Venice, 1618–1750*. Baltimore: Johns Hopkins University Press, 2001.

———, Thomas Kuehn, and Silvana Seidel Menchi, eds. *Time, Space, and Women's Lives in Early Modern Europe*. Kirksville, MO: Truman State University Press, 2001.

Seifert, Lewis C. *Fairy Tales, Sexuality and Gender in France 1690–1715: Nostalgic Utopias*. Cambridge, UK: Cambridge University Press, 1996.

Shannon, Laurie. *Sovereign Amity: Figures of Friendship in Shakespearean Contexts*. Chicago: University of Chicago Press, 2002.

Shemek, Deanna. *Ladies Errant: Wayward Women and Social Order in Early Modern Italy*. Durham, NC: Duke University Press, 1998.

Silent But for the Word. Ed. Margaret Hannay. Kent, OH: Kent State University Press, 1985.

The Single Woman in Medieval and Early Modern England: Her Life and Representation. Ed. Dorothea Kehler and Laurel Amtower. Tempe, AZ: MRTS, 2002.

Smarr, Janet L. *Joining the Conversation: Dialogues by Renaissance Women*. Ann Arbor: University of Michigan Press, 2005.

Smith, Hilda L. *Reason's Disciples: Seventeenth-Century English Feminists*. Urbana: University of Illinois Press, 1982.

———. *Women Writers and the Early Modern British Political Tradition*. Cambridge: Cambridge University Press, 1998.

Snook, Edith. *Women, Reading, and the Cultural Politics of Early Modern England*. Aldershot and Brookfield: Ashgate Publishing Co., 2005.

Sobel, Dava. *Galileo's Daughter: A Historical Memoir of Science, Faith, and Love*. New York: Penguin Books, 2000.

Sommerville, Margaret R. *Sex and Subjection: Attitudes to Women in Early-Modern Society*. London: Arnold, 1995.

Soufas, Teresa Scott. *Dramas of Distinction: A Study of Plays by Golden Age Women*. Lexington: The University Press of Kentucky, 1997.

Spencer, Jane. *The Rise of the Woman Novelist: From Aphra Behn to Jane Austen*. Oxford: Basil Blackwell, 1986.

Spender, Dale. *Mothers of the Novel: 100 Good Women Writers Before Jane Austen.* London and New York: Routledge, 1986.

Sperling, Jutta Gisela. *Convents and the Body Politic in Late Renaissance Venice.* Foreword by Catharine R. Stimpson. Chicago: University of Chicago Press, 1999.

Steinbrügge, Lieselotte. *The Moral Sex: Woman's Nature in the French Enlightenment.* Trans. Pamela E. Selwyn. New York: Oxford University Press, 1995.

Stephens, Sonya, ed. *A History of Women's Writing in France.* Cambridge: Cambridge University Press, 2000.

Stephenson, Barbara. *The Power and Patronage of Marguerite de Navarre.* Aldershot and Brookfield: Ashgate Publishing Co., 2004.

Stocker, Margarita. *Judith, Sexual Warrior: Women and Power in Western Culture.* New Haven: Yale University Press, 1998.

Straznacky, Marta. *Privacy, Playreading, and Women's Closet Drama, 1550–1700.* Cambridge: Cambridge University Press, 2004.

Stretton, Timothy. *Women Waging Law in Elizabethan England.* Cambridge: Cambridge University Press, 1998.

Strong Voices, Weak History: Early Women Writers and Canons in England, France, and Italy. Ed. Pamela J. Benson and Victoria Kirkham. Ann Arbor: University of Michigan Press, 2005.

Stuard, Susan M. "The Dominion of Gender: Women's Fortunes in the High Middle Ages." In Renate Bridenthal, Claudia Koonz, and Susan M. Stuard, eds. *Becoming Visible: Women in European History.* Third edition. Boston: Houghton Mifflin, 1998.

Summit, Jennifer. *Lost Property: The Woman Writer and English Literary History, 1380–1589.* Chicago: University of Chicago Press, 2000.

Surtz, Ronald E. *The Guitar of God: Gender, Power, and Authority in the Visionary World of Mother Juana de la Cruz (1481–1534).* Philadelphia: University of Pennsylvania Press, 1991.

———. *Writing Women in Late Medieval and Early Modern Spain: The Mothers of Saint Teresa of Avila.* Philadelphia: University of Pennsylvania Press, 1995.

Suzuki, Mihoko. *Subordinate Subjects: Gender, the Political Nation, and Literary Form in England, 1588–1688.* Aldershot and Brookfield: Ashgate Publishing Co., 2003.

Tatlock, Lynne, and Christiane Bohnert, eds. *The Graph of Sex* (q.v.).

Teaching Tudor and Stuart Women Writers. Ed. Susanne Woods and Margaret P. Hannay. New York: MLA, 2000.

Teague, Frances. *Bathsua Makin, Woman of Learning.* Lewisburg, PA: Bucknell University Press, 1999.

Thomas, Anabel. *Art and Piety in the Female Religious Communities of Renaissance Italy: Iconography, Space, and the Religious Woman's Perspective.* New York: Cambridge University Press, 2003.

Tinagli, Paola. *Women in Italian Renaissance Art: Gender, Representation, Identity.* Manchester: Manchester University Press, 1997.

Todd, Janet. *The Secret Life of Aphra Behn.* London, New York, and Sydney: Pandora, 2000.

———. *The Sign of Angelica: Women, Writing and Fiction, 1660–1800.* New York: Columbia University Press, 1989.

Tomas, Natalie R. *The Medici Women: Gender and Power in Renaissance Florence.* Aldershot and Brookfield: Ashgate Publishing Co., 2004.

Traub, Valerie. *The Renaissance of Lesbianism in Early Modern England.* Cambridge: Cambridge University Press, 2002.

Valenze, Deborah. *The First Industrial Woman.* New York: Oxford University Press, 1995.

Van Dijk, Susan, Lia van Gemert, and Sheila Ottway, eds. *Writing the History of Women's Writing: Toward an International Approach.* Proceedings of the Colloquium, Amsterdam, 9–11 September. Amsterdam: Royal Netherlands Academy of Arts and Sciences, 2001.

Vickery, Amanda. *The Gentleman's Daughter: Women's Lives in Georgian England.* New Haven: Yale University Press, 1998.

Vollendorf, Lisa. *The Lives of Women: A New History of Inquisitional Spain.* Nashville, TN: Vanderbilt University Press, 2005.

Walker, Claire. *Gender and Politics in Early Modern Europe: English Convents in France and the Low Countries.* New York: Palgrave, 2003.

Wall, Wendy. *The Imprint of Gender: Authorship and Publication in the English Renaissance.* Ithaca, NY: Cornell University Press, 1993.

Walsh, William T. *St. Teresa of Avila: A Biography.* Rockford, IL: TAN Books & Publications, 1987.

Warner, Marina. *Alone of All Her Sex: The Myth and Cult of the Virgin Mary.* New York: Knopf, 1976.

Warnicke, Retha M. *The Marrying of Anne of Cleves: Royal Protocol in Tudor England.* Cambridge: Cambridge University Press, 2000.

Watt, Diane. *Secretaries of God: Women Prophets in Late Medieval and Early Modern England.* Cambridge, England: D. S. Brewer, 1997.

Weaver, Elissa. *Convent Theatre in Early Modern Italy: Spiritual Fun and Learning for Women.* New York: Cambridge University Press, 2002.

Weber, Alison. *Teresa of Avila and the Rhetoric of Femininity.* Princeton: Princeton University Press, 1990.

Welles, Marcia L. *Persephone's Girdle: Narratives of Rape in Seventeenth-Century Spanish Literature.* Nashville: Vanderbilt University Press, 2000.

Whitehead, Barbara J., ed. *Women's Education in Early Modern Europe: A History, 1500–1800.* New York and London: Garland Publishing Co., 1999.

Widowhood and Visual Culture in Early Modern Europe. Ed. Allison Levy. Aldershot and Brookfield: Ashgate Publishing Co., 2003.

Widowhood in Medieval and Early Modern Europe. Ed. Sandra Cavallo and Lydan Warner. New York: Longman, 1999.

Wiesner, Merry E. *Working Women in Renaissance Germany.* New Brunswick, NJ: Rutgers University Press, 1986.

Wiesner-Hanks, Merry E. *Christianity and Sexuality in the Early Modern World: Regulating Desire, Reforming Practice.* New York: Routledge, 2000.

———. *Gender, Church, and State in Early Modern Germany: Essays.* New York: Longman, 1998.

———. *Gender in History.* Malden, MA: Blackwell, 2001.

———. *Women and Gender in Early Modern Europe.* Cambridge: Cambridge University Press, 1993.

———. *Working Women in Renaissance Germany.* New Brunswick, NJ: Rutgers University Press, 1986.

Willard, Charity Cannon. *Christine de Pizan: Her Life and Works.* New York: Persea Books, 1984.

Wilson, Katharina, ed. *Encyclopedia of Continental Women Writers.* 2 vols. New York: Garland, 1991.

Winn, Colette, and Donna Kuizenga, eds. *Women Writers in Pre-Revolutionary France.* New York: Garland Publishing, 1997.

Winston-Allen, Anne. *Convent Chronicles: Women Writing about Women and Reform in the Late Middle Ages.* University Park: Pennsylvania State University Press, 2004.

Women and Monasticism in Medieval Europe: Sisters and Patrons of the Cistercian Reform, ed. Constance H. Berman. Kalamazoo: Western Michigan University Press, 2002.

Women, Crime and the Courts in Early Modern England. Ed. Jenny Kermode and Garthine Walker. Chapel Hill: University of North Carolina Press, 1994.

Women in Italian Renaissance Culture and Society. Ed. Letizia Panizza. Oxford: European Humanities Research Centre, 2000.

Women in Reformation and Counter-Reformation Europe: Public and Private Worlds. Ed. Sherrin Marshall. Bloomington, IN: Indiana University Press, 1989.

Women in Renaissance and Early Modern Europe. Ed. Christine Meek. Dublin-Portland: Four Courts Press, 2000.

Women in the Inquisition: Spain and the New World. Ed. Mary E. Giles. Baltimore: Johns Hopkins University Press, 1999.

Women in the Middle Ages and the Renaissance: Literary and Historical Perspectives. Ed. Mary Beth Rose. Syracuse: Syracuse University Press, 1986.

Women Players in England, 1500–1660: Beyond the All-Male Stage. Ed. Pamela Allen Brown and Peter Parolin. Aldershot and Brookfield: Ashgate Publishing Co., 2005.

Women, "Race," and Writing in the Early Modern Period. Ed. Margo Hendricks and Patricia Parker. London and New York: Routledge, 1994.

Woodbridge, Linda. *Women and the English Renaissance: Literature and the Nature of Womankind, 1540–1620.* Urbana: University of Illinois Press, 1984.

Woodford, Charlotte. *Nuns as Historians in Early Modern Germany.* Oxford: Clarendon Press, 2002.

Woods, Susanne. *Lanyer: A Renaissance Woman Poet.* New York: Oxford University Press, 1999.

——— and Margaret P. Hannay, eds. *Teaching Tudor and Stuart Women Writers.* New York: MLA, 2000.

Writing the Female Voice. Ed. Elizabeth C. Goldsmith. Boston: Northeastern University Press, 1989.

Writing the History of Women's Writing: Toward an International Approach. Ed. Susan Van Dijk, Lia van Gemert and Sheila Ottway Proceedings of the Colloquium, Amsterdam, 9–11 September. Amsterdam: Royal Netherlands Academy of Arts and Sciences, 2001.

INDEX